The Many Worlds of Sarala Devi
&
The Tagores and Sartorial Styles

The Many Worlds of Sarala Devi
A Diary

Translated from the Bengali *Jeevaner Jharapata*
Sukhendu Ray
With an Introduction by **Bharati Ray**

&

The Tagores and Sartorial Styles
A Photo Essay
Malavika Karlekar

Routledge
Taylor & Francis Group
LONDON AND NEW YORK

First published 2017
by Routledge
4 Park Square, Milton Park, Abingdon, Oxon OX14 4RN
605 Third Avenue, New York, NY 10017

First issued in paperback 2023

Routledge is an imprint of the Taylor & Francis Group, an informa business

© 2017 Sukhendu Ray, Malavika Karlekar, Bharati Ray and Social Science Press

The right of Sukhendu Ray, Malavika Karlekar and Bharati Ray to be identified as authors of this work has been asserted by them in accordance with sections 77 and 78 of the Copyright, Designs and Patents Act 1988.

All rights reserved. No part of this book may be reprinted or reproduced or utilised in any form or by any electronic, mechanical, or other means, now known or hereafter invented, including photocopying and recording, or in any information storage or retrieval system, without permission in writing from the publishers.

Trademark notice: Product or corporate names may be trademarks or registered trademarks, and are used only for identification and explanation without intent to infringe.

Publisher's Note
The publisher has gone to great lengths to ensure the quality of this reprint but points out that some imperfections in the original copies may be apparent.

Print edition not for sale in South Asia (India, Sri Lanka, Nepal, Bangladesh, Afghanistan, Pakistan or Bhutan).

British Library Cataloguing in Publication Data
A catalogue record for this book is available from the British Library

Library of Congress Cataloging in Publication Data
A catalogue record for this book has been requested

ISBN-13: 978-1-138-29571-1 (hbk)
ISBN-13: 978-1-03-265295-5 (pbk)
ISBN-13: 978-1-315-10056-2 (ebk)

DOI: 10.4324/9781315100562

Typeset in Book Antiqua 10/12
by Eleven Arts, Delhi 110 035

Contents

Introduction   1
  Bharati Ray

Jeevaner Jharapata   27
  Sukhendu Ray

Glossary   201

The Tagores and Sartorial Styles   203
  Malavika Karlekar

Introduction

• *Bharati Ray*

C an autobiographies be considered history? If literature be regarded as a form of history[1] then Sarala Devi Chaudhurani's autobiography, *Jeevaner Jharapata*, can claim to be an important part of Bengal's social history of the late nineteenth and early twentieth centuries. Society is an umbrella term that includes every aspect of civil life which is free from direct control by the State. Society includes all the ingredients that go into making it—art, culture, values, manners, customs, religion, myths, memory, food, dress, health, education, gender, family and even politics and economy. The way we live defines our society. In this sense, the society of the Hindu-Brahmo upper class and the upper middle-class way of life is mirrored in fascinating detail in this volume.

I have argued elsewhere that in a sense all of us are historians—practising or not—of our times. We register in our minds the facts of our lives and circumstances, contemporary society and polity,

---

[1] This is true of novels also. To quote Murasaki Shikibu of Japan, 'Without it what should we know of how people lived in the past? ... For history books ... show us only one small corner of life; whereas these diaries and romances ... contain the most minute information about all sorts of people's private affairs'. Cited in Sharon Sievers, 'Women in China, Japan and Korea', in Barbara N. Ramusack and Sharon Sievers (eds.) *Women of Asia*, Bloomingdon and Indianapolis: Indiana University Press, 1999, pp. 178-9.

2 *Introduction*

and make our own observations. Only a handful of us put down in writing what our memory holds.[2] Since events are seen through the looking glass of one individual and often inscribed without any verification, memoirs should be examined critically. But then, all accounts, even if verified or analysed, are basically subjective. Established hard-core history, narrative or theory, also needs careful investigation. Seen in this light, autobiographies do not stand outside history. They represent contemporary history from the authors' standpoint.

To give but one or two examples, historian Udaya Kumar in a recent article has dealt with the relation between the discourse of social reform in Kerala and certain forms of autobiographical articulation in Malayalam. These reform initiatives, taken primarily between the 1880s and the 1930s (roughly the same period during which Sarala Devi lived and worked), involved a reformulation of the ideas of caste and community and the autobiographies themselves were written by active participants in these efforts. Beginning with a discussion of some of the earliest autobiographies in Malayalam, e.g. by Yacob Rama Varma Thampuran and Vaikkom Pachu Moothathu, Udaya Kumar moves on to analyse the self-narratives of V. T. Bhattathiripad and Kanippayyur Sankaran Nambudiripad, C. V. Kunjuraman and C. Kesavan and, in the process, gives insights on how autobiographies, if scrutinized with care, represent vivid contemporary history.[3] In Bengal, the autobiographies of men like Akshay C. Sarkar, Nabin Chandra Sen, Chandranath Basu and Shivnath Shastri highlight contemporary social structures, customs and behaviour patterns, and to a great extent, fill in the gap in narratives culled from archival and other sources.

Historian Tanika Sarkar in her recent publication on the autobiography by Rasasundari Devi (b.1809), *Amar Jiban* (1868), shows how this earliest autobiography written by a woman in the nineteenth century is, at once, 'a very early text of modernity' and underlines the lives and activities of women in rural Bengal.[4] Indeed, women's autobiographies are increasingly being regarded

---

[2] See 'Introduction,' in Bharati Ray, ed. *Different Types of History,* New Delhi, Pearson Longman, 2009.

[3] See Udaya Kumar, 'Subjects of New Lives: Reform, Self-Making and the Discourse of Autobiography in Kerala', in Bharati Ray ed. op.cit.

[4] Tanika Sarkar, *Words to Remember: Rasasundari Devi, Amar Jiban, A Modern Autobiography,* New Delhi: Kali for Women, 1999.

Bharati Ray 3

as highlighting many vital aspects of social history missing in official records and papers. Seen from this perspective, *Jeevaner Jharapata* is an important autobiography authored by a woman.

THE CONTEXT

Sarala was born at her mother's family home at Jorasanko, Calcutta, in 1872. In order to contextualize her, we have to recall the age as well as the family she was born in. She belonged to the Hindu-Brahmo community, which played a leading role in the nineteenth century reform movement in Bengal, and was related to the Tagores of Jorasanko, unquestionably the most illustrious family in contemporary Bengal. Her mother Swarnakumari Devi (b.1855), a renowned author, was the daughter of Maharshi Debendranath Tagore and the elder sister of Rabindranath Tagore.

Much has been written on the nineteenth-century social reform movement in Bengal.[5] For our purpose we need to mention two developments that spanned the late nineteenth and early twentieth centuries. First, the period saw a fabulous outburst of cultural activity, in art, literature, music, and indeed, in all spheres of Bengali social life. Rammohun Roy was one of the pioneers, and a galaxy of great men like Iswar Chandra Vidyasagar, Bankim Chandra Chattopadhyay and Swami Vivekananda appeared one by one.. The Tagore family, as will be mentioned later, occupied a unique place in the cultural efflorescence of the time.[6] Second, social reforms, especially in favour of women, were introduced. For instance, sati was abolished, and education for women was introduced after a gap of many centuries. The tremendous impact of education in women's lives, and indeed on the whole society, was quite beyond the reformers' imagination.

While social reform progressed, nationalism grew and Bengal witnessed the Swadeshi movement that burgeoned forth as a protest against Lord Curzon's partition of Bengal in 1905. Bengal took the pride of place in India both in inaugurating the anti-

[5] For reform movement, see David Kopf, *The Brahmo Samaj and the Shaping of the Modern Mind* Princeton, 1977; Charles Heimsath, *Indian Nationalism and Hindu Social Reform,* Princeton University Press, 1964; Tapan Raychaudhuri, *Europe Reconsidered,* New Delhi, Oxford University Press, 1988.

[6] See Prashanta Kumar Pal, *Rabi Jiboni* (Life of Rabindranath), Calcutta: Ananda Publishers, 5 vols, 1397 *BS*/1990 CE.

4   *Introduction*

colonial movement and in producing political leaders of the first order.[7] Sarala was privileged in being an integral part of both the cultural and the political stirrings. Her father Janakinath Ghosal was a staunch supporter of the early Indian National Congress and her mother Swarnakumari Devi became one of the first women delegates to the organization. Her family home, Jorasanko, had become as much a centre of creative culture as of emerging nationalism. Swarnakumari moved out of Jorasanko, a joint-family household, after her marriage, only to return when her husband went abroad for his studies.

JOINT FAMILY

Any attempt at an analysis of the history of family patterns in Bengal must reject a unilinear interpretation, and take into account the complexities and contradictions that prevailed in Bengali social life. Through the processes of integration and disintegration, the joint family became an established institution by the latter part of the eighteenth century in Bengali society. Family annals contained in district histories and biographies of nineteenth century personalities establish this fact.[8] The typical Bengali middle class home came to be occupied by a joint family.[9]

The joint family structure was not a monolithic one. The number of members depended on how many people a particular family accommodated. Besides the three biological generations, a household would often accommodate, in terms of the relationship to the *karta*,

[7] Sumit Sarkar, *The Swadeshi Movement in Bengal, 1903–1908*, Delhi: People's Publishing House, 1973. For a succinct account of the political movements, see Sekhar Bandopayopadhyay, *From Plassey to Partition*, New Delhi: Oriental Longman, 2004, pp. 251–62, 284–321.

[8] There are many such biographical records. To name only a few, see the autobiographies of Kartikeya Chandra Roy, Girischandra Vidyaratna, Rajnarain Basu, Sharadasundari Devi and Jadavchandra Chattopadhyay, in Naresh Jana et al. (eds.) *Atmakatha*, 3 volumes, Calcutta: Ananya Prakashan, 1981–94; Swarnakumari Devi, 'Sekela Katha' (Tales of Old Days), in *Bharati*, Gyanadanandini Devi, in *Puratani*, Bipin Pal, *Autobiography*.

[9] The term joint family has been interpreted in various ways by different scholars. Here we take it as the Bengali concept of *ekannavarti* (sharing the same kitchen). Roughly, it denotes a household where at least two generations of agnatically related married males form a commensual unit, accept the controlling authority of the eldest male or *karta* and abide by a set of mutual rights and duties.

Bharati Ray 5

widowed aunts, grand aunts, siblings, siblings' children, cousins, their children, widowed daughters-in-law of siblings or cousins, distant relations, and sometimes even friends or acquaintances in need of a home. Listen to Hemalata Tagore (b. 1873) married to Dwipendranath Tagore, nephew of Rabindranath Tagore, describe the Tagore household at Jorasanko:

After my marriage, I entered our house at Jorasanko. It is an understatement to say that it was a huge family. My fathers-in-law (i.e. father-in-law and his brothers) were seven in number, aunts-in-law (sisters of father-in-law) were four. All of the aunts' husbands were *ghar-jamais* (lived-in-sons-in-law). Maharshi (i.e. Debendranath Tagore) had sixteen servants... In his household, there were altogether 116 people. All were ekannavarti. Nobody could dream of separation.[10]

Sarala, too, tells us in her autobiography that Jorasanko was:

...a place of great magnificence, every corner teeming with people, humming with endless activities. The sons and daughters of my maternal grandfather had their separate quarters where they lived with their respective families... A dozen Brahmin cooks were kept busy since early morning in the central kitchen cooking for the entire family and other residents. Cooked rice would be piled high almost touching the ceiling on one end of the huge kitchen.

In this joint household Maharshi was the karta. Usually, the Maharshi's children with their children participated in various celebrations, and performances. Sarala recalls:

[10] Hemlata Tagore, 'Purano Katha' (Stories of Olden Days), in Abhijit Sen and Abhijit Bhattacharya (eds.) *Sekele Katha: Shatak Suchanay Meyeder Smritikatha* (Stories At the Turn of the Century: Memoirs of Women), Kolkata, Naya Udyog, 1997, pp. 191, 196. Sarat Chandra Chatterjee (b. 1876) in *Nishkriti*, a popular household novel, graphically depicts a middle class joint family: 'The Chatujyes of Bhowanipore belonged to a joint family. Two brothers, Girish and Harish, and their younger cousin, Ramesh, lived together. Girish and Harish, both became advocates, made plenty of money, built a house' and acquired huge property. Girish's widowed, elderly mother, his wife Siddheswari, Harish and his wife Nayantara, Ramesh and his wife Shailaja lived together along with four sons and one daughter of Girish, one son of Harish and two sons of Ramesh. Girish, the eldest brother, was the karta, and Siddheswari was the ginni. Girish and Harish earned the money, and cousin Ramesh, a spendthrift irresponsible young man, earned nothing but wasted his brothers' money on futile business ventures. Yet for all practical purposes, his wife Shailaja, the most efficient among the three sisters-in-law, controlled the household, as well as the children.

6 *Introduction*

Counting the children of my many aunts and uncles, we cousins formed quite a large contingent. Understandably, there were age-wise groupings among the children. My elder sister Hironmoyee's group was just above ours, but even though my elder brother Jyotsna's group consisted entirely of boys, we were on friendly terms with them...without inhibition, we often used to engage ourselves in fights with the boys in my brother's group.[11]

Hironmoyee Devi (b.1870), the elder daughter of Swarnakumari, also recalls a joyous childhood in the company of cousins. The children used to organize their own dramas:

...without telling any of the elders... They all acclaimed our acting as well as the stage decorations... On the drop scene was painted the face of uncle Rabindranath surrounded by a garland. Each flower was the face of a child actor. [12]

Clearly such rich environment, not available to a child from a middle-class family, greatly enriched the Jorasanko children.

A few words about the Jorasanko family may not be out of place here, because the Tagores left an indelible stamp on the social and cultural history of Bengal. Indeed, few Bengalis could claim to have contributed as much to the cultural efflorescence of Bengal as the Tagores did. Dwarakanath Tagore was a pioneer industrialist. His son Debendranath was the leading Brahmo figure after Rammohun Roy. Almost all of Debendranath's sons rose to fame. The eldest Dwijendranath was a philosopher, author, nationalist, and a patron of *Hindu Mela*;[13] the second, Satyendranath, was the first Indian member of the Indian Civil Service, and a champion of women moving out of the confinement of their homes;[14] the third son, Hemendranath, was a businessman; and the fourth, Jyotirindranath, was a man of many talents, a writer, musician, industrialist and nationalist. However, outshining all brothers, reigning over the Indian cultural domain of that era, was Rabindranath, a Nobel

[11] Sarala Devi Chaudhurani, 'Amar Balyajibon' (My Childhood), *Bharati, Baishakh* 1312 *BS,* CE 1905.

[12] Hironmoyee Devi, 'Kaifayat' (An Apology), *Bharati, Baishakh,* 1323 *BS,* CE 1918.

[13] Under the patronage of the Tagores and some others, Hindu Mela functioned from 1867–80, held annual exhibitions to display indigenous products, and sought to shape a nationalist entity.

[14] Satyendranath's letters to his wife bear testimony to this. See Indira Devi Chaudhurani, *Puratani,* Calcutta: Indian Associated Publishing Company, 1957.

laureate in literature, creator of a new genre of music, Rabindra Sangeet, an excellent painter, and an ardent nationalist. His nephew Abanindranath was a most celebrated painter. Thakurbari, as the Tagore family home at Jorasanko was known, became then the meeting point of many a brilliant contemporary mind.

The women of the Tagore family also made history.[15] Debendranath's wife Sarada Devi was literate and fond of reading books. Their daughter Saudamini, went to Bethune School at the age of five, and became one of the earliest Bengali upper class girls to go for formal education. Debendranath's daughter Swarnakumari was a celebrated author, daughter-in-law of Gyanadanandini, one of the most 'modern' women of her time, went to live with her husband first in Bombay,[16] and later in England, innovated the 'modern' style of wearing saree[17] and started a children's magazine. Another daughter-in-law, Kadambari Devi, used to ride on horseback in especially tailored clothes and was a highly talented actress participating in family plays. She was a source of inspiration to the young Rabindranath.[18] It was among such extraordinarily gifted men and women, that Sarala had the fortune of growing up. No wonder, she could have the best of education and opportunities freshly opened to women.

EDUCATION

Sarala's autobiography throws interesting light on the contemporary system of women's education.[19] It is known that despite strong

[15] For a sketch of their lives, see Chitra Deb, *Thakurbarir Andarmahal*, Calcutta: Ananda Publishers, 1993.

[16] On her return from Bombay, she publicly alighted from a carriage at the family home, moving the family retainers to tears. Swarnakumari recalls that the scene of shame and sorrow at Jorasanko was beyond description. Swarnakumari Devi, 'Sekele Katha', *Bharati, Chaitra*,1322 *BS*, 1915 CE.

[17] A Bengali woman used to wear only a saree. No undergarment was worn. The clothing was comfortable for the hot climate in Bengal, but not suitable for going out. For the significance of sartorial reform, see Himani Bannerji, 'The Discourse on Shame *(lajja)* and Clothing of the Bhadramahila' in Bharati Ray, ed. *From the Seams of History: Essays on Indian Women*, New Delhi: Oxford University Press, 1995.

[18] There are many references to Kadambari Devi in the innumerable writings on Rabindranath. One of the latest is Uma Das Gupta, *The Oxford India Tagore*, New Delhi, Oxford University Press, 2009, pp. 25–64.

[19] Meredith Borthwick, *Changing Role,* pp. 60–108 is a good history of women's education in Bengal in the nineteenth century. For a short summary,

8 *Introduction*

resistance from the orthodox,[20] women's education had made steady advance since the nineteenth century. Initially zenana education had been launched,[21] but Bethune School was founded in 1849; its Collegiate department was started in 1880.[22] So while mother Swarnakumari had been taught at home, daughter Sarala entered Bethune School. It was, at the time, the centre of learning for the girls from 'progressive' families. Hindu reformers like Madanmohan Tarkalankar and Brahmo leaders like Rajnarayan Bose, Shivanath Shastri and Durgamohan Das sent their daughters to Bethune School. Rajnarayan's daughter, Lajjabati (b.1874) became a poet and essayist and Shivanath Shasri's daughter, Hemalata (b. 1868) later founded Maharani Girls' School in Darjeeling. Kamini Ray (b.1865), the latter-day celebrated poet, Abala Bose (b. 1864), daughter of Durgamohan Das became renowned as a committed educationist and the founder of Nari Shiksha Samiti and Kumudini Khastagir (b. 1865), who later became the principal of Bethune College, were all Sarala's contemporaries. These were the privileged first generation of women who received formal institutional education. They met, became friends and enriched one another. After finishing school, where Sarala made name as a bright student, she proceeded to graduate from Bethune College with honours in

---

see 'Introduction', Bharati Ray, *Sekaler Narishiksha: Bamabodhini Patrika,* Calcutta: Calcutta University Press, 1994, pp. 19–34. Aparna Basu, 'History deals with the History of Women's Education at the All-India Level' in Karuna Chanana ed. *Socialisation, Education and Women: Explorations in Gender Identity,* New Delhi: Orient Longman, 1988, looks at the question from women's perspective.

[20] See Shivanath Shastri, *Ramtanu Lahiri O Tatkalin Bangasamaj,* Calcutta. The popular perception of assertive women found the most powerful representations in Kalighat *patachitra* representing the visual satire on educated women, especially the English-educated *babu's* abject surrender to his 'modern' wife and neglect to his mother.

[21] In most families, women were taught at home by their male relations, and in some, they were educated by women teachers or 'Vaisnavis', women belonging to the Vaisnava Hindu religious sect. For instance, Rokeya Sakhawat Hossain was taught by her elder brother, and Kailasbasini Devi by her husband.

[22] Author Lila Majumdar describes amusingly the happiness—and self awareness—of her cousins, who could make it to Bethune College. 'Almost all the college going girls were at Bethune College. All of them knotted their hair in a big bun, wore colourful *sarees* from Dhaka, a gold chain round their necks, gold bangles of a particular design then popular, and gold earrings of almost uniform style. They would occasionally flare up for no apparent reason, or they would be highly amused again for no reason; they would needlessly run up and down the stairs with a song on their lips equally for no reason at all.'

English in 1890, only a few years after Kadambini Ganguly and Chandramukhi Basu had graduated in 1883.[23]

Although most reformers were supportive of female education, bitter debate raged over the issue and extent of their education.[24] Few were inclined to consider the related theme of the development of a woman's individuality. On the other hand, fearful that too much education would make women westernized, promote disruptive individualism, and foster disrespect of tradition, they preferred different syllabi for men and women. Men were encouraged to take up science, and women, to opt for humanities. As a result, Sarala was denied her chosen field of study — science. The amusing anecdotes related in *Jharapata* reveal her frustration as well as that of many like her.

The implications of education for different sectors of society have been analyzed in recent debates.[25] One point is clear, however. Notwithstanding the patriarchal bias in the entire educational framework, education brought to many women awareness of gender inequality, and a realization that the value of education lay not merely in equipping themselves with domestic skills as advised by social reformers,[26] but in the cultivation of the mind and in the promotion of an all-round personhood. These new ideas found outlet in various arenas.

MARRIAGE

Sarala's autobiography throws interesting light on the prevalent system of marriage and, in the process, on the relationship between

[23] Kadambini Ganguly (b. 1861) and Chandramukhi Basu (b. 1860) were the two first women graduates under Calcutta University. Kadambini Ganguly became a physician, while Chandramukhi secured her Master's and became the first principal of Bethune College.

[24] For a summary of the debate, see Bharati Ray, 'Introduction' in *Sekaler Narishiksha*, pp. 29–34.

[25] See, for example, Andre Béteille, 'The Reproduction of Inequality: Occupation, Caste and Family', in *Contributions to Indian Sociology*, 25:1, 1991; D. Drury, *The Iron Schoolmaster: Education, Employment and the Family in India*, Berkeley, 1992. The force of education in maintaining the dominant belief systems and its divisive are recognized today.

[26] Of the didactic literature for women, mention may be made of: Bhudev Mukhopadhyay, *Paribarik Prasanga* (On Family Matters, 1884), Girija Prasanna Roy Chowdhury, *Grihalakshmi* (The Lakshmi of the Home, Calcutta, 1887) and Jay Krishna Mitra, *Ramanir Kartavya* (Duties of a Woman, Calcutta, 1890).

10 *Introduction*

the Hindus and Brahmos. On a visit to Krishnanagar to inaugurate the establishment of the Brahmo Samaj, Debendranath met the young Janakinath and was immediately attracted to this young, handsome and well-educated son of a local zamindar of Nadia. Debendranath chose him as the husband for his favourite daughter Swarnakumari. His eldest daughter Saudamini had been married according to the Hindu rites, but since the marriage of his second daughter Sukumari, all the sons-in-law were initiated into the Brahmo faith, and made to reside in their in-laws' home. Janakinath refused to oblige Debendranath. To him, there was no fundamental contradiction between the Hindu and Brahmo beliefs, and so, no need for initiation into the Brahmo faith. Nor would he live in his wife's home. Debendranath had to yield to his wishes.

This marriage drove a wedge between Janakinath and his father. A Hindu, Janakinath's father would not accept as his daughter-in-law, the daughter of Brahmo Debendranath. In fact, he was so upset that he not only refused to recognize this marriage but also disinherited Janakinath. This incident is a pointer to the deep antipathy that the traditional Hindus had for the Brahmos. Amiya P. Sen in his well-researched study analyses the complex relationship between the two communities during the period.[27] Perhaps it was the 'deviations in rituals and customs' which more than the differences in religious interpretations that drove a wedge between the two. Most importantly, the Brahmo Marriage Bill brought into sharp focus the issue of community identity. A separate Marriage Act for Brahmos was obviously seen as a permanent weaning away of the Brahmos from the parental Hindu society. Swarnakumari's marriage took place in 1867, at the height of the Marriage Bill controversy that raged animated between 1865–72, when the Bill became an Act.[28] Little wonder that Janakinath's father refused to approve of the Hindu-Brahmo marriage. Fortunately, the breach was later healed, and the father condescended to occasionally visit his son's home, to the delight of his grandchildren.

Sarala's autobiography sheds illuminating light on another crucial aspect of the institution of marriage. Since the mid-

[27] Amiya P. Sen, *Hindu Revivalism in Bengal, 1872–1905*, Delhi: Oxford University Press, 1999, pp. 23–48.

[28] According to the Act III of 1872, the contracting parties were to formally declare that they did not profess the Hindu faith. It permitted separation and divorce, a positive threat to traditional gender relations in Hindu society.

Bharati Ray   11

nineteenth century, a few 'choice' marriages (marrying by one's own choice rather than having an arranged marriage) had begun to take place in Bengal,[29] but they became more frequent during the freedom movement.[30] Yet, whether a family was Hindu or Brahmo, labelled 'conservative' or 'progressive', the custom of traditional marriage arranged by parents within the caste group was favoured. The case in point is that of Sarala herself. Sarala's autobiography describes how she was compelled to marry Rambhuj Dutta Chaudhuri. In the crucial matter of marriage, she had to bow to her parents' wishes. It is known from related literature that Sarala had a number of suitors; she had a particularly close relationship with Prabhat Mukhopadhyay, an eminent author,[31] who was persuaded by his mother to go abroad and study law. Swarnakumari became concerned that her daughter was going to bring bad name to the family and forced the marriage upon her. The question that must be asked is: was it right for Swarnakumari to marry off her brilliant daughter to an elderly widower and pack her off to the Punjab, thus putting an end to a career full of promise? One wonders why Sarala yielded to the pressure. Sarala does not fully explain. She only tells us that her 'hands and feet were tied' — there was no space for any movement. Perhaps daughters had not learned as yet to make their own decisions regarding their marriage. The institution

[29] It first appeared among the Brahmos. In 1881, noted journalist Krishna Kumar Mitra, married Lilabati, daughter of the Brahmo reformer Rajnarain Bose. Nirmala Majumdar met the latter day eminent doctor Nilratan Sircar, at a Brahmo gathering. They were married in 1897. See Meredith Borthwick, 'The *Bhadramahila* and the Changing Conjugal Relations in Bengal, 1850–1900', in M. Allen and S.N. Mukherjee (eds.) *Women in India and Nepal*, Canberra, 1982, p. 117. Such marriages brought severe censure. Jogendra Chandra Basu made courtship an object of satire in his novel *Radhanath*, serialized in the periodical *Janmabhumi*, December-January 1890–91, March-April 1891, June-July 1891 and October-November 1891. See also Amritalal Basu, *Bibaha Bibhrat Prahasan* (1894) and *Babu* (1894), Bhuban Mohan Sarkar, *Daktar Babu* (1875) and Rakhaldas Bhattacharya, *Suruchir Dhwaja* (1886).

[30] The marriage of Shanti Das with Humayun Kabir, the bride a Hindu, and the bridegroom a Muslim, created a stir throughout Bengal. Sucheta Majumdar married J.B. Kripalani and Aruna Ganguly married Asaf Ali. Caste distinctions as well as religious differences melted away under the banner of a common struggle against a foreign enemy.

[31] Sukumar Sen calls him 'the best known short story writer after Tagore'. Sukumar Sen, *History of Bengali Literature*, New Delhi: Sahitya Academi, 1960, p. 326.

12   *Introduction*

of marriage in India obstinately clung to tradition; it would need another fifty years to be transformed in a major way.

MOTHERHOOD

It is acknowledged that mothers traditionally had held a place of honour in Indian culture. However, glorification of motherhood as an article of faith emerged in India around the middle of the nineteenth century, as the nationalist movement and nationalist ideology began to take shape.[32] Women were assigned a specific and crucial role in rearing a special breed of men, patriotic, brave and nationalistic.[33] In middle-class families, mothers were repeatedly advised to be 'good' mothers, to look after their children and be their 'moral guide' and 'first teacher'. To quote a contemporary journal:

A child emulates the mother in everything she does. The way she moves, the way she speaks, the manner in which she conducts herself, the child quietly observes. The inner feelings of the mother, as expressed in her words and deeds, the child internalizes.[34]

However, the heavy responsibility of properly rearing a child seems to have been assigned to middle-class mothers only. Mothers from aristocratic families do not seem to have been burdened by it, however patriotic they might have been. A convention in affluent homes was that newborn children were nursed not by mothers, but by professional wet-nurses. Immediately after birth, the child was separated from the mother and was handed over to the custody of a wet nurse and a maidservant. Maidservant's arms replaced the mother's, and the child had little or no connection with the mother, thereafter. This aristocratic convention was followed at Jorasanko. Sarala complains in *Jharapata:*

We had no conception of what a mother's love could be, for no mother ever kissed us or fondled us affectionately. Our aunts, my mother's sisters,

[32] 'In India,' said Vivekananda, 'the mother is the centre of the family and our highest ideal. She is to us the representative of God, as God is the mother of the Universe.' *The Complete Works of Swami Vivekananda,* Mayavati Memorial Edition, 1962, vol. 2, pp. 506–7.

[33] See Indira Chowdhury, *The Frail Hero and Virile History: Gender and Politics of Culture in Colonial India,* Delhi: Oxford University Press, 1998.

[34] *BBP, Falgun-Chaitra,* 1313 *BS/*1906 AD, cited in Bharati Ray, 'Introduction', *Nari O Parivar,* p. 11.

were of the same mould, believed to be an inherited trait of indifference from their mother. Such, apparently, was the patriarchal canon of the daughters of rich aristocratic families. It was not so with the wives of their sons; they came from not so elevated backgrounds and arrived with plebian hearts. Their relation with their children was distinctly more intimate.

And she continues:

Lack of any assuaging gesture from my mother when I broke my teeth after a fall did not surprise me because that was not expected.

A reader of *Jharapata* would share the sadness of this second and neglected daughter of Swarnakumari. However, Sarala's was not a case out of the ordinary in the Tagore household. Rabindranath was equally neglected by his mother.

We were under the control of the servants... I wonder why we were so cruelly treated by servants... The true reason was that our entire burden was placed on them.[35]

In this context, one cannot but recall Isaac Newton's childhood. His mother left him when he was barely three. It seems then, despite the prescriptive literature of the time, that nurturing by mothers is not a requisite for the shaping of a brilliant child.

GAINFUL EMPLOYMENT

Gainful employment, denied to middle-class women for centuries, was simultaneously an effect of, and an impetus for, reshaping women's lives and thoughts in Bengal. In the nineteenth century, a few women, like Kadambini Ganguly and Kamini Ray (b. 1864), had taken up paid jobs and a handful had worked as teachers for zenana education. In the early twentieth century, indigent women, especially widows, were advised to work, but from within the home. Krishnabhabini Das wrote a series of articles detailing paying jobs that could be performed at home, while Hemantakumari Chaudhury urged needy middle-class women to take up nursing.[36]

[35] 'Jibansmriti', in *Rabindra Rachanavali*, vol. X, Govt of West Bengal, 1368 BS, pp. 9, 15.

[36] See Krishnabhabini Das's articles entitled 'Striloker Kaj' (Women's Work) in *Bamabodhini Patrika*, 1911 and Hemantakumari's piece on nursing in the journal *Antahpur*, August 1900.

14   *Introduction*

Though written by women, these were echoes of men's voices. Only one woman dared to sing a different tune; as early as 1905, Rokeya Sakhawat Hossain (b.1880)[37] demanded the right to work for women:

Why should we not have access to gainful employment? What do we lack? Are we not able-bodied, and endowed with intelligence? In fact, why should we not employ the labour and energy that we expend on domestic chores in our husbands' homes to run our own enterprises?[38]

Sarala made an attempt to chart a course different from that of other members of her family. She took up a paid job in Maharani School in Mysore, to get a feel of gainful employment, and to earn a living. However, she soon gave it up. It is believed that the reason for this was a threat of molestation;[39] *Jharapata is* silent on the point. However, we get a glimpse of the social attitude towards women's work outside the home from Chitra Deb's well-researched volume *Antahpurer Atmakatha* (An Autobiography of the Women's Quarter). She cites the sharp criticism of Sarala's attempt at paid employment by contemporary press. The magazine *Bangabasi* asked:

What was the need for women from such families to travel alone to distant places to take up a job? Surely they are not wanting in food and comforts. Why create problems for one self?[40]

Sarala was content only to experiment. She did not exhibit any concern—as Rokeya of her generation did or the *Kallol*[41] group of

[37] Rokeya Sakhawat Hossain, a brilliant author, thinker and educationist, was born in Rangpur, now in Bangladesh. Denied formal education by her father, she was taught by her brother secretly during the night. She wrote a number of articles and books, sharply criticized Muslim men for keeping women subservient, and at once scolded women for ignorance and inspired them to be educated. She founded a school in Calcutta which still survives and has grown. She is an inspiration to the women's movement in present day Bangladesh as well as in India. For details, see Bharati Ray, *Early Feminists of Colonial India: Sarala Devi Chaudhurani and Rokeya Sakhawat Hossain,* New Delhi, Oxford University Press, 2002.

[38] Rokeya Sakhawat Hossain, 'Strijatir Abanati' reprinted in Abdul Qadir, ed. *Begum Rokeya Rachanavali,* Dhaka: Bangla Academy, 1993, p. 21.

[39] Sunil Ganguly hints at this in his popular novel *Pratham Alo.*

[40] See Chitra Deb, *Antahpurer Atmakatha,* Calcutta: Ananda Publishers, 1984, p. 165.

[41] It was a journal that represented the 'new thinking' in Bengal. Gokul Nag, Buddhadeb Bose, Premendra Kumar Mitra, Achintya Sen Gupta, and a few other courageous authors belonged to the *avant garde.*

Bharati Ray 15

women began to articulate from the 1930s — for establishing women's right to gainful employment. However, in an essay published in the journal *Bharati*, Sarala justified her endeavour:

> To know oneself one must be away from the cloying atmosphere of one's home. I came to realize this when I was away and living on my own in Mysore. ... No longer am I restless like a caged bird, for I have seen the outside world and come to understand myself.[42]

Can this be taken as foreshadowing the desire of the next generation of educated women?

WOMEN'S LITERARY ACTIVITIES

Unlike paid employment outside the home, there was no frowning on women's engagement with literary activities. Writing was a gentlewomanly occupation; one could write at home; and it was not difficult to attend to domestic duties even for a serious author. For women of the time the opportunity to write and publish was of great import. First, it fulfilled their creative urge and, in the process, gave them public recognition. Second, most women's writings were read by women. Women wrote for women and shared ideas with women. Third, literature is a genre of communication which permits littérateurs to articulate ideas which one cannot express, or translate into action in real life. It offers, therefore, a hot bed for planting and germinating new, even radical, thoughts.

Of the women authors during the era, the most notable were Swarnakumari Devi — the earliest successful woman author — and Sarala Devi, her daughter. Saratkumari Chaudhurani (b. 1864) — better known as Lahorini — Krishnabhamini Das (b. 1864), who travelled to England in an unusual venture those days; Anurupa Devi (b. 1882) who became famous as the Queen of Literature and Nirupama Devi (b. 1883), a writer of great charm. Then there were women poets: Kamini Ray and Priyambada Devi (b. 1871), Girindramohini Dasi (b. 1858) and Mankumari Bose (b. 1861). Sailabala Ghosejaya (b. 1893) and Ambujasundari Dasgupta (b. 1870) were the other notable writers. They mostly published novels, essays and poems.

It is interesting to ask at this point: what did the first generation of women write about? Obviously, they all came from the middle

---

[42] Sarala Devi, 'Janmaswar', in *Bharati, Jaishtha*, 1323 *BS*, 1916 CE.

16 *Introduction*

class, and the majority of them, at the receiving end of male patronage, internalized male concepts of womanhood and echoed male views, emphasizing the nurturing role of women and the basic differences between men's and women's roles. Their writings declared almost unanimously that women should be able to read and write, learn household skills, aspire to become competent housewives and good mothers and be patient and self-sacrificing. Most of the compositions by reputed female authors such as Anurupa Devi and Nirupama Devi put across the presiding point of view and cast women in sexually defined roles. Anurupa's novel *Ma,* a bestseller, was a celebration of motherhood, and Nirupama's popular work, *Annapurna's Mandir* lauded self-sacrifice. Perhaps because they wielded powerful pens and also because they were proponents of the predominant philosophy that their works gained wide acclaim. However, some resistant voices appeared, at the end of the nineteenth century and gained stronger force in the twentieth.[43] A few women started asking questions challenging the male-oriented values. Sailabala was one of them, as was Kamini Ray.

Muslim women had also taken up the pen. Eclipsing others by far was Rokeya Sakhawat Hossain, who published the collection of outstanding articles, *Motichoor,* in 1904 and the widely read *Sultana's Dream* in 1908. Her novel *Padmarag* (1924) is an excellent piece of literature that describes her ideas and idylls. Nawab Faizunnessa Chaudhurani (b. 1847), who began to write even before Rokeya, published *Rupjalal,* partly written in prose and partly in verse, in 1876. Azizunnessa, Khairunnessa (b. 1870) and Shamsunahar Mahmud (b. 1908) were the other known names. Shamsunahar's *Rokeya Jiboni* (Life of Rokeya) was perhaps her best work.

Another category of literature, women's journals edited by women, came on the scene 1900 onwards.[44] *Antahpur* (1898) edited by Banalata Devi (b. 1880), *Bharatamahila* (1905), edited by Sarajubala Dutta, *Suprabhat* (1907) edited by Kumudini Mitra (b. 1882), followed one another in quick succession. In these journals, ordinary housewives, or first generation women learners, expressed themselves. Only occasionally well-known writers, such as Mankumari Basu, Swarnaprabha Basu, Krishnabhabini Das, and Shailabala Ghoshjaya

---

[43] To hear some of them, see Bharati Ray, 'Introduction' in *Naari O Parivar.*

[44] In the nineteenth century a few journals, edited by men, and targeting female readers, were published in Bengal, the most important of these being *Bamabodhini Patrika.*

contributed articles or poems. Established women writers, such as Nirupama Devi or Anurupa Devi, Swarnakumari or Sarala did not contribute to these journals meant primarily for zenana women. Swaranakumari herself edited the 'progressive' and prestigious journal *Bharati* for several years. *Bharati* was also edited by Hiranmoyee Devi and Sarala Devi jointly for some time, and then by Sarala Devi alone for a few years.[45] It gave free rein to Sarala's beliefs and doctrines, often unconventional.Through *Bharati* Sarala spread the message of courage and nationalism to the youth of Bengal. One must not be afraid to die, she wrote, since life was for courage, for adventure, for service to others. Mind and body were closely connected, and so a healthy, strong body was a component of a fearless mind. If and when insulted by the British, she strongly advocated, one should take action oneself and immediately, without waiting to go to a court. Such writings inspired many a young man and helped her form a young men's club imbued with these ideas, as we will see later.

MUSIC

During the period covered by *Jharapata,* there was an efflorescence of Bengali culture, not only in the realm of literature, but also in other arenas like music. Although there are a number of texts on the theory of music, not much is known about the performing techniques of those times, because, as Amlan Das Gupta has argued, the survival of sound is a 'tenuous business'.[46] Obviously, very little is known about women musicians. There is evidence, however, that classical music which was associated with places like Gwalior, Delhi, Lucknow and Benares in the late nineteenth and early twentieth centuries, moved to metropolises like Calcutta and Bombay where trade and political power created a class of patrons. Amiyanath Sanyal has written a first-hand account, *Smritir Atale,* of the musical

[45] It was in course of her editorship that she came into close contact with Swami Vivekananda, who greatly admired her, and requested her to go abroad to represent Indian womanhood and spread the message of the East to the West. 'I am a humble mendicant, an itinerant monk; I am helpless and alone. What can I do? You have the power of wealth, intellect and education; will you forego this opportunity?' wrote Vivekananda to her. *Letters of Swami Vivekananda,* Almora, 1948, p. 371.

[46] Amlan Das Gupta, 'Women and Music: The Case of North India', in Bharati Ray ed. *Women of India: Colonial and Post-Colonial Periods,* New Dehi: Sage, 2005, p. 454. I owe this paragraph to Das Gupta.

18   *Introduction*

setting of Calcutta. We know from him that Gauhar Jan and Malka Jan Agarwali were the two leading exponents of classical music during this time.

In Calcutta, the noveau riche or newly emergent babus organized musical soirees and dancing or theatrical performances during festivals like the Durga Puja and Jhulan. Most of the participants were 'baijis' or professional women artistes.[47] Gradually *kirtan, tappa* and *kavi-gan* also gained popularity. Brahmo Sangeet, patronized by Rammohun Ray and Debendranath Tagore, became increasingly popular.[48] When Rabindranath came, however, music in Bengal underwent a transformation. Of course classical music was not ignored in any way, nor that Brahma Sangeet was forgotten, but Rabindranath created a new kind of music, Rabindra Sangeet, that was a fusion of several different musical strands: Brahma Sangeet, tunes from the classical, *baul, kirtan* and even western music. His niece Sarala was extremely devoted to music. She could mesmerize people with her singing; not just that she also created enchanting music. In *Jharapata,* she claims that Rabindranath set only the first two lines of Bankim Chandra Chattopadhyay's 'Vande Mataram' to music; the rest was set to music by her.

I was passionate about music, and singing was my obsession. Deep in my heart somewhere dwelt the presiding deity of this muse to whom I paid daily homage, and in all this, guiding me as high priest was my Rabimama. Wherever I went I picked up new melodies, new musical forms. From street singers I learned their music by inviting them to sing... When my maternal grandfather occasionally resided in his Chinsura house, I would often visit him and collect from his boatmen many *baul* songs. Whenever I picked up any new song, I could not rest until Rabimama heard me.

She says that Rabindranath had a great gift of adopting her melodies, modifying them, putting words into them and creating new songs.

Musical notes created by Sarala have been compiled, but her voice has not been captured. The Gramophone Company commenced operations in India in 1902, and from the beginning of recording in India, the field attracted women artistes. One of the first to record

---

[47] See Utpala Goswami, *Kolkatar Sangeetcharcha,* Kolkata: Paschim Banga Rajya Sangeet Academy, 1991.
[48] Rammohun, too, learned and composed music. ibid, p. 71.

Bharati Ray 19

was Bai Gauhar Jan, who was quickly followed by sixteen other women. Sarala, unfortunately, was not one of them.

POLITICS

We come to politics, which was the primary interest in Sarala's life and the central theme of *Jharapata*. As is known, and as *Jharapata* accentuates, at the opening of twentieth century, Bengal witnessed two strands of nationalism — the premier and the established one, chalked out by the Indian National Congress, and the other still underground but quietly materializing, *biplabi* consciousness. Janakinath and the Tagore family were supportive of the Congress. Sarala's heart was with the *biplabis*.

One must pause here to take a quick look back, and recall that the nineteenth century social reformers and the early twentieth century nationalist leaders conceived an interesting strategy in order to meet the western cultural challenge. They devised a political contrast between the past and the present, between the East and the West. The design had three traits. First, India had a magnificent past, even if a colonized present, and 'glorious' women of admirable accomplishments and exemplary moral virtues held a high place in the 'glorious' ancient society. The 'grand' past was construed as the age of the Aryans and the 'great' women were none but the Aryan women of the upper castes. It did not matter whether or not the claim was premised on historical evidence. No one questioned if it was possible that *all* Aryan women *equally* and faithfully conformed to those *selected* qualities; it was simply asserted that they did so.[49] Second, the western civilization was materialistic

[49] We must remember, however, that in times like this when traditions are invented for fashioning, reworking, recovering, authenticating an imagined community, nation, culture or religion, proper historical evidence is not called for. It is the necessity of the invention that decides what is to be invented. Romila Thapar argues in 'Imagined Religious Communities: Ancient History and the Modern Search for a Hindu Identity', *Modern Asian Studies*, vol. 23, number 2, 1989, pp. 209–31, that the past is selectively used and interpreted when imagined religious communities are recreated. It is necessary to note that along with gender, other aspects of national life were also being reworked, and the narrative was dyed in terms of 'tradition' and indigenousness. Poetry, music, art, education, economics, all came under this umbrella. We have only to turn to the two Tagores, Rabindranath and Abanindranath, and the Hindu *Mela* for confirmation of this point.

20 *Introduction*

while the Indian was spiritual. In the material world, western civilization might be superior, but in the spiritual domain the East outshone the West. The West dominated the outer world, the beauty of the Indian soul resided inside, within the family. There lay the identity of the Indian nation. It was the Indian 'family' that had encapsulated this identity since the Aryan times, and it was the Indian women who constituted the core of the family. The *griha* (home), the seat of the family, was conceived in terms of an emotional and moral rather than a physical construct,[50] and women were valorized as the presiding deities — *grihalakshmi* — of the homes.[51] Thus an upper caste Hindu Aryan identity of Indianness was formulated which had far-reaching consequences in later history of the country [52] Third, the nationalist leaders converted their political struggle into *deshpuja* and used Hindu idioms to inspire the nation The nationalist imagining of the country as 'motherland' — opposed to the western concept of fatherland — was perhaps formally created by Bankim Chandra Chattopadhyay through his memorable song 'Vande

[50] Partha Chatterjee, 'The Nationalist Resolution of the Women's Question', in Kumkum Sangari and Sudesh Vaid, *Recasting Women,* pp. 235–43, esp. pp. 237–8.

[51] The new model of *grihalakshmi* (goddess of the home) was developed in a mixture of the old and the new to suit men colonized intellectually, but emotionally rooted to the Indian tradition. A truly good wife, it was repeatedly hammered, would be so auspicious as to mark the eternal return of the cosmic principle embodied in the Goddess Lakshmi, the goddess of domestic well-being, by whose grace the family, the extended family and the whole clan would live and prosper. In an interesting essay, Dipesh Chakravarty analyzes the concepts of Lakshmi and Alakshmi. Lakshmi symbolized *dharma* (right conduct), Alakshmi *adharma.* Lakshmi was an ideal housewife, Alakshmi either a *bibi* (westernized woman) or a *veshya* (prostitute). See Dipesh Chakravarty, 'The Difference-Deferral of a Colonial Modernity: Public Debates on Domesticity in British Bengal', in David Arnold and David Hardiman (eds.), *Subaltern Studies* VIII, Delhi: Oxford University Press, 1994.

[52] See K.N. Panikkar, 'The Intellectual History of Colonial India: Some Historiographical and Conceptual Questions', in S. Bhattacharya and Romila Thapar, eds. *Situating Indian History,* Delhi: Oxford University Press, 1986. Uma Chakravorty, 'Whatever Happened to the Vedic Dasi? Orientalism, Nationalism, and a Script for the Past', in Kumkum Sangari and Sudesh Vaid, (eds.) *Recasting Women: Essays in Colonial History,* New Delhi, Kali for Women, 1989; Partha Chatterjee, 'The Nationalist Resolution of the Women's Question', in *Recasting Women,* pp. 235–43, esp. pp. 237–8 and Dipesh Chakravarty, 'The Difference-Deferral of a Colonial Modernity: Public Debates on Domesticity in British Bengal', in David Arnold and David Hardiman (eds.), *Subaltern Studies* VIII, Delhi: Oxford University Press, 1994.

Bharati Ray 21

Mataram' (now a national song of India), which meant 'hail our mother, motherland'. The song was sung by Rabindranath at the Calcutta session of the Congress in 1896 to great effect. Abanindranath Tagore's painting of *Bharatamata* — India, a mother goddess — encapsulated this image.[53]

Sarala was a firm believer in this new creed, and *Jharapata* brings to the fore its impact on her and other Indians. Simultaneously, she was a believer in the *biplabi* tenets. She opened an *akhara* (a club-cum-gymnasium) in the compound of her own home. In order to inspire the members with ideals of heroism, she created Birashtami Utsav, Pratapaditya Utsav and the Udayaditya Utsav, one after the other.[54] For instance, during the Birashtami Utsav (started in 1902), she tells us in *Jharapata,* young men were to gather around a sword and chant a poem which contained the names of a number of heroic men, starting with Krishna. As each name was pronounced, the participants were to shower the sword with flowers. After the ritual was over, there were demonstrations of various forms of physical training and competitive games. Interestingly, the prizes for the winners were awarded by a Muslim woman, the wife of Sujatali Beg, and the teacher of the physical exercises was Professor Murtaza, also a Muslim. Sarala's initiative here was but an attempt to make a bond between the Hindus and the Muslims and to initiate the Bengali youth into the philosophy of armed revolution.[55] Her

[53] Bharati Ray, 'The Freedom Movement and Feminist Consciousness, in Bengal, 1905–29', in Bharati Ray, ed. *From the Seams of History: Essays on Indian Women,* Delhi: Oxford University Press, 1995, pp. 182–4; see also Tanika Sarkar, 'Politics and Women in Bengal — the Conditions and Meaning of Participation', *The Economic and Social History Review,* 21:1, 1984.

[54] It may be mentioned here that Pratapaditya was the last independent Bengali Hindu zamindar of Jessore, who had ventured to resist Mughal arms, and met the challenges from the Portuguese pirates. Sarala believed that the Bengalis needed to cherish this heritage of courage. Udayaditya, Pratapaditya's son, had also repeatedly fought against the Mughal army, and had died in the field of battle. Pratapaditya Utsav, however, created a rift between Sarala and her uncle Rabindranath who refused to accept Pratapaditya as the model of a hero and had indeed portrayed him in a rather uncomplimentary role in his novel *Bau Thakuranir Haat* (1882).

[55] I have argued elsewhere that Sarala was the first woman of Bengal to be involved in the *biplabi* movement, for even before the emergence of the *biplabi* movement in Bengal, she took the initiative to prepare the stage. See, for a brief analysis, Bharati Ray, *Early Feminists of Colonial India: Sarala Devi Chaudhurani and Rokeya Sakhawat Hossain,* New Delhi: Oxford University Press, 2002, pp. 8–12.

22   *Introduction*

enterprise was cut short in Bengal by her marriage with Rambhuj and sojourn into the Punjab.

Rambhuj, however, was a firebrand nationalist, and Sarala co-operated with him in his political work and helped him to edit the nationalist Urdu weekly, *Hindustan*. This phase of her life is not mentioned in *Jharapata*. Jogesh Chandra Bagal has recorded for us a few of her anti-colonial activities in the Punjab[56] and her sudden conversion to Gandhian philosophy. It is history that Gandhi appeared on the Indian scene, casting a spell of his own extraordinary variety over the classes and masses of India, who joined in thousands, the freedom movement under his leadership. Non-violence and the spinning wheel were perhaps the two most distinctive features of his philosophy. Sarala, the *biplabi*, became a votary of non-violence and the *charkha*. It is now public knowledge, thanks to Rajmohan Gandhi's book, that Gandhi became a guest at her home after the Jallianwalla Baag massacre and that a very warm relationship developed between the two.[57] It is highly likely — though no more than a conjecture can be made — that Sarala's unexpected withdrawal from the public life in 1935 was owed to some extent to Gandhi's withdrawal from her life.

GENDER

Simultaneously, with the politics of anti-colonialism, another kind of politics was, as it were, getting ready to arrive. This was the politics of the gender. Education, as mentioned earlier, stimulated the power of thinking and the urge of writing in a number of women. Some, albeit very few, of the newly educated women began to question the rules of patriarchy without, of course, comprehending its structure or nature. I have analysed elsewhere how the freedom movement made many conscious of the subjection to the colonial power as well as the subordination at home.[58]

Writing was not all. Action was being taken to advance women's position by the endeavour of women themselves (the term used

[56] See the notes by him in *Jeevaner Jharapata*.

[57] Rajmohan Gandhi, *Mohandas: A True Story of a Man, His People and an Empire*, New Delhi: Penguin Books, 2007.

[58] See 'Freedom Movement and Feminist Consciousness in Bengal', in Bharati Ray ed. *From the Seams of History: Essays on Indian Women*, New Delhi, Oxford University Press, 1995.

Bharati Ray 23

today is 'women's agency'). In nineteenth-century organizations for the 'progress' of women, such as Bamabodhini Sabha (1863) or Uttarpara Hitakari Sabha (1864) had been formed of and by men. The Arya Nari Samaj (1879) and Banga Mahila Samaj (1879), though women's associations, were spearheaded by men, and flavoured with both patriarchy and patronage. Swarnakumari Devi was the first woman to have formed a women's Samiti. Structured on the ruins of the women's branch of the Theosophical Society, the Sakhi Samiti (1885) was, however, small and short-lived. It was left to her daughter Sarala to lay the foundation of an all-India women's organization, formed by women, of women and led by women. This was the Bharat Stree Mahamandal, literally, The Great Circle of Indian Women, formed in 1910 in the Punjab, with branches in several towns of India, including Calcutta. *Jharapata* does not relate the story, and it was after Sarala's Mahamandal that women's organizations, such as the Women's India Association and All India Women's Conference at the all-India level, and Nari Shiksha Samiti or Dipali Sangha at the regional or local level were formed. However, by 1905, what we may describe as a 'womanist consciousness' was evolving. Through her articles in *Bharati,* Sarala emphasized the power of women and urged them to harness it for themselves and for all women. She was, however, in this respect, a follower of nationalist philosophy and saw contemporary women as successors of the women of ancient India, strong and capable.[59] Although the present day women's movement has serious reservations on the issue, it has to be noted that in the context of the time, such assertions contributed to women's self-confidence and mutual bonding.

RELIGION

Religion, always a complex issue, seems to have been crucial during *Jharapata* days. The Hindu-Brahmo conflict over communal identity has already been mentioned. Far more significant was the unfolding gap between the Hindus and the Muslims, although communalism had not reared its ugly head as yet. As the nationalists were invoking the Hindu imagery of motherland, among the Muslims was emerging, what I have earlier called, the 'Bengali Muslim nationalism'.[60] The

[59] See for instance, Sarala Devi, 'Bangali Paraye', *Bharati, Baishakh* 1309 *BS,* 1902 CE.

[60] See Bharati Ray, *Early Feminists,* pp. 48–50.

24 *Introduction*

movement led by Nawan Abdul Latif and Syed Amir Ali in Bengal deeply affected the mentality of the Bengali Muslims.[61] Like their Hindu-Brahmo counterparts, the new generation of western-educated Muslim men also directed their attention to reforms of the evils in the existing social system and to the revival of the Islamic heritage in its pristine form. A number of journals — *Nabanoor* (1903), *Masik Muhammadi* (1903), *Islam Pracharak* (1900), *Kohinoor* (1898), *Mihir O Sudhakar* (1889) — articulated an inspired redefinition of Islamic history and culture. A galaxy of brilliant men, such as Mir Mussaraf Hossain (b.1847), Ismail Hossain Shirazi (b.1880), Abdul Karim (b.1863), Kazi Imdadul Huq (b.1882) and Nausher Ali Khan Yusufzai (b.1864) wrote profusely and Islam formed the keynote of their writings. Nevertheless, it must be emphasized that there were men among both the Hindus and the Muslims who were committed to their unity. Sarala belonged to this group. Her autobiography is replete with such references. She regularly wrote articles in the *Bharati* urging Hindu-Muslim unity, arguing that although India had been invaded by foreigners starting with the Aryans, Indian civilization transformed outsiders into insiders. The Muslims were now insiders. Only the reactionaries among the two communities were trying to sow discord among them. They needed to engage in a joint struggle against the foreign colonial power.[62] She enlisted the support of Muslim men and women like Murtaza and Begum Sujatali in her semi-revolutionary endeavours. At the personal level, she enjoyed warm friendship with educated Muslim families — Sujatali of Bangalore, Akbar Hydari of Bombay and Syed Amir Ali of Bengal. She started learning Persian from the maulavi who taught the children of the Hydari family, with a view to reading the works of Omar Khayyam in the original Persian. She spoke Urdu fluently. She also sought Muslim support for her Mahamandal, which was open to all religions.

Sarala, was however, always attracted towards Hindu philosophy. We must remember that the movement, which for lack of a better name we need to refer to as 'Hindu Revivalism', had not died in Bengal. Ramakrishna and Vivekananda held tremendous sway over

---

[61] See Anisuzzaman, *Muslim Manas O Bangle Sahitya*, Calcutta: Muktadhara, 1971, esp. pp. 3,6, 66 and 384; Wakil Ahmed, *Unish Shatakee Bangali Muslmaner Chinta Chetanar Dhara*, Dhaka: Bangla Academy, 1983, vol. I, esp. pp. 33, 36 and 49 and vol. 2, pp. 17 and 165.

[62] See, for instance, *Bharati, Bhadra*, 1310 *BS*, 1903 CE.

the Bengali mind. Sarala was attracted by Vivekananda's philosophy, especially that of courage and moral strength. She was in Almora in the Himalayas when her sister's letter called her to Deoghar in Bihar on the pretext of their mother's illness, but really to get her married off. Later when she withdrew from public life, although born in a Brahmo family and married to an Arya Samajist, she chose a Hindu, Bijoykrishna Goswami, as her guru. This perhaps illustrates her father Janakinath's point that there was no basic dichotomy between the Hindu and Brahmo religious beliefs.

Sarala died in 1945, by which time she was almost forgotten by her contemporaries.

CONCLUSION

Jharapata thus captures for us slices of Bengal's history from political activities to the custom of marriage, from images of joint family to concepts of motherhood, from Hindu-Brahmo tension to Hindu-Muslim relationship, from the nationalist ideology regarding the youth of India, to the Indians' age-old attraction for the Himalayas. One can agree or disagree with Sarala's views and statements, one can feel that she propagated herself too much, one can criticize her for willful exaggeration or marginalization of facts, one can fault her for lack of a historical sense (hardly ever dates are mentioned, or chronology maintained), but one has to value *Jeevaner Jharapata* as a description of contemporary society and polity as seen from the 'vantage point' of a woman. It can even be read as an *oeuvre* of sociology.

All said and done, *Jharapata* can claim a threefold importance in Indian literary productions — as a piece of literature, as an autobiography of the first woman national leader of India and as an intimate history of the time. In all respects, it is a meaningful, indeed invaluable, contribution to the culture of Bengal.

THE MANY WORLDS OF SARALA DEVI

A DIARY

TRANSLATED FROM
JEEVANER JHARAPATA

SUKHENDU RAY

*In memory of my loving brother Rabi,
who left us two years ago.*

One

My life story has been reconstructed by stringing together the fallen leaves of my life. The leaves may have fallen, but they never withered and remained evergreen with the touch of human life that enlivened them.

My long journey through life, in all directions, north and south, east and west; in the morning and at night; at festive times and others; in company or by myself; during happy spells and dark days; has given me a rich and rewarding experience, shifting by turns like the wheel of fortune. This story is a record of the many people who have touched my life and left an indelible imprint, enriching my otherwise unworthy existence, and made it memorable.

On a day in the month of Bhadra — it happened to be the seventh day of the New Moon — another female grandchild of the Maharshi, daughter of a daughter, was born — me. I saw the light of the day in the usually set aside lying-in-room, used for all births in the family. It was an isolated room, located on the second floor of the huge mansion, a sort of timber structure now weather beaten with many cracks from long exposure to the elements. My birth was not greeted with any particular warm response or notice; newborn babies, at any rate, were a regular event in this large and extended family. Nevertheless, all the conventional ceremonies were ritually observed; certain other rites newly evolved for the followers of Brahmo faith including special prayers were simultaneously performed. The old custom of celebrating the eighth day of the birth

32 *The Many Worlds of Sarala Devi*

was also not ignored; sweets and other delicacies were distributed to children and their loud cheers welcomed the newborn.

Each day, according to the practice of the times, the new baby was anointed with mustard oil all over its body and laid out under the sun on a balcony adjacent to the natal room. Affluent western women apparently spend a prodigious fortune to travel to distant sea shores to indulge in what is known as sun-bathing after applying fanciful and aromatic lotions all over their bodies — all this to acquire a darkening of the skin known as 'tan'. This Indian child received the gift of this 'tan' with little expense and no trouble at all!

A convention of affluent homes those days was also rigorously followed in the Tagore home at Jorasanko — the newborn children were nursed not by their mothers but by professional wet nurses. Immediately after birth, the infant was separated from the mother and handed over into the custody of a wet nurse and maidservant. The child thereafter had little or no connection with the mother. Neither did I.

Despite many mandatory regulations in the Tagore home, a singular exception was made in the case of my mother. Before his marriage my father had made it a condition that he would not concede to the traditional custom of the Tagore family that was, to be a domiciled son-in-law in the wife's home. Earlier, on a visit to Krishnanagar to inaugurate a centre of the Brahmo Samaj, my maternal grandfather Debendranath had chanced to meet my father. He had been immediately attracted to the young, handsome and well-educated son of a local zamindar of Nadia. My father, associated with Umesh Gupta, was deeply involved in reforming a society, ridden with time-worn and blind superstitions. My grandfather chose him to be my mother's husband. His eldest daughter Saudamini had been married much earlier, according to Hindu rites, but since the marriage of his second daughter Sukumari, all the sons-in-law were inducted into the family after initiation into the Brahmo faith, and made to reside in their in-laws' home. My father refused to accept either of these conditions. A man of strict principles, he averred that there was no fundamental contradiction between the Hindu faith and Brahmo beliefs, regardless of whether one prayed to a formless God or worshipped a god in the shape of an image. Neither did he see any need for his initiation into the Brahmo faith. He also resisted vigorously the proposal to go and live in his wife's home. Grandfather relented on both these counts, and permitted my mother to live with her husband away from his home, even though my mother happened to be his most adored child.

This marriage, unfortunately, spawned another quandary for my father. His father, my paternal grandfather, was strongly opposed to his son marrying a daughter of Debendranath. He refused to recognize this marriage and disinherited my father. This was a grave predicament—both father and son were equally strong willed and hot tempered. Their family had the dubious fame of being the 'volatile Ghosals'. The heroic family was known to have bravely confronted marauding bandits. When incensed, they would fly into a violent rage, and were unbending, not accepting any compromises.

As my father had an older brother, he, the younger son, was given away in adoption to a rich uncle, an older brother of his father. But young Janakinath could not stick there even for six months; the humiliation of being adopted was too much for him. One day, without telling anybody, he left his foster family and walked back to his natal home. As a consequence, he lost the inheritance of his adopting family, but the unexpectedly premature death of his older brother made him the heir to his father, Jayachandra Ghosal. It is another matter that he lost this inheritance upon his marriage to Debendranath Tagore's daughter, who belonged to the lowly clan of Pirali Brahmins, not good enough for him. Deeply aggrieved by my father's inappropriate marriage, my paternal grandfather went on a reckless spree of squandering his fortune so that not a penny went to his renegade son.

In time, however, this tension eased, and we children did not know when and how they were reconciled. All that I remember is the picture of a fond paternal grandfather, whose occasional visits to our home were a source of great joy and happiness for us.

For nearly five years after our parents' marriage we lived in a separate home away from the Jorasanko house, but the two homes were in regular touch. Not a day went by when either my parents did not visit Jorasanko or people from Jorasanko did not come to see us.

When I was six months old, my *annaprasan* was celebrated with much display and show at the Panihati Garden House. Situated on the bank of the Ganges, the garden house then belonged to Debendranath Tagore. For that occasion, the entire Jorasanko clan moved there for the summer. The current owner of that house,

34 *The Many Worlds of Sarala Devi*

Gopaldas Chaudhuri, is a zamindar of Serpur in Mymensingh. He transferred this property to a Trust and founded a home for orphans there. It was named 'Gobindamohini Bhavan' to commemorate his late mother. Many years later after my *annaprasan* of which of course I had no memory at all, I accompanied my uncle Rabindranath when he inaugurated that home. I was visiting the house linked with my *annaprasan* for the very first time, after more than half a century. It was a wonderful place, right on the riverside, with an elegant *ghat* on which sat a sehnai troupe making music. My imaginative eye was trying to seek out that six-month-old girl dressed in a red silk sari, her forehead sporting decorative designs made with sandalwood paste. I fancied that I could almost hear the sehnai music played on that occasion. For my uncle Rabindranath, however, it was all part of his memories, not any fanciful delusion. This house, where the organizers of the inauguration ceremony had earlier made my uncle ceremonially plant a mango sapling, took him back to the recollections of an 11-year-old boy. Gone for the time being from his thoughts were the warm welcome by young girls, the presentation of the scroll of honour, and his conventional reply. It was presently replaced by the curiosity to revive the memorable day of my *annaprasan* by visiting each room, the nooks and corners of the garden, in search for a long lost 11-year-old boy. And keeping company with him was that once six-month old child relative, now grown into a mature woman with greying hair. She was the lone sympathetic listener of the animated evocations of that lost page of history.

Although my *annaprasan,* understandably, has no place in my memory, two incidents that occurred when I was about two and a half years old still remain very alive in my mind. Both these episodes were emotional — one of pleasure and the other of fear. The neighbourhood of our Sealdah home was largely dominated by the Anglo-indian community. From the bathroom of our house, through a hole in the wall that served as the drainage for outflow of water, lying on my stomach and screwing my eyes as if viewing through a telescope, I saw a young white child in the house opposite frolicking in a tin bath full of soap suds. I found that scene delightfully charming, but sadly as nothing pleasurable lasts, my *ayah* catching me thus engaged, dragged me away from this voyeuristic pleasure!

The other incident occurred when I was somewhat older, still at our Sealdah home, and this incident is deeply etched in my memory. Every evening, the children, after a wash and getting into fresh clothes, were taken for an outing in the company of servants, usually across the Sealdah railway station. Then the station was not as big as it is now, with just a few tracks, on some of which stood empty carriages waiting to be shunted. A bodyguard who always accompanied us when we went out occasionally seated us in some of the empty carriages. Once, when we three siblings were thus seated, our carriage suddenly started to move. I immediately panicked. Why was the car moving? Where were we going? To which unknown destination? My elder sister always had a wise head, and so did my brother; they did not appear to be bothered, but I, an absolute ignoramus, died with fear. They saw my horror stricken face, were highly amused and began to laugh. Our bodyguard too walked calmly alongside with a smile on his face. In a minute or two the car stopped, soothing my palpitating heart, and dousing my fright for the time being, but I never did get over this scary experience.

Our family moved from the Sealdah house to another in the locality of Simla (not the Hills but an area in Calcutta). Our house was in a lane close to what is the present day Minerva Theatre Hall. I still remember a horrific episode in that house. When I was about four years old, I slipped and rolled down the stairs from the roof down to the ground floor. In the process I broke two front teeth and my gums bled profusely. I also suffered some painful bruises on my arms and legs. Scared of the attendant maidservant I could not cry out loudly, as she had already started proclaiming her innocence at the top of her voice. It was not due to her negligence, but because of the child's recklessness, she claimed. Forget about receiving any sympathy, I was on the receiving end of much reproach and derision. My elder sister warned me somberly that I shall remain toothless all my life, and to add to my misery, the maidservants of the house portentously announced a horrendous future for me. 'You will never have a husband. Whoever wants a toothless bride?' My mother remained passive as usual; and my father came down to apply arnica to my injuries.

I have already said that almost immediately after birth, the children in our home had no connection with their mothers. Mothers were aloof, inaccessible queens. Maidservants' arms replaced mothers' arms, and we were no exceptions. We had no conception of what a mother's love could be, for no mother ever kissed us or

36   *The Many Worlds of Sarala Devi*

fondled us affectionately. Our aunts, my mother's sisters, were of the same mould. This indifference was believed to be an inherited trait from their mother. Such, apparently, was the patriarchal canon of the daughters of rich aristocratic families. It was not so with the wives of their sons; they did not come from such elevated backgrounds and had plebian hearts. Their relation with their children was distinctly more intimate. But that is another story

Lack of any assuaging gesture from my mother when I broke my teeth after that fall did not surprise me because that was expected. But, later, another incident hurt me painfully. Children do not just laugh and cry; they also develop quite early in life a sense of fair play or the lack of it. My younger sister Urmila had still not arrived in our midst, and at that point of time we were only three of us—my elder sister Hiranmoyee, my elder brother Jyotsnanath and I. My elder sister was the self-appointed leader of the pack, and full of mischievous ideas. In one of her motivated pranks she told me, 'Your hair has grown too long, let me trim it.' From nowhere she procured a large pair of scissors, and without a by-your-leave, snipped off chunks from my lovely curls. My head was now almost shorn of hair looking like an uneven patch of turf. Our parents were not at home then, and when they returned and saw me they were horrified. My furious father admonished me, 'For next seven days you must not go out of home. People will laugh when they see the state of your hair.' My mother seemingly did not disagree with him.

As a child I could not comprehend the disastrous implication that might follow people's laughter provoked by my ruined hairstyle, but the sheer injustice of my punishment hurt me deeply. My sister, who was the culprit for messing up my hair, escaped unscathed. She continued, as before, to go out in the evenings, dressed daintily, escorted by the maidservants, with her head held high. My brother kept her company, although he had also, without permission of our parents, surrendered his head to our sister. Her hairstyling skills had left equally visible signs in his unevenly cropped hair! But he was also let off, because a boy's ungainly hair was of little importance. It was only the girls who must at all times maintain decency and decorum. And of the three, I was the only one adjudged guilty, and was confined to an attic on the roof for seven days—all by myself, feeling uncommonly sorry for myself.

As the first child my elder sister was the darling of our parents,

Sukhendu Ray 37

and so was my brother as the first son, but sadly, I arrived as an unwanted daughter. I carried around me a cloak of neglect, which was lifted gradually as I came more and more in contact with the outside world.

Yes, I grew up in an atmosphere of rigid discipline and repression, not of love and affection. Even so, beyond the strictly regulated life, our Simla home remains associated with the tender memory of our paternal grandfather Jayachandra Ghosal. I have said earlier that he was a powerful rural zamindar, and whenever he came to visit us, he brought with him a fresh whiff of country air. And to our utter delight he always came bearing gifts for us—succulent jackfruits, for instance, and in the cold weather, the mouth watering delicacies of date palm molasses either in solid cakes or in jars of liquid nectar. His arrival unfolded for us that unique image of him—sitting on a bath stool, his whole body glistening with smeared oil, having an open-air bath. His arrival revived for us the tales of his derring-dos, of battling bandits bare handed. His arrival thrilled us with his adventures of foxing the police force, making his escape by boats, zigzagging through many canals, just to avoid being served with a summons to appear before a court of justice on charges of a murder in his estate. What, of course, touched me the most, deep in my heart, otherwise an arid corner, was when he addressed me as—'didi, didi'. This sweet musical sobriquet created an oasis for me in our otherwise desert-like home. Writing today I am able to analyse my feelings of those days with a fine tooth-comb, but I did not then have any sense of percipience, just a blissful aura of engulfing affection.

We had another regular visitor to our home—Pareshnath Mukhopadhyay—an uncle of ours, married to a sister of my father. He was a medical doctor in the employment of the Tripura Raj. On occasions he was accompanied by a nephew of his, Phani Bhusan Mukhopadhyay, who later married my sister Hiranmoyee.

During a particular visit of this uncle, I attained the age of five years and the traditional ceremony of *hatekhari*—initiation into reading and writing—was performed. We had a resident pandit at our home, Satish Mukhujye, whose ancestral home happened to be at the same place as our uncle. I started taking lessons from him, and in a single day, I went through the whole of the first book of primer, the Barnaparichaya. My uncle usually kept some loose change in the receptacle of his *hookah*, and on appropriate occasions

38   *The Many Worlds of Sarala Devi*

he used to reward us from this cache. My brother and sister often earned a few *annas* by pulling out his grey hairs, but lacking such skill, I was not so lucky. When my uncle was told of my feat of mastering the first primer in a single day he was so impressed that he emptied the cache in my hand. In reality it was my maidservant who was the gainer as I had to hand over my reward, all of it, to her. Until now the maidservants attached to my sister and brother had been the only beneficiaries. It was customary that any bounties that we children received were eventually confiscated by the maidservants; for some reason this was an accepted form of extortion!

Two

Just near the first floor landing of the inner quarter of our Simla home was our mother's bedroom which had a huge four–poster bed. This bed was the daily meeting place of our various Jorasanko aunts and female cousins who regularly gathered there, and whose sessions started from noon onwards. In the midst of card games they munched spicy *muri* and mouth-watering *pakoras*. It often occurred to us that perhaps this was the main purpose of these gatherings. On occasions, some variety was introduced in their programmes, such as, someone singing a song or my mother reciting her poems. We three siblings made occasional unwanted forays into her room in the hope that someone would be kind enough to pass us a fistful of *muri* or may be a *pakora* or two. Frankly they hardly ever noticed us, and in any case, we were not supposed to tarry there long. Indeed, we had to slip out almost immediately for children to be seen at the gatherings of elders was not the done thing.

This four–poster assembly of my mother's firmly implanted in my mind the idea that such bedsteads were the natural habitat of mothers in general. Mothers, I believed, never squatted on the floor. When our maidservants talked about their homes, I fancied that their mothers also rested on big beds with their legs stretched out. After all, why should their mothers be any different from ours? Of course, for fairy tale princesses and their queen mothers, it must have been altogether another world.

Even ignoring my fertile imagination of mothers of impoverished families holding forth sitting on majestic four-posters, there is no

40   *The Many Worlds of Sarala Devi*

denying that four-posters served as crucial social focus points for intimate associations of women. In fact, gatherings of women never properly bond unless they collectively sit on a bed. And this is just not true of Bengal; it is the same story all over the north and west of India

When we were at our Simla house it was decided that my father would travel to England. Shortly before he left we moved to Jorasanko to live there. Since then Jorasanko, which was my birth place, had been inextricably entwined with my life.

What does the Jorasanko House stand for? For me as well as many others? Is it merely a mansion of bricks and mortar, with doors and windows fashioned from seasoned timber, boasting of a large courtyard and a huge roof? Does it have any individual entity, an existence of its own? Does a spark charged with long-lost memories, weaving through this otherwise insensate edifice, ever animate it? With its omniscience does it at all keep a benign watchful eye on the children who are born there, play and grow up there? Does this house have any recall of those illustrious men and women, who were born and lived there, and who in their lifetime, brought glory to their family and their country and are now gone? And does it have any thoughts to spare for those others who may not have been well known but who must have basked in the glory of their illustrious ancestors, and lived here as children? Equally, does this house have any sense of gratification for those outstanding members of the family who spread their wings of leadership and influence far and wide throughout the country? And does it look with any feelings of compassion and revulsion at those whose negligence and indifference ultimately led to its near oblivion?

How sad it is to reflect upon the decline of that majestic Jorasanko mansion! In the old days this place hummed with continuous activity; it was the birthplace of new thoughts and creative ideas; a hive of intellectual liveliness; and always resonated with incomparable music. Today it is a derelict pile—bereft of any descendants of Debendranath living there—an empty shell, fouled with pigeon droppings. If any of the past residents were to return and look at the dilapidated ruin, their eyes moist, will this house also shed a tear or two in sympathy? What a magnificent edifice it was; now it is reduced to tumbledown structure, and how long will this relic also last?

Jorasanko was a place of great magnificence when as a child of five I went to live there; teeming with people, busy with endless

Sukhendu Ray 41

activities. The sons and daughters of my maternal grandfather had their own separate quarters where they lived with their respective families. And, of course, there were countless domestics, both male and female, to take care of the residents. A dozen Brahmin cooks were kept busy since early morning in the central kitchen cooking for the entire family and other residents. Cooked rice would be piled high almost touching the ceiling on one end of the huge kitchen. Also cooked were masses of vegetable dishes. Rice was the staple for midday meals, replaced by *luchis* for the evening meals.

Jorasanko had another curious system. Whenever a new child arrived, a new set of white Jaipur stoneware plates, bowls, etc., was acquired for the child. When in the process of usage and breakages this set was depleted, it was replaced by a set of black Munger stoneware. All of us ate off such stoneware plates. Shiny and polished bell metal utensils were considered infra dig, fit only for the estate employees and servants. Western style crockery made of china clay was unknown to us those days. There were no tea cups as tea was not drunk in that home. Instead we all drank milk, fetched from the common milk pool in silver bowls, especially earmarked for each child and kept in the custody of the respective child minder.

The food items that the cooks delivered at each quarter were common for all the residents, but in addition, the wives would prepare some special dishes, in their own corners, according to their own ideas or to suit the taste of their husbands. No wonder, the culinary quality of the especially prepared food was vastly superior to the food that came from the central kitchen. Later in my life whenever I heard students moaning about the insipid food at their hostels, my mind invariably went back to the food doled out from the central kitchen.

On the northern side of Jorasanko house was a large open space which was used as the granary to store rice, paddy, pulses and lentils, and other grains. Ghee, cooking oil, salt, sugar, etc., were stored elsewhere, in the charge of specially designated staff, who measured out these items to the cooks as deemed necessary. Vegetables, fruits and sweetmeats were the sole responsibility of the ladies of the house.

A gong summoned everyone at seven in the morning to assemble for prayers. The wives and married daughters would appear in their special outfit, the *cheli*, they were given at marriage. At an appropriate age unmarried grand-daughters received a gift of such *chelis* which they put on to attend the prayers. This was the symbol

42   *The Many Worlds of Sarala Devi*

of their initiation. It was not compulsory for small girls to come for the prayers, but they could if they wished to, and without the compulsion of *chelis*. Grandsons were debarred from such sessions until and unless they were initiated with the sacred thread ritual. They were, however, allowed to listen to the devotional songs, which many did. The singer those days was the legendary Bishnu *babu*.

When our maternal grandfather happened to be present, these prayer meetings and the sermons became notably lively; otherwise they were reduced to just routine chores. After the prayers, the ladies returned to their rooms, and having changed into their usual day clothes, reported for their duties at the pantry. These morning gatherings of the ladies, comprising many *mamimas* and *mashimas*, were quite congenial. Whilst the ladies would be busy chopping vegetables in the pantry which was on the first floor, down below, near the kitchen, maidservants would cut and clean the fish.

The regulars at these vegetable cutting sessions were the eldest, the third and the youngest *mashimas*, as well as the eldest, the fourth and the fifth *mamimas*. Cousins Saroja-*didi* (married eldest daughter of our eldest mama) and Sushila-*didi* (eldest daughter of our third *mashima*) also joined them. Occasionally my eldest sister joined them, but my mother, never.

Just as temples have two chambers, the outer where everyone can enter, and the inner sanctum to which only the temple's priest has access, the pantry of our aunts had divisions. The outer chamber was the place to get the vegetables ready for cooking, where anyone could go in whether they lent a hand or not in the work. The inner chamber was the exclusive domain of our eldest *mashima*. We youngsters often visited our elders in the outer chamber, where our entry was not restricted. We watched with great curiosity what went on there and listened to their talks. All the time, however, we kept our eyes open to see what was happening in the inner sanctum over which our eldest *mashima* presided. There, away from our prying eyes, were stored in jars after jars a host of tasty treats, and on certain days, the eldest *mashima* would generously distribute some of these put-away delicacies, thus winning our hearts. Her lifelong motto had been, 'never deprive anyone, give something howsoever small to everyone'. No wonder, she was so adored by all!

Whenever our maternal grandfather was in residence, some special dishes were always cooked for him in the outer chamber of the pantry. Our third *mashima* was a reputed cook. All our aunts were normally engaged in housework, but not my mother. She was always involved in her writing. Except for ceremonial occasions my mother was hardly ever seen near the pantry.

One half of the second floor of the outer quarter was my mother's domain, but the domain of her children — that is us — was far removed from there to the second floor of the inner quarter. There we existed under the absolute surveillance of maidservants. The other half of the second floor of the outer quarter was occupied by my *natun-mama* and his wife. Both these wings were ultimately inherited by Rabi-*mama* (Rabindrananth), in whose will this property passed on to Viswa-Bharati after his death. Towards the end of his life, our maternal grandfather lived in a room on this floor, and his mortal life also ended there. Long before that, another person lost her life on the same floor, and that was my *natun-mami*, much adored by Rabindranath, who tragically took her own life. My *sejo-mama* Hemendranath had also died earlier at the same place. All five children of Rabindranath were born there, of whom Rathi and Mira now live in Santiniketan; the other three are no longer alive.

All those rooms so charged with wonderful memories now remain permanently shut, devoid of any human connections, mute. The walls of these rooms have been witness to so much joy and sadness, fear and depression, love and heartbreaks. Do these sentiments, I wonder, ever try to break through these walls with a heart-rending wail? Do they wish to speak out at all?

We had no direct touch with our mother, but when we went to play with other children on the roof of her quarters we had a brief glimpse of her from a distance like an unapproachable divine being. That our mother never gave us any motherly love, never gave us any time, did not, in reality, make us unhappy. There were more reasons to be unhappy at our small Simla house, where we lived in comparatively close proximity to our parents. At Jorasanko, there was greater physical distance between our mother and us and that perhaps ameliorated the misery of separation. Nature mediates between God and the living mortals. Mortals weep or laugh, move about, mechanically, to God's wishes, but the hand that operates the machine inheres in men's nature, albeit latent, perhaps as God's agent. In a similar way, our lifestyle was regulated by our parents' ideas, but the main players there were the ambience of the Jorasanko house, the roles performed by the private tutors, hordes of male and female servants, and the company of other children. Living with them, playing games with them, maybe also fighting with them, going through many different moods, we hardly ever felt

44   *The Many Worlds of Sarala Devi*

the lack of our parents' presence in our lives. And yet, we did not grow up into boneless weaklings lacking mother's love, nor did we suffer from any self-inflicted agony of deprivation. On the other hand, we grew up into strong and able individuals.

There were two major differences in the lifestyles of us three siblings and that of the other children in the extended family. The other children did have their own assigned servants and maidservants to take care of them, but we three children were left in the absolute charge of our servants. In any event it would not have been possible for our mother to look after us even had she wished it, for the simple reason that, her own domain was in another physical part of the house. It must be admitted that our three individual attendants, in their own way, did their job well. Each attendant's aim was to seek the most preferred treatment for his or her own charge, to procure the choicest of food for their consumption, bathing them, keeping them clean and tidy, but depending on their individual nature, there were some discrepancies in the treatment of their charges in terms of severity or leniency.

My first attendant, Jadu-*dai*, did not accompany us when we moved to Jorasanko. She was a comely looking woman with a tender heart. She was very attached to me, and often visited Jorasanko to look me up, and whenever she came she always brought some delicacies for me and gave me a fond hug and kisses. As a result I became a victim of much ragging by our cousins, so much so, that I started avoiding meeting Jadu-*dai* and ran away when she came to see me. My next attendant Mangala, in contrast, was very dark hued, and spoke only Hindi. She belonged to the community of the milkmen. She took care of me, but that did not stop her from giving me severe thrashings when she felt the need to do so.

Well, all this occurred in the inner quarter of the house where we lived. In the outer quarter, in our study room, getting thrashed by our tutor was a daily event. No other children except the three of us had any resident private tutor. Our tutor lived in the premises, room and food provided. Inside the house my guardian was my maidservant, and outside, it was the private tutor, both prone to administer corporal punishment with little provocation. Mangala used her hands, whilst the torture instrument of Satish Pandit was a cylindrical ruler. If any of our cousins and I fell out, they would immediately threaten me with, 'well, we are going to speak to Mangala', or, 'wait till we report to Satish Pandit'. I, a seven year old, had warily to thread my way through these two menacing perils.

Three

Next to our study was the study of our *baro-mama*, Dwijendranath's children. Here one found Nitu-*dada*, Sudhi-*dada*, Usha-*didi* and his youngest son Kriti. Their tutor was a school 'Sir' — Brojo-*babu*, the incumbent Headmaster of Metropolitan School; witty, full of fun, and always with a smile. He was not severe with his wards; on the contrary, he would often reward them for no apparent reason at all. His quota of sternness was perhaps restricted to his schoolboys, and did not extend to his private students at our place. Whatever penalties he extracted from the erring boys of his school, such as pen knives or colour crayons, went into his pockets, and from this cache, he rewarded his private pupils. Just to see them happy was a great source of satisfaction to him.

From time to time Brojo-*babu* would walk into our study and talk to our teacher, which gave us some respite from our lessons, and we were also sometimes rewarded with his impounded treasure trove. Once, our Panditmashai, instead of making us stand in a corner, asked us to go and hide under the table. 'When Brojo-*babu* comes in, you two will pinch his feet. That will be great fun.' Forget about the humiliation of being punished, what we found most despicable was being asked to indulge in such shameless conduct. With his warped sense of humour our Panditmashai would often relate to us how in earlier times, the fertile brains of the pandits of village schools would evolve all manners of punishments compared to

46 *The Many Worlds of Sarala Devi*

which we were let off very leniently. Being struck by the ruler was no harsher than being struck by a bunch of flowers!

Besides us another set of cousins was also exposed to very rigid discipline — they were the children of our *sejo-mama*, Hemendranath. They were disciplined by their parents themselves, not by any servants or tutors. Their lives with their studies and music lessons were strictly regulated, and any deviation invited severe punishment at the hands of their father. These children had hardly any scope to mix with other children, and perhaps in their early life, were not much inclined to do so. The doors of their quarter were always firmly shut, and no one had easy access to them. As the years passed, some of them started to come out, but not all. The barriers started to break down when their eldest daughter Prativa got married to Asutosh Choudhuri. Prativa-*didi* was one of seven sisters, but none of them was close to any cousins of their own age.

Three of us girls were great friends; Suprova-*didi* — the second daughter of our *sejo-mashima*, Usha-*didi* — the youngest daughter of our *baro-mama* and I. In the evenings we would join the boys for games in the verandah next to the large hall. In that group were the two sons of our *baro-mama*, Nitu-*dada* and Sudhi-*dada*, my elder brother Jyotsnanath, and Biman-*mama*, a cousin of our mother's. Nitu-*dada* was the self-appointed leader of the pack, and he had patented a series of swear words which went like this — 'stupid — gadha (ass) — damn — shoowar (pig) — paji (wicked) — rascal — fool'. One had to say this quickly as if it were one word. The artistry in the arrangement of these words sounded like music to our ears, and we were ever tempted to shoot out these words! These swear words rained whenever there was a fight or dispute. The older boys would recite this as they rolled their iron hoops along the verandah and even sedate persons like Suprova-*didi* and Usha-*didi* were also not above occasionally reciting this 'rhyme'. But if ever I had the audacity to mouth it, I was immediately threatened by my cousins, 'What? Using foul language? Wait till we report to Satish Pandit!'

Satish Pandit was just not our tutor; in a way he was also our guardian. The first thing in the morning after we got up and had our milk was to report to him. Even if we were able to escape from the eagle eyes of our maidservants, it was impossible to evade our tutor. We may get over the hurdles inside the house, but we invariably tumbled at the hurdle of the outer house. His first job was to examine our teeth to see if we had properly brushed them. If we passed this test, well and good, otherwise a hit of the merciless ruler or some other punishment awaited us.

The pressure on our course of studies kept mounting as we approached admission to a school. Once school started we had very little time for after school games. As soon as we came home we found our Sanskrit teacher, Sashi Pandit, waiting for us. I liked my Sanskrit lessons because at this stage, we were spared the dry and tiresome drill of grammar. The stories in our primer, 'Rijupath', were taught as pieces of literature. Soon after Sashi Pandit left in came Bhim-*babu*, our music teacher. Satish Pandit ushered him into the house, for it was under his strict supervision that our entire education process was conducted.

My singing lessons commenced under the tutelage of Abja-*babu*, who succeeded Bishnu-*babu* as the principal singer of the Brahmo Samaj. Abja-*babu* had a device to explain musical beats and timings. He drew a sketch on a blackboard, and instructed us how to follow his scheme. My elder brother and sister took some time to come to grips with his training, but somehow I was quicker to grasp his ideas. I was able to sing the notes correctly as taught by Abja-*babu*, which greatly pleased him. He sent in a good report about me to mother, and for the first time, mother started to take some notice of me, but that did not mean that I was any closer to her.

Bhim-*babu*, who taught at Saurindra Mohan Tagore's school, had also some good words for me, which somehow reached my mother's ears. Thus, some aspects my education now came directly under her supervision. Mother had a piano in her room, and a European lady was engaged to give me piano lessons two days a week, which had to be, of course, in my mother's room. I enjoyed the lessons, but my mother had made a strict rule that I must practise for an hour after my lesson. This I found very tedious. My fingers began to ache, my concentration flagged, but the hour never seemed to end. It was at that point of time that Suprova-*didi* came to my rescue.

In the family, Suprova-*didi* was a unique person of great charm. Her mother, my *sejo-mashima,* was not too bothered about her children's education. I doubt if Suprova-*didi* went beyond the first primer, but in worldly matters, though untaught, she had vast wisdom and experience. She had the great gift of keeping herself informed of what was happening in the whole of this huge mansion, right from the top floor where the elders had their rooms down to the ground floor, the domain of the domestic servants. Tirelessly she roamed everywhere in the house, up and down, lord knows

48   *The Many Worlds of Sarala Devi*

how many times! Like her father, Jadunath Mukhopadhyay, she was a bundle of fun. She had no equal when it came to making gatherings lively with her repartees and sense of humour. After her marriage to a deputy magistrate, she ran some sort of a salon at her home where the local ladies assembled. Perhaps under the influence of her friends there she abandoned the Brahmo faith of her birth and became a believer in idol worship, severing her link with the Brahmo creed of non-idolatry. She eventually became a devotee of Shiva.

Suprova-*didi*'s in-laws were adherents of the Brahmo faith, and she had been married according to the Brahmo rites to Sukumar Haldar, son of Rakhaldas Haldar. This did not prevent her from following her own dictates when she broke away from the faith she was born into. To her credit, this never embarrassed her a bit and she kept up her regular visits to Jorasanko.

Our Iru-*didi*, the eldest daughter of *baro-mashima*, turned into a regular worshipper of Shiva-Durga at her in-laws' home in Kashi. She was married to Nitya Ranjan *babu,* son of Niranjan Mukhopadhyay, all of whom were devotees of Shiva-Durga. They had a Shiva temple in their home. For the first sixteen years or so after her marriage, Iru-*didi* did not visit her home in Jorasanko. When after this long gap she did step into the Jorasanko house, it was a memorable day for all of us.

Suprova-*didi* was our leader before her marriage, but she often used to get into trouble with her own mother. Having noticed my distress over piano lessons, she once told me, 'If you do not like to practise so long, then why do you do it?'

'What option do I have?' I moaned.

'Of course you have. Just advance the clock time,' she suggested.

I was too scared. 'No, I cannot do it.'

'Then I will,' she retorted.

And once during my practice session when my mother was away somewhere, Suprova-*didi* put the clock ahead by twenty minutes.

When my mother returned and looked at the clock, she immediately saw through the deception. She also knew that I could not reach the clock, and so it was not I who had tampered with it. Having spotted Suprova-*didi* earlier she surmised correctly that it was her handiwork. But Suprova was not her daughter, so she could not take her to task, and in truth, I was the guilty person, so I had to be punished. There were some others present in the room, and she asked them to leave as it would not be appropriate to discipline me in their presence. Then she gave me a slap, ever so lightly, nothing like Mangala's hard knock. For the first time I discovered how delicate my mother's nature was. She knew that to punish children in presence of other people was damaging to the children's self respect. Later in life I observed many such instances of my mother's refined gracefulness.

Nevertheless, Suprova-*didi*'s kind effort on my behalf was effective, as my mother reduced my practice time to half an hour.

I have already said that the pressure on us for school and other lessons kept mounting progressively. After school, we had Bhim-*babu* for music lessons, and when that was over it was the turn of our resident tutor to take over and coach us for our school work. This went on till nine o'clock in the evening when the gatehouse gong announced the hour, and we were released. With our eyes heavy with sleep we somehow reached our respective maidservants, who fed us and put us to bed.

Getting back to our rooms at that point of time in the evening meant that we had to skirt the sitting room of our *sejo-mama*. We were rather scared to walk past his room because it was alleged that he had once been studying to be a medical doctor and that he used to dissect cadavers in his room. He was also rumoured to keep a human skull there. So his room was believed to be haunted by spooks. Our omniscient Suprova-*didi* happened to know the antidote for phasmophobia. She told us that if we recited 'Ram, Ram', then ghosts could not harm us, and if we had something made of iron on our body, then no ghosts would dare come near us. My elder sister was safe from ghosts because by then she had started putting up her hair in a bun for which she needed hair pins. My brother, fearless as he was, was not scared of ghosts. So the only person left was poor me; I just somehow ran across the passage to my safe haven, back in my room.

Not that we always went to bed after we returned to our rooms. That was the time when our *mashimas* got together and played cards. We often trespassed into their rooms and watched them playing. In this process we also picked up some of the card games, and were occasionally allowed to play a hand or two with the *mashimas*. This was the 'night club' of the ladies until their husbands returned to their respective quarters. By my forays into this club I acquired some proficiency in a few of the card games, particularly the games known as 'Das-Pachis' and 'Binti', but did not go much beyond that. The intricacies of the card game called 'Graboo' still

50 *The Many Worlds of Sarala Devi*

remain a mystery to me. This game is somewhat like the game of 'Bridge', and in neither of these card games I acquired any skill. In any case, I never had any inclination for card games, either as a young girl or when I had grown up.

Amongst the children of the family I was closest to Usha-*didi*, the youngest daughter of our *baro-mama*. All Jorasanko children had their own groups. Amongst my contemporaries, Nitu-*dada*, Sudhi-*dada*, Bolu-*dada* belonged to one group, and the girls Sushila-*didi* and my elder sister to another. Suprova-*didi*, Usha-*didi* and I belonged to a younger group. In reality, Suprova-*didi* belonged to all the groups, which made Usha-*didi* and me close friends. I was really very attached to her. Though not a livewire like Suprova-*didi*, she was unassuming, of quiet disposition, and with no angularities. Grown ups seldom appreciate that the bond between children can be as strong as among them; Usha-*didi* and I were indeed close.

Usha-*didi*'s personal maidservant was Sankari, as Mangala was mine. Sankari was a repository of fairy tales. Whenever I could slip away from Mangala, I escaped to Usha-*didi*'s room, and climbing on to her large bed, under a mosquito net, hugging Usha-*didi*, listened entranced to Sankari's tales. Getting up early in the morning we would go to the inner garden to collect fallen *shiuli* flowers. The dried flowers were soaked in water, which was then used to dye clothes. By then Suprova-*didi* and Usha-*didi* had been promoted to *saris* while I was still in frocks. There was also another plant, *natkonay*, which grew in our garden and which was also used as dye, but for some reason, only the elders could pick them — not us children. Light *natkonay*-dyed *saris* were often the evening wear of the grown ups. We never ventured into the garden alone, always in a group, usually with Suprova-*didi* leading the way. Beyond one of the walls of the garden was Singhibagan, and we were always scared of a thief jumping over the wall from there. Apparently, according to our all-knowing Suprova-*didi*, such an incident had happened once.

On holidays, Usha-*didi* and I often shared each other's food. Her *luchis* and potato fries and my *luchis* and treacle. What great satisfaction it was when we put into each other's mouths, our mutual comestibles And one day this deep attachment of these two young girls found expression in a bizarre statement of mine. Not quite realizing the implications of what I was saying, I told Usha-*didi*, rather emotionally, that when her parents were gone she need not then stay in her room and could come and stay with us. In which case, we would always be together. I do not know how, but what I had said reached the ears of Usha-*didi's* elder sister Saroja-*didi*, and it immediately spread rapidly, and comments were flying around. 'How awful! What a wicked girl! How could she ever think of saying something like this?' and so on. No one could fathom the emotional urge that was behind the unguarded statement, an expression of unadulterated love by a child who was merely anticipating a time when they would not be separated even for a moment. I was condemned from every quarter, bringing home to me that I had done something unpardonable. It was past anybody's belief that a small child like me could even conceive of such frightful thoughts; that was the reproach on everybody's lips. For me it was nothing but an outward expression of my deeply entrenched hunger for affection. It was not surprising for someone who had no access to her mother, could not snuggle into her mother's arms, to search for a substitute anchor to which she could attach herself.

In the big house of Jorasanko the elders had everything—their sources of entertainment and amusement, their own favourites among the children, such as, our *natun-mami's* love for our younger sister Urmila. I never had the sort of love that *natun-mami* had for Urmila. If I did, then my fondness for Usha-*didi* would never have found an outlet in such a weird fashion. For the life of me, at that point of time, the gravity of my transgression was beyond my conception. It never occurred to me that my statement 'in the absence of your parents' could be taken to mean the frightful prospect of their death. How could it possibly enter my immature imagination that someone's absence might also be construed as death? Yes, I now realize death must have some tragic consequence, as underlined by the saying, 'No one even wishes death for his worst enemies!'

Death, indeed, did cloud my young life when we unexpectedly lost our little sister Urmila at a very tender age. She was the darling of our *natun-mami*, who looked after her. Being childless, her starving maternal love was heaped upon Urmila as if she were her own child. Urmila lived in their rooms and not ours.

The only time when Urmila was with us was when we went to school together, riding in the same palanquin. Other than that we hardly had any connection with her. She was two years junior to me. Very shortly after she started going to school she met with an

52 *The Many Worlds of Sarala Devi*

accident. While climbing down a spiral staircase she slipped and fell, and died of a brain concussion. Our father was then away in England.

Her death cast a dark shadow over the entire Jorasanko house. Mother remained confined to her rooms, and we were not allowed to visit her. On that dreadful day, Satish Pandit took care of us. None of the children came out to play; they all kept to their own rooms. Satish Pandit was asked to keep our mind distracted, not to tell us about the death. We were told Urmila had gone away on a holiday, and much later did we realize that she would never return.

Four

I was admitted to Bethune School when I was seven and half years old, in the juniormost class. I also happened to be the youngest of the students in my class. Lajjabati, Rajnarain Basu's daughter, who was in my class, was at least four years my senior. She became very attached to me, and treated me as if I were a plaything, like an adored doll. As I progressed each year to next higher class, I also became increasingly popular with the girls. It became embarrassing when the girls from various sections successively fell in love with me.

When we started using the school bus after the services of our family transport was withdrawn, it was a competition among my junior fellow travellers as to who would carry Sarala-*didi*'s books. During tiffin breaks in school or when we were waiting for our turn for bus trips home, the girls demanded that Sarala-*didi* either played games with them or told them English fairy tales. There were occasions when many of the girls would invite me to their homes and treat me with their favourite items of food.

I entered Bethune School at an age when we were taught from primers like *Kathamala*, and I left the school with a Bachelor of Arts degree at the age of seventeen. During these years I was fortunate enough to have countless fond friends, many of them had since become my long term companions. My association with the school continued long after I left it. I was invited regularly for many years to coach the girls in music and drama on the occasion of the school's

54 *The Many Worlds of Sarala Devi*

prize distribution ceremonies and also to dress them up for their stage presentation. My teachers were very fond of me, and after my graduation, they felicitated me with a gift of books by well-known English poets.

I have somewhat gone ahead of my story; let me get back. From our Jorasanko house we travelled to school in palanquins. The route to our school took us to Chitpore Road, from there to Baranasi Ghose Street and then to Manicktala Street. On Manicktala Street, we made the bearers halt at a particular confectioner's shop where we would buy gem biscuits and lozenges—our first thrilling shopping spree!

Palanquins were closely associated with our lives those days. A few of our own family palanquins were always standing at the outhouse, ready for use. All one had to do was to summon the bearers from their quarters.

Off Baranasi Ghose Street there was another street, Chasa-Dhopapara, where resided our mother's *mama* and *mami* with their children. One of our favourite outings was to visit them on holidays by hiring a palanquin for a sum of two annas. As soon as we could lay our hands on this bit of money, prospects of a merry time beckoned us to their house, and once there, we soaked ourselves in the convivial atmosphere of that place. It was a small two-storey house, with a small courtyard, a small pavilion for *puja,* a small roof—everything was small in this house—and presiding over all this, was our mother's *mami-ma*—a large-hearted, simple-minded woman who was not particularly good-looking but who was always smiling, and was a great aunt for us. Mother's *mama,* who belonged to the Pirali clan of Jessore, was a handsome man with very fair complexion. He kept to himself in the ground floor room. Their eldest daughter, Binoda-*masi,* was of the same age as our youngest *masi,* Barnakumari, and they were great friends. Their eldest son was of the same age as our Nitu-*dada.*

But what did we do there? We romped and rollicked, sang songs and made music, aped the dramatic performances of our elders. We had with us another distant female cousin, and we derived wicked pleasure by ragging her to sing for which she had no talent at all. We used to laugh at her performance, taking care that she should not stumble on to the truth. In all of this, our usual leader was Saroja-*didi,* or someone else in her absence. This distant cousin of ours needed very little urging to break into songs, and when she was at it, everyone present went into fits of mischievous laughter. We had a good cover-up too: the initiator of the mischief feigned that one of the younger boys had played a prank by tickling her, and pointed an accusing finger at the innocent lad, which excused her laughter at the cost of the poor singer, who had, of course, no clue that she had been the butt of all this malicious fun. There is something else that I remember about this family. We, the younger children, somehow received the impression that they were not well off, and that it was rather difficult for them to maintain this large household on their meagre income. Clearly, we gained this knowledge from what our elders told us, and so, even as children we had the sense of responsibility that we must in no way impose any financial burden on them. Whenever we visited them we carried some foodstuff, bought with our own money, to save any embarrassment to our great aunt. These visits to Chasa-Dhopapara home were a regular part of our life during our school days. Of course, as we grew older this bond slackened. This great aunt was later replaced by another great aunt, and she was the mother of our *mejo-mami*. We often visited this great aunt with the children of *mejo-mami* after she returned from England.

I was not a particularly industrious student, but because of the coaching that we received at home from our *Panditmashai*, I did reasonably well in school. My schooling opened the door for some contact with my mother. I recall one particular incident. To test my proficiency in English grammar my mother asked me. 'Is Ganga (the river Ganges) a common or proper noun?' I promptly answered, 'A common noun.' Mohini-*babu*, Saroja-*didi*'s husband who happened to be present there, said, 'Wrong. You do not seem to have learned anything!'

I was rattled. I knew that I did not make a mistake, and so asked, 'But how am I wrong? Ganga means a river, so it has to be a common noun?'

The maidservants at home used the word Ganga as a generic term for a river, and that was deeply entrenched in my mind. I could not, however, make this point clear to my mother, and so when I was told that I had made a mistake, I was quite unhappy. I was confident that my answer was correct, and yet they said that I was wrong!

Later, when I went to Punjab after my marriage, I found that the women there also used the term Ganga for any river. So, in a

56 *The Many Worlds of Sarala Devi*

sense, I was not wrong, because Ganga could both be a common noun and a proper noun, and arguably, therefore, neither were my seniors when they had said that I had made a mistake!

Although not too bad in studies I had no inclination for needlework and stitching. In my later life I regretted my mistake of neglecting sewing lessons. For sewing lessons, the entire class moved to a lecture room with a gallery, where the girls assiduously bent over their assignments. I climbed to the top of the gallery, hardly paid any attention to the lessons, and kept talking. On one occasion I was chatting animatedly with another girl when the teacher, Miss Mukherjee, came up and before I knew it, gave me a ringing slap to punish me for indiscipline. Like my Mangala maid, this Christian lady teacher was well known for her blows and slaps. Once she had slapped a girl so hard that she had left the marks of her fingers on the victim's cheek. On a complaint to the School Committee by the girl's guardians the poor teacher lost her job. No one else had ever punished me in school; on the contrary I had received a lot of love and affection from all. May be because of that I did not do so badly at school even though I did not concentrate all that much on my studies. It was also possible that the insensitive attitude of our sewing teacher deterred me from taking any interest in that subject.

Later, in a higher class, the arrival of a studious girl opened my eyes to what application could achieve. This girl was Hemaprabha, a sister of Jagadish Chandra Bose. She topped the class from the time she came; there was no question of anyone out-performing her. Soon she and I became great friends. Occasionally, with the permission of her elder sister Labanya-*didi*, she used to come to our home to spend some weekends, away from her school hostel where she was a boarder. We had just about moved to our Kashiabagan home from Jorasanko. We also had other visitors to our home, namely, my elder sister's friend Shaila, also known as Khusi, a daughter of Durgamohan Das; Hem, Shibnath Shastri's daughter; and another schoolmate of mine Hemanta, daughter of the Lahore resident Nabin Ray. Indeed, we had a large circle of friends.

Five

By the time we moved to our Kashiabagan home from Jorasanko, our *mejo-mami* and her family had already returned from England. My *mejo-mama*, Satyendranath Tagore, was the first Indian member of the Indian Civil Service, and was posted to Bombay Province. Their children, son Suren and daughter Bibi, spoke in English, their manners were also English, and with them came their servant, Rama, rigged up in livery. All this caused great deal of curious amusement for us. Indira's nickname, Bibi, was also an import from Bombay.

With them had arrived another companion, and that was a lovely little Japanese lapdog, which they had acquired in the French city of Nice. It was a white furry creature, and we all fought to take him up in our arms and fondle him. He used to protest by baring his teeth but would soon calm down.

Suren and Bibi were always dressed in English clothes that they had brought from England, but the mode of dress for Jorasanko children had remained traditional—shorts and a loose upper garment, both made of cotton. For school, we had special frocks stitched by our local tailors, of no style at all. The earlier practice of Afghan type breeches was discontinued after Iru-*didi* and Indu-*didi,* daughters of our *baro-mashima*, grew up.

Our usual relaxation in the evenings was to go up to the terrace of the outer house. But Suren and Bibi who, having just returned from England, were taken out to the Eden Gardens by Rama. By

58   *The Many Worlds of Sarala Devi*

turns, one child would be allowed to accompany them. Then my turn came one day. My sister and I had two new dresses; mine was of Swiss muslin adorned with coloured ribbons. My sister had had some occasions to put on her new dress, but so far I had had none. For this outing to the Eden Gardens, I put on my new outfit, and waited in the veranda of the south wing of the house for Rama to collect me. Suddenly, Satish Pandit spotted me.

'Where are you going dressed up like this?' he asked.

'To the Eden Gardens with Suren and Bibi.'

'And who permitted you?'

'My mother', I said.

'Is that so? But I was not asked. And without my permission you cannot go. Return to your room, to your maidservant, and change your clothes,' he commanded.

With tears in my eyes I returned to my room. It never occurred to me that Satish Pandit could not have any authority to countermand my mother's decision. When much later I told my mother, she said, 'But why did you not come and tell me then?' Perhaps my brother and sister were aware that our mother was the Supreme Court where one could appeal against the verdict of Satish Pandit. I now ponder and wonder how, even with the cruel dispensations of a despotic dictator, we were still able to make space for ourselves to have a joyful childhood. May be the innate stability of a child's mind accounts for the ability to overcome heartaches.

Suren and Bibi were admitted to English medium schools, Suren to St. Xaviers and Bibi to Loreto Convent, while my brother and I were sent to Indian schools. Even so, both the pairs of siblings became good friends. Our cultural affinity was formed by the ambience of our Jorasanko home. At the beginning, though, there were a lot of differences between their tastes and ideals and ours. Bethune School inculcated in me a love for our country. *Natun-mama* once offered to take us to a circus. Two circus shows were on at the same time in town, one by a Bengali troupe and the other run by a foreign party. I suggested that we go the Bengali show, but our freshly returned-from-England cousins protested. 'We believe it is rather a dirty place,' they sniggered. 'So what?' I said rebutting them, 'a group of Bengalis has, with so much difficulties, put up a show, surely we ought to support it.' *Natun-mama* being a nationalist took us eventually to the Bengali circus. Later, when Suren and Bibi grew up, they progressively absorbed the Indian culture;

the creation of the Hindustan Co-operative Insurance Company was Suren's nationalistic venture.

Meanwhile, our nationalistic feelings were increasingly fanned under the guidance and influence of some senior girls in the school. Notably among them were Kamini-*didi* and Abala-*didi*—later Kamini Ray, the poet and Lady Abala Basu (wife of Jagadish Chandra Basu). Their instructions were filtered to us through my elder sister and her classmates. Not that we always understood the point of such instructions, nevertheless we faithfully obeyed them. When Suren Bannerjee was sentenced to a term in prison, we all tied black bands on our sleeves. Why I really did not know then, but when I saw similar black bands sported by many other school children, I experienced a spark of empathy with them. And it gave us the feeling that we were involved in some very momentous activity.

I was selected as one of the 'flower girls' who were to welcome Lord Ripon on his arrival at Calcutta. All the selected girls, wearing similar uniforms, supplied by the Reception Committee, were lined up at the Howrah Station, each carrying a basket of flowers. When the train carrying Lord Ripon arrived and he got down, the flower girls showered flowers on him. At the age of nine, it was my first participation in a public function. The main moving spirit behind this show was the barrister, Girija Sankar Dey, whose younger sister was a classmate of mine. His elder sister Mohini Devi is presently a Congress leader.

With *mejo-mami* and her family our Rabi-*mama* also returned home from his first ever visit to England. He came to my life through our mutual interest in music. I quote below, with minor alterations, from an article that I wrote in this connection.

Rabi-*mama* is gradually assuming a leading role at our home in the field of music, song, drama, etc. Earlier it was *natun-mama*—Jyotirindra Nath Tagore—who was the principal torchbearer for such activities. During Rabindranath's absence away in England, Basontotsav, a dance-drama written by my mother was staged under the direction of Jyotirindranath. A massive musical wave then held sway throughout our home, and, even we children, in imitation of our seniors, regaled in our efforts to sing snatches of some of the songs of that dance-drama. Looking back, I realize that Basontotsav was indeed a unique creation. It was not a product of someone like Rabi-*mama*, structured from the various streams of European music that he had the opportunity to imbibe abroad. It was, on the other hand, the creative work by a home-bound woman who composed it all

60 *The Many Worlds of Sarala Devi*

sitting at home. It is comparable only to the best of compositions by earlier poets of India. The sponsorship of well wishers that helped Rabindranath from his young age was missing to lend support to this production. Sadly this dance-drama was denied its due recognition in the country. Many years later when I visited Tripura, invited by Raja Birendra Manikya, I was most moved by a special performance of this play in the private chambers of the palace, in which the ladies of the court appeared in the various roles and which was produced under the direction of the Raja himself.

The ground was ready for Rabindranath; all that he had to do was to sow new seeds for fresh creative activities. The very first effort was the staging of a dance-drama, in which the roles of Indra and Sachi were enacted respectively by *natun-mama* and *natun-mami*, and Rabindranath played the character of Basanta. The name of this new dance-drama was Manmoyee, authored by *natun-mama*.

Our next programme was to organize a cultural get-together on the occasion of the Saraswati Puja. A makeshift stage was erected on the terrace, and in the presence of a large number of invited guests, Rabindranath's 'Balmiki Prativa' was mounted to much applause. This was the first public unveiling of Rabindranath's talent.

Although the seniors in the family were generally behind the literary and musical ventures, we juniors were forever eager to drink at the fountain of all such cultural activities. Often imitating our elders, we youngsters would band together and put up our own shows. Our leader in all such efforts was Sudhi-*dada*, son of our *baro-mama*, Dwijendranath Tagore. He used to take the role of Balmiki, successfully emulating Rabindranath. He was able to model his handwriting on Rabindranath's with a fair degree of competence. Remember, Rabindranath was not, at that point of time, the famous present-day Rabindranath with thousands of young admirers trying to copy his calligraphy.

Thus, progressively we came under the influence of Rabi-*mama* for our interest in music, though not necessarily directly, except when we participated in the celebration of the 11th Magh Festival. Until then, musical rehearsals for this festival were held under the joint supervision of *baro-mama*, *natun-mama*, and when he could come from Bombay, *mejo-mama*. After his return from England, Rabindranath took over as the sole leader of this function. Along with his elder brothers he continued to write new devotional songs, set the lyrics to music based partly on what he learnt from music masters, and partly on his own devised melodies, which he then taught others. Yes, this was our all-comprehensive Rabi-*mama*. From

Sukhendu Ray 61

this time onwards the youngsters of the family were included to participate in the music on the occasion of the 11th Magh Festival. Until then, only veteran singers like Akhshay-*babu* and others like him sang at this festival; the only exception being Pratibha-*didi*, daughter of our *sejo-mama*, who occasionally found a place in it. We had an early indication of the painstaking thoroughness and skill that marked Rabindranath's later life. No longer did we have to wait for the printed sheets of music, because he would laboriously copy in his own hand the relevant songs, and distribute the respective piece to each participant to commence rehearsals. Meanwhile, he would get to work with the Adi Brahmo Samaj Press and arrange to procure a number of proof copies of the songs, to be used by the singers. The rigorous process of training then followed under his tutelage.

The religious songs of the Brahmo Samaj those days were in praise of monotheism, literally emulating the verses of the Upanishadas, which were far too inscrutable for our young minds to appreciate. Rabi-*mama*'s regime wrought a transformation. His music, solemnity combined with harmony, had an indescribably stirring effect in the hearts of young persons like us. We may or may not have fully comprehended the significance of his songs; nevertheless the songs were a source of surging joy for us. I recall a particular song that moved me the most when I was a child of nine years, which went like this, 'Must I then turn back with a weary mien, my friend/To return once again to this dismal existence.'

Not just devotional songs, but songs conveying many moods, many sentiments, came to be a part of our musical repertoire. Along with the Indian music that we were taught at home, Rabi-*mama* was the moving spirit behind our instruction in western music by European lady teachers. Just about then I developed a natural flair to set Bengali lyrics to western melody by applying the theory of harmony. Rabi-*mama* then set a task for us: to turn his poem 'Nirjharer Swapnabhanga' into a piano piece. Only I succeeded in doing this. I still recall with what intense absorption he drilled me into this task. He explained to me, with focused profundity, the significance of the poem, and then guided me to structure the rhythm and the music. It was an unforgettable experience that took me to ecstatic heights!

On my twelfth birthday Rabi-*mama* arrived unannounced at our Kashiabagan home, carrying with him a book of blank western music score sheets. The cover had the legend in large bold letters:

62 *The Many Worlds of Sarala Devi*

'SOCATORE — COMPOSED BY SARALA'. 'Socatore Oi Kandichhe sakale' [Mournfully they are all lamenting] — is a devotional Brahmo song composed by Rabi-*mama*, which I had turned into a western musical piece. This could be played on a piano or by an orchestra. Those who are not familiar with this particular song would never believe that it is really an Indian song, but those who are would be simultaneously surprised and delighted to recognize the identity of the original melody expressed via a harmonic blend of contrasting western music.

The western score of this music had stuck deep roots in my memory, and I could play it by the ear whenever I had the occasion to do so. Rabi-*mama*, in presenting the notation book, told me, 'Write it down, or you may forget it.' I did copy down the score, but with the passage of time I also forgot all about it. Finally, somewhere down the line, I lost the book, like so many other losses in my life.

Thereafter I set many other lyrics of Rabindranath to the western style of music, as I did for some of my own lyrics. Though basically Indian songs, they presented a harmonious blend with a touch of western musical form. All these songs were taught to many others and were sung at various musical gatherings. The difficult task of transcribing the songs into western notations was undertaken by Indira, daughter of our *mejo-mama*. These notations were never published either because no suitable printers were available or, may be, due to lack of any great enthusiasm on my part.

Until early teen-age, children are like oil lamps, that need to be tended by grown-ups to keep them going. No young person with burning ambition can achieve the desired goal without the active encouragement of the elders, regardless of how inspired she or he might be. If the inspiration is not sustained and fades away, then the individual ceases to be motivated. In my case, my parents did nothing to encourage me to come out of my shell, to promote my aptitude for music and writing, or show any enterprise to get my music and writings published. This will explain why all my writings still remain confined to the pages of the *Bharati* magazine, and my songs in manuscript form in my notebook, except when they are sung.

My literary outputs were printed in all manners of journals — dailies, weeklies, monthlies — but never came out between two covers to find a place in homes. The exceptions are: a collection of my short stories called 'Nababarsher Swapna' [New Year Dreams], brought out by the publishers Gurudas Chattopaddhya & Co, priced at eight *annas*; some of my talks in English and Bengali at

Sukhendu Ray 63

various meetings and conferences; two pamphlets in the 'Heroes of Bengal' series and a couple of recently published spiritual books. When at Lahore I made some unsuccessful efforts to get some of my writings printed. I also wasted some money when a book of my poetry was partly printed and then abandoned.

I was passionate about music, and singing was my obsession. Deep in my heart somewhere, there dwelt the presiding deity of music to whom I paid daily homage, and in all this, guiding me as the high priest, was my Rabi-*mama*. Wherever I went I picked up new melodies, new musical forms. From street singers I learned their music by inviting them to sing for me and remunerating them for their trouble. Even now I retain that interest.

When my maternal grandfather occasionally resided in his Chinsura house, I would visit him and collect many *baul* songs from his boatmen. Whenever I picked up any new song, I could not rest until Rabi-*mama* had heard me, for there was none to match him in his knowledge and appreciation of music. He had the great gift of adopting my melodies, modifying them, putting words into them and creating new songs.

Later, when I returned from Mysore after my teaching job, I had a rich haul of uniquely different types of music, and I was impatient until I could present my collection to Rabi-*mama*. And he in his own inimitable style, re-arranged these melodies and set the music to his own lyrics, and many of his now popular songs are based on my Mysore collection. Indeed, most gratifying for me!

At the core of my collection of music was the urge to offer it to Rabi-*mama*, because no one appreciated such gifts as he did. It is futile to waste a precious gift on someone who hardly values it.

The first two lines of the song 'Vande Mataram' were set to music by Rabi-*mama*. He asked me to score the music for the rest of this song, which I did. He was very pleased, and since then this song has gained in popularity.

My taste in literature also was initiated and inspired by Rabi-*mama*. It was he who opened up for me the magic windows of Mathew Arnold, Browning, Keats, Shelley and many others. I remember well a long stay at our house in Darjeeling, when in the evenings, he would fascinatingly read to us from Browning's 'Blot in the Scutcheon (sic)', and expound it word by word. Around that time, he was bedridden with a painful blister on his back when he began composing his dance drama 'Mayar Khela'. Each day he would pen a lyric or two, and immediately coach me to render those songs.

Six

I recall accompanying Rabi-*mama* to a meeting, which was my first ever attendance at a public meeting. I was really excited. Others who also were at the meeting included Suren, Bibi, Sudhi-*dada,* Bolu-*dada,* et al. The venue of this meeting was the hall of the Adi Brahmo Samaj; the purpose was for Rabindranath to protest against an observation of Bankimchandra. Bankim was then in the high noon of his name and fame, whilst Rabindranath was just about getting to be known. This meeting had raised considerable interest among the public. Rabindranath those days was known, if at all, for his songs, but at this meeting, the way he drew the attention of the audience with cogent arguments of his talk was astonishing.

The dispute, in brief, was this: Rabindranath's contention was that under no circumstances could truth be compromised, regardless of certain scriptural sanctions allowing for prevarications in certain situations, which Bankim accepted but Rabindranath did not. Rabindranath's two elder brothers sided with Bankim on this issue, and so they did not go to his meeting, but the younger generation after listening to him, began to hero-worship him.

The theme of this debate is indeed most sensitive, and remains perpetually a controversial issue. With an uncompromising stand in his speech, Rabindranath seemed to have discovered Bankim's 'Achilles' Heel' where he tried to target Bankim. This talk of Rabindranath came out in an issue of *Bharati*, and I am sure it must have found place in some collections of his writings published by Viswa-Bharati. Sadly, there is no organization to keep alive Bankim's contributions for the Bengalis. He was not just a great novelist; he was, in the truest sense, a 'modernist' who rose above the then contemporary beliefs and conventions. With his prodigious intellectual and profound analytical power, he was truly a man of the advanced age. The present generation may not be aware of it, but he was, in a sense, Rabindranath's 'guru' and his path-finder.

Rabindranath's uncompromising attitude to truth, expounded in his speech, made a profound impression on the younger generation like us, and loyalty to the truth became indelibly etched deep in our hearts. This lesson must be inculcated early in the minds of children, and they must be instructed in this code of conduct. To talk to them about exceptions will mislead their unformed minds to seek shelter under this latitude and take recourse to untruths and deceptive stances. A story goes that Vidyasagar once caught a student of his school lying. He told the student, 'Child, this school is no place for you. You better go and sit with the lawyers in Alipore Court.'

Regardless of age, all human beings have certain high ideals deep inside them. I recall having read in a British military manual: 'Soldiers must not be directed by commands only. It is important to appeal to their instinctive ideals to motivate them to beat the enemies.' In truth lies the ultimate virtue, and yet, there could be circumstances where a departure from the truth can be regarded as another facet of righteous conduct, and so acceptable. This is what some scriptural authorities tell us. The line between truth and untruth is well-defined, even so there may be mitigating situations where some compromises are inevitable and permissible in the interest of certain noble motives. This is the message that Bankim tried to impart to us through his writings on Lord Krishna. Later, when I grew up and was able to think for myself, I realized that, swayed by Rabindranath on that occasion, I was unfair to Bankim. My excessive adulation for Rabi-*mama* made me an adversary of Bankim, unnecessarily.

Seven

Bankim came to my life, if only by name, the day when Rabindranath spoke against him, disputing his views. When I was a little older my first initiation into Bankim's literature was through his novel, *Indira*, at our Kashiabagan home. I enjoyed it immensely, and subsequently I was permitted to read his other books. The sparkle of his genius progressively became a source of my intellectual enrichment.

Once at a Maghotsav festival when the children of the family were in the midst of a song, we heard some sort of a commotion behind us. Apparently, someone had arrived. Turning back I observed a person—sharp-nosed, keen bright eyes, with a radiant smiling face, decidedly distinctive. This was Bankim. Till then Bankim was just an image for me whom I knew through his writings, and for the first time that day I met the actual person in flesh and blood.

My subsequent direct contact with him was when he wrote to me after he had read something I had just written. This was no ordinary letter; it was a letter that carried the stamp of his inimitable style. He wrote complimenting me when he read my two pieces, 'Ratibilap' and 'Malabikagnimitra', printed in the magazine *Bharati*. I was then nineteen years old. That letter was his verdict on a writer who then stood at the threshold of literature; in fact more, it was a welcome to a new entrant with extended arms. Rabi-*mama* had also written expressing his appreciation, but at that point of time, I felt more gratified by Bankim's approbation than my uncle's.

Bankim, in those days, was a sort of uncrowned king and the supreme arbiter of Bengali literature. The appreciation of these two persons at that stage of my literary life provided me with precisely the inspiration that I needed to set me off on my journey to a literary career. Tragically, I have lost both these letters. My wish to gift these letters for preservation to an archive has been frustrated. Perhaps the presiding deity who directs my life must have ordained for me, 'Go ahead, enjoy your life to the hilt. Nourish it with all the pleasures that come your way; give no thought to the future.'

During the political turbulence in Punjab all my letters so earnestly preserved were put to the torch. Afraid that I may be arrested, during my absence one day at my home, my many friends and well-wishers in their desire to protect me, destroyed all my preserved letters by burning them. These included letters and writings in Bengali, as well as letters in English which I had kept separately locked in a box. These were from Cambridge University-based Monomohan Ghose, rich in poetic lyricism; the Saint Tirtharam's philosophic letters that had a tinge of patriotic flavour; and also included in them was a bunch of letters from Justice Woodruff — very informative and inspired by his thoughts on *Tantra*. All these were consigned to flames, unknown to me, by my well-wishers. A very large part of my married life in Punjab was like living in a war camp. Move forward, and scorch everything left behind!

To many of his friends, like Srish Majumdar, Bankim had written expressing his appreciative views on my writings, which were in turn quoted by the recipients in their own writings on Bankim. But there is a world of difference between Bankim's letters and the letters from others. Bankim's letters were by themselves gems of literature, written in his own imitable elegance. He did not agree with what I said about the Court Jester. He picked this up and made some very highly amusing witty comments in support of the Court Jester. That letter of his was truly a masterpiece. Sadly, in its battle against the muse of literature the demon of politics succeeded in destroying an object of sublime art!

Along with his letters Bankim also gifted me a set of his books — an unexpected and invaluable token of affection. And I could not even retain these books, inscribed to me in his own hand, till the end of my life. Many Bengali residents in Punjab as well as visitors borrowed these books, and following the universal practice, never returned the books. The wife of the well-known medical doctor Colonel Denham White told us this story of a friend of theirs, on

68 *The Many Worlds of Sarala Devi*

whose tomb was engraved — 'He returned books.' None of my friends who borrowed my Bankim books deserved this epitaph. In the process, I lost my entire priceless Bankim collection.

Following the gift of his books, Bankim came to visit us, invited by my parents. This was my very first contact with Bankim, the man. I recall he liked drinking good tea, and my father happened to be a connoisseur of tea. Bankim relished the tea served at our home, and the very next day, that special brand of tea accompanied by a bouquet of roses went as a gift to him from us. Set against Bankim's books, a packet of Darjeeling tea can hardly be comparable as a gift, but to my mind, in terms of expression of affection and regard, it was on par.

On the very first day we met he asked me to set his song, 'Sadher Tarani', to music. The way this song was rendered in theatre hall performances did not measure up to his idea. I agreed, and later when he listened to the melody I had composed, he was delighted. The notation for this song is included in my book of music, 'Shatagan'.

Shortly thereafter Bankim invited my mother and me — my elder sister had been married by then — to visit their home. This was the beginning of a close friendship with his wife. Bankim's conversation with his wife and his manner of relating to her always created an atmosphere of lighthearted but intimate fun. I thought that we were playing roles as characters in his novel. Very soon accompanied by his two grandsons, children of their daughter, he and his wife became frequent visitors to our Kashiabagan home.

Not just Bankim, many other distinguished persons visited our home. My great admiration for him occasionally fetched the great Vidyasagar to our home. Both my parents being keen theosophists, Madam Blavatsky and Colonel Olcot visited us regularly. Dwijendra Lal Ray often came to see us, as did Asutosh Chaudhury, Loken Palit and many other members of the Jorasanko family with their numerous friends. For me that house is loaded with many happy memories, but where is that house of ours now, the house that was the hub of so many distinguished visitors? Razed to the ground, reduced to dust on its site on Raja Dinendra Street. The garden of that house was a great attraction for our Jorasanko family; its arbours; its flower and fruit trees; its pond to which came the neighbourhood wives and daughters to collect water, with the tinkling music of their ankle bells; the pond in which the poet Rabindranath would plunge for a swim and then get out to compose new poems and

Sukhendu Ray 69

lyrics. And the large attic room in which our eldest *mama* with his profound wisdom sat immersed in tranquil meditation. All of it has now been crushed under the steam rollers of the municipal corporation, and is gone for ever.

Speaking about Bankim it is impossible not to think of 'Vande Mataram', which is a mantra now. My adulation for Bankim did not lead me to that song; my Rabi-*mama* did it. In the early stages of his life Rabindranath was very open to appreciate and accept poetry and music composed by others. If he liked someone's poem, he would promptly compose the music for it, sing it himself and teach others. This was the way he popularized other peoples' creations. He had set to music many verses of *vaisnava* literature, and also many poems of Biharilal Chakravarty. In fact, in his 'Balmiki Prativa', he included a song by Biharilal.

The first two lines of 'Vande Mataram' were set to music by Rabindranath, and still continue to be sung in his tune. One day my uncle asked me to score the music for the rest of the song. I accepted his invitation, and keeping in mind the tenor of the song, and in consonance with the music composed for the first two lines by Rabindranath, I managed to write the music that I was asked to. I taught this song to many others and it has been sung in a chorus at many national events. Ever since, the song in my music score has continued to gain in popularity.

The words 'Vande Mataram' had already gained the status of a cult mantra when I was received at the Mymensingh Railway station by the members of the Suhrid Samiti. They carried me in a procession to the venue of their meeting, shouting 'Vande Mataram' all through the journey. Originating in Bengal, this mantra quickly spread its wings all over the country. This mantra became symbolic from the Himalayas in the north to the Cape Comorin in the south when the then Governor of Bengal embarked upon a reign of terror in East Bengal.

After my marriage I once went to Benares to attend a session of the National Congress. Gokhale was then the president of the Congress. I was sitting separately with the ladies in the upper gallery of a makeshift structure at the venue of the session. Seated next to me was Lady Abala Bose. Gokhale received an unexpected request from some of the attending delegates to ask me to sing the 'Vande Mataram'. Gokhale was troubled. Earlier the singing of 'Vande Mataram' had been proscribed in Bengal by the provincial government. Being a cautious person he did not wish to flout any

70 *The Many Worlds of Sarala Devi*

government injunction; he would rather play safe by observing the law. But he was also helpless; he found it very difficult to resist the intense desire of so many delegates assembled from all corners of India to hear me singing the 'Vande Mataram'. Gokhale eventually sent me a note asking me to sing, but he suggested that due to the paucity of time, I should render a shortened version instead of the entire song. I had no idea if Gokhale had in mind the deletion of any particular parts of the song. In any case I sang an edited version of it as I thought suitable, but replaced the words 'sapta koti' with 'tringsa koti'. (Sapta koti or seventy million referred to the then population of Bengal whereas tringsa koti or three hundred million was the population of India). The song on that occasion created a sensation, and many of the delegates who attended the session and who are still alive remember this song till today.

The Congress has since endorsed a shortened version of this song, and the truncated version in no way has vitiated the shining spirit of the song.

The day I came to know about Bankim's death, I felt that a part of my life had been extinguished.

Eight

'Birthdays', rather observation of birthday anniversaries, were unknown to us until our *mejo-mami* returned from England and started celebrating the birthdays of her children, Suren and Bibi, following the practice in the West. Occasions of birthdays did not call for any celebrations till then for anyone in our extended family. To my knowledge no religious rituals as practised by the Hindus ever marked anyone's birthday at Jorasanko. With the renouncement of idol worship, all forms of *puja* at our home were abandoned. Saraswati Puja was turned into Saraswat Sanmelan, restricted to the men's quarters. The only concession permitted that day was for some of the older girls to wear saris dyed in saffron colour. The occasion of Poush Parban was also observed when the tradition of cooking certain special items of sweetmeats, known as *pithes* and *pulis*, was retained, but no *pujas*. We were, however, allowed the indulgence of celebrating Holi, the festival of colours.

Since no birthdays were observed, no one bothered about who was born when. Our birthdates were apparently recorded in some family documents, which could have been horoscopes, but no one gave any thought to remembering them. The birthday celebrations that our *mejo-mami* organized for her children had no element of *puja* in them, and were entirely copied from the West. Our *mejo-mama* Satyendra Nath Tagore and his wife were both very large-hearted persons. *Mejo-mami*, understandably, was very attached

72 *The Many Worlds of Sarala Devi*

to her children; nevertheless, she had always maintained a very cordial relationship with her many in-laws in the family, and in particular, she was genuinely fond of their children. She always invited everyone in the family for the birthday celebrations of her children; festivities in the evening followed by a feast. The invited children invariably carried some gifts, but it never occurred to them to feel deprived as they never received any gifts to mark their birthdays. These children grew up in the belief that they did not count, but without any sense of rancour. Equally, they were not provoked by any desire to match the status of *mejo-mami's* children.

It just happened around that time that a friend of mine had somehow ferreted out my date of birth, and unexpectedly and to my utter embarrassment, brought me a gift. That friend was Hemaprabha, younger sister of Jagadish Chandra Bose. I have said it somewhere earlier that this friend of mine was a boarder in the school hostel, and often came to our home for the weekends. She would return with us to her hostel when we resumed school on Mondays.

Jagadish Bose's father, Bhagaban Bose, was a deputy magistrate, and by faith, a Brahmo. His eldest daughter married Ananda Mohan Bose, a barrister, and the second daughter, Subarnaprabha, married his younger brother, Dr Mohini Mohan Bose. The three younger daughters remained unmarried, of whom Labanyaprabha was the seniormost. All three of them came from their moffusil home and boarded at the Bethune School hostel. The crème de la crème of the Brahmo Samaj sent their daughters to the Bethune School, mainly in the upper classes. Among them were: Kadambini Bose (later Ganguli); Kamini Sen (later Ray); Abala Das (later Bose); Kumudini Khastagir (later Das); and also Hemalata (later Sarkar), a daughter of Shibnath Shastri.

The presence of Jagadish Bose's sisters in our school brought about certain subtle changes in the character of the school, largely influenced by their Brahmo culture. A more relaxed ambience, a progressive attitude to the course of studies, and in some ways, adoption of English ways was noticeable. In those days many Brahmos modelled their ritual customs in imitation of the western style. At their prayer meetings, the language used was often English and not the mother tongue. At marriages, the bride was usually dressed in white, and where she was clad in a sari and not in western gown, she would wear a veil of net to which was attached the traditional 'orange blossom'. A posse of bridesmaids following the bride was also a must at certain weddings. I was a bridesmaid on two occasions – once at the marriage of Shibnath Shastri's eldest daughter Hem, and the other, at the wedding of Khusi, the younger daughter of Durgamohan Das, and a very dear friend of ours. Hem was married in the temple of the Sadharan Brahmo Samaj, following the practice of church weddings in the West. Hem wore an off-white, a sort of cream-coloured, sari with a veil of net. By the time Khusi got married the fancy for aping western manners was dying out. Instead of a white sari Khusi opted for the traditional red Benarasi sari, and replaced the veil of net with an Indian veil to cover her head. But the custom of bridesmaids was retained, and in this instance, reduced to one – that was me, because Khusi did not want anyone else. The dresses of bridesmaids were traditionally provided by the groom's family, and here I was, attired in my new costume paid for by Dr D.N. Ray. I walked behind Khusi and sat near her in a very solemn manner.

European marriages have the custom of a best man, a close parallel to which is the custom at Bengali weddings of a 'Nitbor' (the little groom), but there is nothing like the best maid equivalent to our custom of having a 'Nitkonay' (the little bride). I did once take the role of a Nitkonay at the marriage of my cousin Pratibha-*didi*. She chose me for this ceremonial duty though she had six sisters of her own. I think she did so because she knew that her would be husband, Asutosh Chaudhury, looked upon me as a dear young sister, and I also happened to be a close friend of his younger sister Mena and his niece Priyambada. Dressed up like a bride in a vivid red Benarasi sari, I accompanied the real bride to the prayer hall of Jorasanko house. My responsibility that day was to keep an eye on the bride and help her out when needed. I was most conscious of my importance and took much delight in it.

I started this chapter talking about celebrations of birthdays. In time this function grew into a popular trend with the Brahmos. In the Christian community such celebrations start with prayers by a clergy, and following that practice, Brahmos also commenced their celebrations with prayers by their Acharya [a teacher or a preacher], followed by refreshments and offer of gifts. Since in the prescribed procedures of Brahmo social functions as enunciated by our maternal grandfather, the observation of birthdays was not included, the birthday observations of the children of our *mejo-mami* did not commence with prayers, but otherwise were a festival of much fun and amusements, get-togethers, and good food.

74   *The Many Worlds of Sarala Devi*

Nothing really had changed in our home when Hemaprabha dug out my date of birth. No one had a clue that it was my birthday. Only my dear friend made it memorable for me with the present of a book of English stories, fondly inscribed, 'For Sarala with love on her birthday'. The name of the book was, I recall, 'Lamplighter' — a wonderful book. I have no idea if girls these days are familiar with this book.

Since then I became conscious of my birthday, and my elder sister Hiranmoyee made it a reality. By then she had, on her own, assumed the role of the head of our family. I had always suffered from a sense of inferiority complex, but not *Didi* who was raised as the darling of our parents. She went about with an air that no one in our family was a big fish — neither our parents and certainly nor any of their children including herself. After we moved to our Kashiabagan house from Jorasanko, she introduced birthday celebrations in our home — starting with mother and then her siblings. And we in turn celebrated her birthday; the exception being our father because we could not elicit from him his date of birth.

I remember my sixteenth birthday well. Stacked on a beautifully decorated large table with flowers were all sorts of eatable goodies, and standing on a shiny silver tray in the centre of the table was a large cake, with sixteen lit candles around it. Sixteen candles to match the age I had attained that day. To introduce this delightful foreign custom was the innovation of my *Didi*. As far as I could recall our *mejo-mami* never did this for her children.

I have already said that no birthdays were observed at Jorasanko until our *mejo-mami* returned from England. These days Rabindranath's birthday is celebrated throughout the country, but in his early years, even after he returned from England with *mejo-mama*, his birthdays went unnoticed. Arising from my great admiration for him I was instrumental in initiating his birthday celebration. He along with our *natun-mama* was then resident at 49 Park Street, the home of our *mejo-mama*. In this context I will quote from what I had earlier written on this topic:

I was the first person to observe Rabi-*mama*'s birthday. He and our *natun-mama* then lived at 49 Park Street, the home of our *mejo-mama*. Very early in the morning I slipped out of our Kashiabagan house, and tip-toeing into his bedroom placed near his bed a garland that I myself had strung with Bakul flowers collected from our garden along with some more flowers and a garland made of Bel flowers which I had procured at a

Sukhendu Ray 75

florist. I also placed at his feet a pair of *dhoti* and *chadar*, and waking him up, touched his feet. By then others had woken up and everyone started talking of Rabi's birthday. Ever since Rabindranath's birthday remained a regular event in our family.

We came to know later that *natun-mama's* birthday and Rabi-*mama's* were very close, Rabi-mama's on the seventh of May and *natun-mama's* on, probably, the fifth of May. At the prompting of our *mejo-mami*, we also introduced observation of *natun-mama's* birthday the following year. After he lost his wife some years ago *natun-mama* made his home with *mejo-mama*. Much later the practice of observing the birthday of our maternal grandfather was also inaugurated, which was held at Jorasanko and with prayers.

Women are the home makers, and they reinforce the family bond by maintaining the family rituals and traditions. Though originally confined to women only, progressively many of these rituals developed into larger social occasions. The ritual of observing birthdays initiated by *mejo-mami* for her children spread in time to other members of the Jorasanko family, when birthdays of other children began to be celebrated, either privately or openly, finally evolving into a regular family feature. And from children the practice moved to seniors, and in a forward leap within a generation, birthday celebrations covered everyone in the family.

To *mejo-mami's* credit goes another innovation, not just in our family, but it spread to other parts of the province of Bengal. And that is the style in which the sari is worn by the women. Early in our maternal grandfather's days there had been much debate, and experimentations, concerning dress forms suitable for the women in the family. We were told that after many tests grandfather had recommended a version of the 'salwar-kameez' for unmarried girls when they went out. There is a lovely portrait of Iru-*didi*, the eldest daughter of our eldest *masi*, dressed in that fashion, hung in Abanindranath's house.

However, the more convenient western style frocks soon replaced the 'salwar-kameez', but it did nothing to change the mode of donning the sari for the married women. The women in our family were reluctant to adopt the western gowns, preferred by some married ladies elsewhere, such as, the wife of barrister Manomohan Ghosh. The traditional method of wrapping the body utterly lacked any grace. During her stay in Bombay, *mejo-mami* had been intrigued by the way Parsi and Gujarati women donned their saris. This

76 *The Many Worlds of Sarala Devi*

particular style was in vogue only among the women in western India, a style captured in many old Indian paintings. *Mejo-mami* embraced this form except that she retained the mode of wearing the loose end of the sari in the traditional Bengali fashion. After a visit to Bombay my mother accompanied by *mejo-mami* returned home, both wearing saris in the newly adopted mode. And soon this mode became the trend adopted by all women in the family. In time, following them, some Brahmo ladies of discernment assumed this reformed method. This style later came to be known as 'Thakurbari sari', and after it gained in popularity, was labelled as 'Brahmika sari' (Brahmo Ladies' sari).

The second evolution in the Bengali way of putting on saris was ushered in after the Delhi Durbar, where many ranis and maharanis had assembled from all over India. The Maharani of Coochbehar Suniti Devi and the Maharani of Maurbhanj Sucharu Devi, who were also present at the Durbar, affected the new mode in wearing their saris in conformity with the other princely ladies. These two maharanis retained this new style when they returned home. It was claimed that the new style was, in any case, already in vogue in both Coochbehar and Mayurbhanj—their in-laws' places—but in their pride as Bengali, they had forsworn this new trend till then.

With the adoption of the graceful style, found very attractive by Bengali women, it progressively became universal among them, and in the process led to a uniform trend throughout India— another national unifying element. *Mejo-mami* was the pathfinder in introducing the adoption of a unified style in donning the sari in the country.

But what about the men? There was no such innovation in their garbs, which remained widely varied in the various regions of the country. The usual attire of Bengali men consisted of a fine dhoti, a punjabi (a collarless shirt), and a chadar (a seamless piece of cloth which was wrapped round the upper body), replaced by a woollen shawl during the cold weather. The normal attire of the men of north-west India was a churidar (a tight pair of leg-wear), a sherwani or achkan (a buttoned-up coat), and a headgear, would be acceptable for Bengalis except for weddings and at funeral services. Men in our family, probably influenced by the aristocratic Muslim culture, had opted for the north-west form of dress for their outdoor lives. The headgear alternated between a turban and a cap, which is evident from the many photographs of Rabi-*mama* and his elder brothers. *Mejo-mami*'s deft hands were often pressed into service to tie the turbans effectively on the heads of her many younger brothers-in-law.

Mejo-mami had been a driving force on many festive occasions to get the Jorasanko family together and in helping in their dressing up. Our *mejo-mama* was a family man in equal measure. Many of our relations visited him when he was located in Bombay and they learnt a great deal from the Gujaratis, Marathis, Parsees and Sindhi citizens of Bombay. When *mejo-mama* came home on leave he brought with him an armful of toys for the children. The toys were displayed at a particular spot, and each child was at liberty to pick his own choice without any restriction. I recall I was once much tempted by a large wax doll but did not dare to pick it up. One of the elders who noticed me asked which toy I fancied, and when I silently pointed at the doll he picked it up and handed it to me. No wonder we all looked forward to *mejo-mama* coming home on leave.

Nine

Memory of my eldest sister, Hiranmoyee, remains with me like the fragrance of a flower; the fragrance of the *Hasnuhana* blossoms in the evenings; the redolence of *Bel* and *Juin* flowers that fill the early morning air. Soaring above her physical image it is her evocative tenderness, warmth and love that have kept her memories alive in my heart.

Ever since we moved to our Kashiabagan home, *Didi* assumed charge of the family. I have already told of her initiative in celebrating birthdays in our family. In many other matters she took the leadership and in a way, assumed the role of a guardian of all in the family. Each passing day we saw evidence of her natural gift in looking after all of us with love and devotion. She took particular care in ministering to the needs of our parents. Once an old retainer who had been in the family from our grandfather's days made a malicious attempt to alienate her from our father by talking against her. *Didi* never forgot this episode neither did she ever forgive the offender. How dare a mere servant try to create a rift between a father and a daughter?

Didi's love for me compensated a great deal for my mother's indifference, and for all my needs, I turned to her. For instance, I just happened to mention once to her that I would dearly cherish to have a garland of *Bel* flowers each morning, and she promptly arranged for one to be delivered to me daily by a florist. On another occasion I coveted a gold necklace of an unusual design worn by a girl from Jorasanko. And who saw to it that I got one? Not my mother, but *Didi*. By then she was married, and ruled the roost in her family. She was free to spend money at will, and give away gifts as she pleased.

Didi got married when she was sixteen years old to Phani Bhusan Mukhopadhyay, a nephew of our uncle (husband of our father's sister). He was a frequent visitor to our Simla home, and became attracted to *Didi* whom he wished to marry. To achieve that end he procured a Gilchrist scholarship and went to England for higher studies. He returned home with an appointment in the Indian Government Education Service, and joined as a professor of Botany at the Presidency College. After subsequent assignments at Rajshahi College and then at Hooghly College, he ended his career as the College Inspector for the Burdwan and Presidency Divisions. When stationed in Calcutta *Didi* and her husband usually stayed with us at our Kashiabagan home.

In keeping with the tradition of our maternal grandfather, *Didi* like all granddaughters of the family, was married at the Jorasanko house. All in our family moved there for the occasion. *Didi*'s close friend Khusi was the bridesmaid, and she had put on a delicate green Benarasi sari for the wedding. When told to change into some other colour as the green did not suit her, she was not bothered. 'I like green, and it does not matter if I do not look good in it,' she insisted.

For the wedding, as part of the entertainment programme, Rabi-*mama* composed an opera, calling it 'The Wedding Festival', which was performed almost entirely by the women of the family. Khusi also had a part in it; Saroja took the heroine's role; some girls acted as her companions. There were two male characters — the hero and his comedian buddy. These characters were played respectively by Sushila-*bouthan*, the first wife of Dipu-*dada*, and Suprova-*didi*.

After her marriage *Didi*'s attachment to her natal family deepened, and she started assisting mother in her work. The cult of theosophy was much in vogue those days, and our mother was the President of the Women's Theosophical Society that met at our home. Wives of theosophists and other lady members of their families usually came to these meetings. Gathering of ladies from many locations of Calcutta widened the circle of my mother's friends. Theosophy also brought Madam Blavatsky and Colonel Olcot to our home, and they were involved in initiating many women to the tenets of theosophy.

80   *The Many Worlds of Sarala Devi*

On one occasion when we were all in our sitting room, Colonel Olcot abruptly rose in the midst of talking to us and ran into the next room, normally used as a bedroom for men. He returned a few minutes later, and when we looked inquisitively at him, he told us that the saintly Kuthomi had appeared in that room to give him a message, and then disappeared. We were thrilled and amazed in equal measure. How fortunate, indeed, we were that the saintly Kuthomi had sanctified our home by his presence! I became most interested in theosophy, but was then too young to receive initiation. *Didi* had just been initiated. I kept counting the days when I could qualify. Olcot once showed us a painted portrait of Kuthomi. Extraordinary eyes he had, which appeared to penetrate deep into your heart! Those eyes had kept haunting me for a long time.

One morning as I tried to get up I twisted my neck causing excruciating pain, so much so, that I could not lift my head. Even the slightest of movement was acutely agonizing. My father sought Colonel Olcot's help to cure me by application of mesmerism. Olcot was reputed to be a gifted mesmerist. He made a few passes with his hands, and then asked me to get up. 'No way! How can I get up when I cannot even raise my head, not even turn it?' I said.

'Yes, you can,' he insisted. He held my hand, and I tried gingerly to raise my head. Surprisingly, I was able to do so painlessly. Suddenly something snapped in my neck, and I almost died with pain, but I did manage to sit up. He gave me a glass of water which he had apparently sanctified with some mantra and instructed me to sip this water at regular intervals. He returned the following evening, and told me, 'You are well now, your pain has gone.' And that was indeed true. Since then all at home were sold on the benefits of mesmerism.

Among the lady members of the theosophical society was a sister of Nabin Bannerjee of Bhowanipore. She was usually dressed as a *sanyasin* (a female monk), and along with her, came a niece of hers, who had left her husband though the husband wanted her back. This lady averred that she had renounced the world and that her mission was to attain nirvana. Many members of this family had something odd about them. A son of Nabin Bannerjee turned out to be an expert in the art of mesmerism, and he often demonstrated his skill. He would put a man into sleep, make him see all sorts of reptiles and amphibians, command him to move according to his will, and make him laugh and cry, also at his will.

Sukhendu Ray 81

Our Sushila-*bouthan*, another member of the theosophical society, was discovered surprisingly to possess the faculty of hypnotizing people. She often practised this gift of hers using as a medium, a young girl called Nirmala, daughter of one of her maidservants. This girl could call correctly the taste of the foods that *bouthan* had consumed, bitter or sweet or whatever. We exercised tenacious vigilance to ensure that Nirmala was not cheating. No, she did not, and whatever she said was always under the spell of hypnotism. *Bouthan* would, on occasion, command her to travel to the Himalayas, and to our amazement, she displayed all the signs of suffering from the effects of the bitter cold of the Himalayas. Sushila-*bouthan* was later cautioned to desist from such experiments which could lead to adverse consequences.

By then the charm of theosophy was getting rusty, and so were the influence and regard for Madam Blavatsky. Among many others my mother's theosophical society also broke up. My mother then formed another association with some of the former members of the dissolved theosophical society, which was named Sakhi Samiti (Association of Lady Friends), a name suggested by Rabi-*mama*. This association adopted many reform measures to alleviate the distress of disadvantaged women. Fund education for unmarried women and helpless widows and later find gainful employments for them as teachers; arrange for legal aids by engaging lawyers to help molested women in the muffasils; organize exhibitions to display local handicrafts from the various districts of Bengal; promote stage shows with performance by women at these exhibitions. In time this Sakhi Samiti built up considerable reputation for itself.

The opera (*Mayar Khela*) was first staged by Sakhi Samiti with Suren and my elder brother as stage managers. They created a special effect by fixing invisibly wired lamps on the heads of the dancing girls. Everyone was scared in case this innovation misfired and the girls received electrical shocks. But the two new-age scientists were supremely confident, and nothing went wrong. They created another spectacular electrical mischief at the venue of Ashu Chaudhury's wedding. They laid electrical cables underneath the decorative seat earmarked for the groom, and periodically startled the groom by applying mild electrical shocks to the vast amusement of his many prospective sisters-in-law. These preoccupations and pranks, sadly, greatly interfered with their education.

82   *The Many Worlds of Sarala Devi*

Our Sanskrit teacher, Chandrakanta Pandit, deplored our mother's latitude in allowing her son to indulge in such superfluous activities which was ruining his school studies. And he was right. My eldest brother failed the Entrance (school final) examination that year, although I got through. He was older but still we were contemporaries in school, and as a result of this failure he became a junior. He could not sit for the following year's examination as he was very unwell then, and in the process, he became my junior by two years. By then I had cleared my F.A. exams. Nevertheless, all this loss was made up when he was sent to England the same year, and returned home a few years later after qualifying for the Indian Civil Service.

Before her marriage, *Didi* and I had started a school for the neighbourhood girls of our Kashiabagan home. *Didi* was the head teacher, and I her assistant. *Didi* was around fourteen or fifteen years of age and I was about ten or so, and we were then both in Bethune School. Besides our regular school hours, we had each day, morning and evening, our tuition from Satish Pandit, plus lessons from a Sanskrit teacher, and on top of that, there was music instruction, by an Ustad and a European lady teacher, for proficiency in both Indian and western music. The only time we could spare to run our school was when we came home from our school. After a quick wash and gulping down some food, we conducted our school between 4:30 and 6:30 in the evenings. The subjects taught were Bengali, English, Maths and sewing. There were around 20 girls, some married, some child widows. We sat the girls on the steps of the portico, as if they were ranged on a gallery of a big school. The idea of starting a school for the local girls evolved when we saw them come to our home to fetch water. Many of our Jorasanko relations often visited us, and we pressed some of them into service by asking them to test the students. And the highlight of this venture was when we got Rabi-*mama* to give away the prizes. After *Didi* got married I tried to run the school on my own, but had to give up when I had to take my Entrance exams. The school, sadly, had to be closed down.

Didi, unfortunately, lost her early children, and her empty heart hungrily sought out children to whom she could give her love. She was keen to look after some orphaned children who were under the care of the Sakhi Samiti. These girls looked up to her as their mother, and she did everything for them as if they were her own family. Around then she came to know about a home for widows,

Established by Sashipada Bandopadhyay. Meanwhile, with passing time, Sakhi Samiti, founded by our mother, lost its early lustre and became a dying institution. *Didi* tried to keep it alive through many transformations of its structure and aims, and finally turned it into a home for the rehabilitation of widows. She built up this home with her dedicated service, with untiring toil and perseverance, through many ups and downs.

The inspiration to serve the motherland stemmed from her intense love for our mother. The home for widows that she founded was an offshoot of her efforts to keep mother's achievements unimpaired. She was trying to reshape the Sakhi Samiti into a humanitarian institution. The depth of her attachment to her creation was matched by her revulsion towards anyone who was bent on harming it. She displayed a singular resolve in protecting what she regarded as her own. She was a curious amalgam of tenderness and toughness; those who came within the ambit of her grace remained her long time friends; others suffered.

Mother was planning to travel to Karwar with *mejo-mama*; a tailor was engaged to stitch some new dresses for her, and a few dresses were also made for *Didi*. A couple of days before mother's departure *Didi* was found depressed. Mother was her close companion, and the thought of the forthcoming days without mother filled her with sadness. Mother's presence or absence made little difference to me, because I never had the benefit of her companionship. Away from her, my days were confined to the care of the domestic servants, tutors, teachers and the pandits. And, of course, I was busy with lessons. My mother's impending departure created no emotional ripple in me. After *Didi*'s marriage when she went to live with her husband, and our brother was away in England, I had a somewhat closer contact with mother. But on the day mother left, *Didi*'s tears and my dry eyes brought out the truth — that I was incapable of love.

But was *Didi* concerned about everyone without any discrimination? I think not! She could be quite indifferent to others. I recall a visit to an exhibition in Calcutta, to which mother took us and also invited a friend of hers. She told this friend to stick close to *Didi* who could then take her around and explain the exhibits. It was a big show, with so many attractions and diversions, so much to see, that *Didi* had no patience to keep an eye on her charge. With geat energy she rushed through the various booths and displays. The poor friend, unable to keep pace with *Didi*, sat down on benches

84   *The Many Worlds of Sarala Devi*

from time to time, to rest her weary feet. *Didi*, of course, was blissfully unaware that she had lost her charge. The friend suddenly spotted me and clung to me. I helped her lean on me as she hobbled on her feet, and at her request, stayed on with her. I do not claim that I did anything extraordinary; after all I could hardly abandon her. When we returned home, my mother's friend was very critical of *Didi* and heaped praises upon me. This had a counter-effect on me; I felt as if had let down both mother and *Didi*. Till the end of her life, this friend of mother's never lost her affection for me and her pique for *Didi*.

I have already spoken about *Didi*'s leadership qualities; she also happened to be a very efficient organizer. Planned by her, we used to go on her 'conducted tours' to various places each year during Phani-*dadd*'s college vacations. *Didi* had to drag her reluctant husband along on these trips. Single-handedly, she assumed total responsibility for all arrangements — from railway reservations, collecting luggage from the brake van at destinations, to getting the servants to cook. She was the unchallenged boss. Phani-*dada* tagged along like a tug boat hitched behind a large boat, grumbling all the time till we reached our destination when he heaved a sigh of relief. I did help *Didi* out to the extent I could. With our brother away in England and our father unwilling to travel, it was left to mother and me to join *Didi* in those excursions because she would be miserable if we did not.

Didi occasionally wrote for the *Bharati* magazine, which was edited by mother. She contributed no original pieces, but translated from some English language publications on socially useful topics in simplified Bengali for lay readers. She did, however, compose a few sonnets, which were delicate but melancholic.

After I earned my bachelor's degree, with some difficulty I persuaded my father to allow me to accept a teaching job in faraway Mysore. I was soon favoured with a gift of two sonnets *Didi* composed specially for me and *Bharati* printed them. But that was not enough; she tied me up by offering me the joint editorship of *Bharati* so that I retained my contact with home from distant Mysore.

Earlier I had said how *Didi* lost her first children in their infancy, and that her empty heart was hungry for motherhood. This void in her life was eventually filled when her later children survived. At the time of her death she left behind three delightful children — two boys and a girl.

Ten

We never had the luxury of 'thirteen festivals in twelve months' as was the norm for most Bengalis. For Jorasanko children there was only one festive occasion, and that was the celebration of 11th Magh. This, for us, was the equivalent of the Durga Puja, but these two festivals hardly had anything in common. No modellers ever shaped a clay image of a deity at our place to ceremonially install that image on a platform, apply paint on it and sketch its eyes. No such diversions for the Jorasanko kids! The conflict between the worship of idols and worship of a formless supreme being split the Tagore clan. Dwarkanath Tagore's house at No. 6 and the other Tagores went their separate ways; even the next door house at No. 6/1. That used to be the main quarter for men in the family during Dwarkanath's time, which at the time of the partition of properties between our grandfather Debendranath and his brothers, went to one of his brothers and his children.

Gunendranath was a first cousin of our mother. He was the father of Gaganendranath, Samarendranath and Abanindranath. The Tagores at No. 6/1 went along with the rest of the Tagore clan elsewhere, and continued with the practice of traditional Hindu *pujas.* No. 6 was the only exception and became isolated. Not only did the difference in religious faiths and other family customs segregate Maharshi's home from the rest of the Tagores, there was a virtual ban to any social contact. Fortunately, because of a strong

86   *The Many Worlds of Sarala Devi*

fraternal bond between Gunendranath and our uncles, the men of the two families were still on good terms, but sadly not the women. Men usually take the lead in formulating and propounding the family culture, but it was left to women to maintain and sustain this culture and related customs. Family traditions go for a toss if women take no hand in them. The women in our home were held back from attending any religious functions in the next-door family, and there was no way the divergent cultures of the two homes found any common ground in the absence of participation by the women. Oddly enough, idol worshipping Hindus did not consider worship of a formless god unacceptable, and so members from the other Tagore clans came regularly to our 11th Magh festival, particularly to listen to the music. Senior men from the families of Raja Jatindramohun Tagore of Pathuriaghata and of Kalikrishna Tagore often made their brief presence in the afternoon of the Magh festivals in response to the invitation of the Maharshi. Women never, as they were never invited. The men also visited our home on the occasion of Bejoya Dashami, but their visit did not progress beyond the outer precincts.

Women in our family would eagerly watch out for the arrival of men from other Tagore clans, peeping through the blinds. Even so, the relationship sadly continued to deteriorate. The rupture between the Maharshi family and the other Tagore clans intensified in subsequent generations, but the gulf between his brother's family next door and ours was progressively bridged. The connection between house No. 6/1 and the Pathuriaghata Tagores came to be tightly knit through marriages, but house No. 6 remained aloof and firm in its belief. It stayed isolated, holding its head high, freethinking and singular in its distinctive culture. But, came a day, when the pioneering innovations and progressive ideas adopted by the members of the Maharshi's family became the role model for the other families of the Tagore clans. In those families the custom of isolation of women was discontinued, and their education was encouraged; music lessons for girls came to be a part of their cultural life. The one and only difference that remained was in the religious faiths and practices — idol worship versus prayers, festival of Brahmo Maghotsav versus the festivals of the Hindu Durga Puja and the Holi.

Those days we had, of course, no idea of any religion-based festivities other than the Brahmotsav held on 11th of Magh each year. Some other sects of Brahmos, belonging to the Sadharan Samaj

Sukhendu Ray 87

or the Naba-vidan Sabha, observed this festival over a longer span of time — some for ten or fifteen days, some others for an extended period of a month. For us the festival was strictly restricted to just one day, the 11th of Magh. In our younger days the advent of this festival was announced a month ahead, when long iron poles, large and heavy — a little push by which would be enough to crack your skull — were brought in and laid down side to side for a few days before being driven down deep holes to stand upright. On the 10th of Magh decorations started when strings of marigold flowers were festooned like a chain from pole to pole. Lamp-holders were then clamped on each pole. Chandeliers were fixed on the walls as well as hung inside the verandas. Wax candles were, however, not screwed in until the last day for fear of theft.

A large marquee was erected covering the entire courtyard, which effectively screened the outer house and shut out the daylight. It was this very darkness that excited us in anticipation of the event. The advent of electricity dispensed with the need for erecting iron poles, and a big chunk of our pleasure in the festival was ruined. To get used to lighting up by electricity and finally, to accept it took some time.

There was a major difference between the 11th Magh festival at our home and the Puja festival at the house next door, and that was the issue of new clothes. There was no customary practice to be dressed in new clothes on the occasion of Maghotsav. All that we did was to dress well. On the other hand in Hindu Bengali homes '*puja* shopping' was a major event. Much in advance people would go out shopping for new dresses and gifts for each member of the family as well as for the retainers. Affluent families showed off in despatching *puja* gifts to the in-laws of the daughters carried in a sort of ceremonial procession! None of these rituals were applicable to us. Once in our preparatory class when we were asked to compose an essay on 'A comparison between X'mas and Durga Puja', I just had no clue what to write. Our teacher, finding me pensive, threw out a few hints; at Christmas the English people wait anxiously to get together with friends and relations, and similarly Bengalis look forward to meeting friends and relations. Christians exchange gifts as do Bengali Hindus to celebrate their respective festivals. With such broad hints I knocked up my essay, but I did not think much of it as what I wrote was outside my personal experience.

Since putting on new clothes was associated with the Hindu Durga Puja, it is likely that my grandfather thought this custom

88   *The Many Worlds of Sarala Devi*

would be inappropriate for our Maghotsav festival. Or it could be that the origin of observing the Magh festival might have dissuaded him to dispense with such a formal custom. For it was on the 11th of Magh that Rammohun Roy formally established Brahmotsav by leading a prayer in Jorasanko house, and the observation of the annual Maghotsav was just the anniversary of that occasion. Fundamentally then, it was not a family occasion and, therefore, there was no call for setting up any rituals that involved the families. This could also be the reason why the tradition of new clothes did not find a place in our festivities. I really do not know what is true, but new clothes were out for us!

Similarly, the custom of greeting each other on the Bejoya Dashami day, or embracing close friends and relations, or the younger people touching the feet of elders, was not a part of the culture in our home. Later, however, Bejoya came to be observed in certain parts of our family following the marriage of the family daughters with Asutosh Chaudhury and his brothers. This was just emulating the practice of the Chaudhury family.

We did have a family occasion, and that was celebrating the Bengali New Year day—the first of Baisakh. On that day we did exchange greetings, embraced each other and touched the feet of elders. The system of donning new clothes on that day was catching up. In a way, New Year day was truly the occasion of the family get–together. Very early in the morning the gong at the main gate would ring out the wake-up call. All the men in the family would rise, get ready dressed in fresh white clothes and assemble in the courtyard for prayers. The women kept indoors, watching from behind the blinds. The end of the prayers was the time to exchange greetings, wishing a happy new year, and juniors touching the feet of elders. This exchange of greetings was also on in the women's quarters. Sweet soft drinks were then served, and later, the entire family ate lunch together.

Even though the new year day celebration was an intimate family affair, for us, the 11th Magh was the real festive occasion. There were other events, such as, the festival of *pithas* on the last day of the month of Poush. That used to be a big do, appropriate for such a large family. Since it was entirely a domestic affair with no external association, it somehow did not appear to be much of a festivity. All that happened was that ladies made the initial preparations of the special sweets for the occasion, finally cooked by the house cooks, and then distributed to each quarter. Just a happy private do!

Sukhendu Ray 89

The core of the 11th Magh festival was prayers and music. In our younger days three *acharyyas* (preachers) sat on the dais, and to listen to their recital of Sanskrit verses from the Vedas, in flawless diction, was an unalloyed pleasure. The venue was filled to the brim with devotees. Occasionally, either Dwijendranath or Satyendranath also acted as *acharyya*. Many came just for the music. Such vedic hymns sung in Bengali had not been heard before, nor had such solemn yet melodious music enchanted the listeners earlier. This music was not at all like the *vaisnavite kirtans. Kirtan* singers got emotionally carried away into a trance when they went prostrate on the ground, but the music in praise of Brahma ecstatically soared heavenwards above the mortal earth. This was particularly so when Rabindranath took the stage to sing devotional songs along with his brothers and their music transported the audience to a divine plane.

The content of Brahmo hymns has gone through some transformation since the days of Rammohun Roy. Diverting from the abstract notion of a formless supreme being, the later songs are addressed to a God with primordial aspects, a Christian concept of a 'Personal God'. It is not easy to conceive of a 'Personal God' in terms of formlessness. So, post-Rammohun, hymns referred to a God endowed with 'Eyes', with a 'Face', with 'Feet'. An analysis of the change in ideas and language of songs since Rammohun Roy's time will demonstrate the validity of the argument of 'no difference' between the concept of a 'formless God' and a 'deity with a form'.

Rabindranath used to be upset when he found people paying homage to images made from clay and straws, metal or stone, or even paintings. It outraged his belief in a 'formless' God in which he was brought up. After marital ties were established between the Jorasanko family and the family of Asutosh Chaudhury, many of us once accompanied his sister, wife of Dr Umadas Bannerjee, to Benares for a holiday. Indira was then just married to Pramatha Chaudhury, and they also came with us. We put up at the palatial home of Maharaja Jatindramohun Tagore in Benares. Hem Mallik of the Bowbazar Mallik house also happened to be there with his family. He made some special arrangements for us to witness the celebrated *arati* at the Visweswar temple. We were allowed the privilege of ring-side seats facing the deity, and pandas were hovering around to protect us from intruders. What a magnificent show this *arati* was! Equally remarkable was the throng of devotees and their shrill cries of exultation! One could not but be thrilled at the sight

90   The Many Worlds of Sarala Devi

and not feel an emotion of veneration. At the end of the *arati*, in that ambience echoing the adulations of devotees for thousand of years, carried along with the current eruption of piety by hundreds of gathered devotees, we also made our obeisance.

On our return to Calcutta when Rabi-*mama* was told of what we did in Benares, he almost exploded. 'How could you stoop to idolatry? How could you play false to your spiritual faith?' he chastised us.

Sadly, it was a fact that many members of the Jorasanko family slowly deviated from the received faith against heretical idolatry and veered to the traditional creed of image worship. This development disturbed Rabindranath enormously.

As youngsters we had a limited role in the music for the 11th Magh festival. We went along as directed by our seniors. A fortnight before the actual day we rehearsed our songs and on the day of the festival we sang and played instruments to accompany the songs. Some years later a part of organizing the music was handed over to us, and we grabbed the opportunity with both hands. Being an inveterate music lover, I was tempted to show myself off in the programme. Between the four of us—Suren, Bibi, my elder brother and I—we could play more than one instrument, not counting the ubiquitous harmonium. We often got up concerts of Western music among ourselves. A couple of sisters of Pratibha-*didi* were also members of our musical group.

We really were most enthusiastic those days. I recall on one occasion, when the morning prayers were over at Jorasanko and after we had had our meals, we moved straight away to Birjitala, the then residence of *mejo-mama*, where we practised our music undisturbed to make it as perfect as we could. Before evenfall we rushed back to Jorasanko carting our instruments and took our place on the dais. And on that occasion we introduced the technique of playing a part of the melody on our instruments as prelude to our songs. I have since observed that wireless broadcasts and gramophone records these days start with a prelude of instrumental music before a song is sung. As far as I am concerned I still believe we were the innovators of this practice.

The children of Jorasanko had very few outlets for entertainment. Other than the 11th Magh celebration they had no other festivities. And, once back from Lahore after my marriage, I discovered to my horror that even that outlet was dying. With Rabi-*mama*'s creation

Sukhendu Ray 91

Santiniketan flourishing, he sacrificed Jorasanko children to favour Santiniketan students. Boys and girls from Santiniketan came to Calcutta fully prepared to sing at Magh festival, and the children of Jorasanko ceased to have any role there. I heard complaints from Pratibha-*didi*'s sisters who had earlier participated at Magh festival and from which they were now excluded. Where would the daughters of Jorasanko turn to? Other than the Maghotsav we had no other festive occasions. Look at the Hindu homes. Observe the spontaneous joy of their children during Durga Puja. New clothes, good food, visits from friends and relations, go round the various puja venues — no end to their source of pleasures. The family feast of Magh festival had ceased long ago, and the tenuous connection that we had through music was now being denied because of Rabi-*mama*. The one and only festival a year was now lost to us. So, what would we do? Should we walk into the camps of Sadharan Brahmo Samaj or the Nabavidhan? If we join the Hindus we will be subject to much abuse. Rabi-*mama* became supremely indifferent to the girls of the Jorasanko family, while girls from outside the family received all his encouragement to participate in the fun and joy of the Maghotsav.

This indeed is a very heart-rending grievance. Even during the lifetime of our maternal grandfather, in order to economize, the 11th Magh celebrations had continued to slide down in scale and become a low key affair. After his death, the present day Maghotsav is a mere shadow of the earlier magnificence. Perhaps as long as the Jorasanko courtyard remains with the family, 11th Magh will continue to be observed in some form in accordance with the provisions of the will left by the Maharshi. But even that courtyard has since become a public thoroughfare. The part of the house inherited by Ritu-*dada*, the younger son of our *sejo-mama*, has now been sold to a Marwari buyer, whose family has the right of way to pass through the courtyard. Oddly enough, just when the 11th Magh prayers and music are on, smoke from the open coal ovens and smell of cooking from the Marwari home come drifting down creating a nuisance. The many houses adjacent to our courtyard are now rented out piecemeal mainly to immigrants from outside Calcutta, and they all have the freedom to walk in and walk out through the courtyard at will, even during the Magh festival. Because of the present deplorable situation students of Santiniketan no longer visit Calcutta to participate in Jorasanko house; they do it in Bolpur now.

92   *The Many Worlds of Sarala Devi*

The celebration of 11th Magh has gradually shifted to many musical schools that have sprung up to teach Rabindra *sangeet* (music). The many Jorasanko festivals that were once intimate parts of Debendranath's family have since his death progressively been converted into institutional affairs connected with the name of his famous youngest son. As none connected with Maharshi's family has any right to the near-ruined pile at Jorasanko, similarly no blood relation of his has any longer any role in the observation of 11th Magh.

The turbulent Padma has relentlessly shifted its course over time and in the process, wiped out many distinguished families and their achievements. In the same way, time has eroded the glory of Debendranath and Jorasanko, and it has shifted to Santiniketan, where under the Chhatim tree has grown up Rabindranath's institution — his 'Taj Mahal'. The ruins of Jorasanko have now come under the protection of Curzon's Act to preserve historic monuments!

Eleven

From the present growing trend and propensity among Bengali women to go in for training in music and making a name for themselves, one would find it inconceivable that when we were young, it was a taboo for women of decent families to take to music. Indeed, it was rare to come across a girl singing openly in her own home. And that probably accounts for the great attraction of our 11th Magh festivals where women participated openly in the musical programmes and sang songs. This was such a novelty for the residents of Calcutta those days that the festivals drew large crowds just for the curiosity of witnessing women singing in public. The songs sung on those occasions were serious and based on classical *ragas.* They were not the light-hearted popular songs now purveyed by women, who have taken up music as a career; these songs have rhythmic beats that eager listeners sway to.

In this context I recall an occasion when I accompanied Rabi-*mama* to the home of Kashishwar Mitra — very close to our Kashiabagan home. The event was the celebration of Brahmotsav. Usually the 11th Magh was strictly observed only in the Jorasanko house, yet there were a few devotees of the original Adi Samaj who regularly celebrated the Magh festival at their homes. Though they belonged to the Adi Samaj they were not formal Brahmos like members of the Sadharan Sabha, nor were they qualified to act as preachers at functions of the Adi Samaj. Whilst they prayed to the

94   *The Many Worlds of Sarala Devi*

formless Brahma at public functions, their domestic and social ceremonies still retained some aspects of the traditional idolatry. In other words, they wavered between theory and practice. Kashishwar Mitra of Nandabagan was a Brahmo of such persuasion.

Outside the boundaries of our Kashiabagan home was a water tank, its periphery inhabited by a few families. This tank was the principal source of water for these families for all their needs except drinking as this water was not considered 'sweet'. For potable water they came to our house to collect from our tank which they apparently found suitable. Kashishwar Mitra's house was on the other side of this outside tank. The wife of his eldest son was a friend of my mother's. Both Rabi-*mama* and I were once invited to sing on the occasion of Brahmotsav in their home. Rabi-*mama* sang with great feeling in his wonderfully melodious voice—vastly superior to the singing of Akshay Babu and his troupe.

That was the one and only participation by Rabi-*mama* at the Mitra home, but repeated invitations came pouring in for me almost every week to sing either at their Sunday sessions or on occasions of their family gatherings. Those days I could go on singing tirelessly for hours. A common practice then for women was to form bonds with each other and give their alliance some sort of a fancy appellation. At Jorasanko my mother had many such friendships, and one of them was the wife of Gyanendramohun Das, the editor of Samay. The solicitor Srinath Das was his father. Their home was a regular venue where I used to sing non-stop for many hours, without any trouble to my voice or getting physically exhausted. I was then no more than 11 years old.

There was a time when my mother's Sakhi Samiti sessions were held at the residence of Barrister W C Bonnerjee's wife. Some of his sisters also happened to be theosophists. At those sittings I was frequently asked to sing. Owing to dearth of women singers demands for my service were far too many. I recall the many evening receptions and dinner parties in the home of Barrister Monomohun Ghose where Bengali plays were often put up. At their large dinner parties they often had prominent European ladies and gentlemen as guests. Mrs Ghose would personally come to invite my parents and me to these dinners at their home, No. 4 Theatre Road. According to strict English etiquette, I was far too young to attend such dinners—I was not even 14 years old and anyone less than sixteen was not really eligible to sit at the table for such formal dinners. But as the adage goes, 'necessity knows no law'. The trend those days was to

Sukhendu Ray 95

entertain with Indian songs, if only to demonstrate to European guests that Indian women were also well versed in music. Regardless of being under-age therefore, I was needed to render Indian songs. It was left to Pratibha-*didi* to sing or play western music. Pratibha-*didi* was an accomplished pianist and sang English songs extremely well. Her musical attainment was so westernized that Indian songs sung by her never seemed to suit her voice. Later she abandoned western music to assiduously pursue Indian classical music in which she gained considerable proficiency.

Another incident, which happened much later, comes to my mind. I was on a visit home from Lahore to be with our family at Calcutta, and soon received an invitation from Sir Rajen Mookherjee to a dinner to say farewell to Sir Harcourt Butler on his appointment as Governor of Burma. Nearly a hundred guests were expected. It was a particular wish of Sir Rajen and Lady Mookherjee that I should sing on that occasion. Just about the time we were ready to set out, my mother's car unfortunately malfunctioned. It was getting late. Western dinner parties are not like our Indian counterparts where one could roll up any time. Sit-down western style dinners have fixed places for each guest indicated by name cards, and any absences at the last moment can cause considerable disarray. We sent for a taxicab, but none could be found immediately. Meanwhile I was getting increasingly nervous. Asutosh Chaudhury's house was near ours, and we could see some kind of a do going on there as many cars were lined up in front of his house. We sent a servant to his house in case he could help out with one of the visiting cars, but it was of no use. The servant could not even enter the house, let alone meet Asutosh Chaudhury. I sat desperately waiting and fidgeting. What would Sir Rajen and Lady Mookherjee think of us? Such travesty of manners? Eventually a taxicab was found, and somehow we managed to arrive, a little late, as the guests were proceeding for dinner, having waited for us. When I told Sir Rajen of my predicament, he said, 'But why did you not telephone me? I could have immediately sent up a car for you.'

I sang after the dinner was over. I was asked to sing Indian songs but harmonized in the style of western music. I chose first 'Ogo Bideshini', and followed it up with 'Sundar Basanta Barek Phirao'. As I left, an extremely courteous Sir Harcourt came to me and with a deep bow thanked me for my melodious songs. He did not really have to do this but did so from his innate sense of decorum.

I have no idea how good Sir Harcourt was as a Governor, but in

96   *The Many Worlds of Sarala Devi*

England theirs was a very illustrious family that had produced many successful men. His younger brother was for a while the Deputy Commissioner at Lahore, and even before he reached that city to assume charge, Lahore was rife with political agitations, and many people were sent to jail. During his administration political agitations continued unabated, but it was not his policy to fill prisons.

I was then living in Lahore after my marriage. A powerful Urdu language journal called *Hindustan* was published from Lahore. Through some circumstantial co-incidences I came to own that paper, and with my husband, was responsible in formulating the policy of this journal. Many toadies of the British Government used to carry tales against my husband and me to the Deputy Commissioner. The day Sufi Ambaprasad, the well-known Urdu writer and some of his associates were released from jail, I engaged Ambaprasad as the editor of *Hindustan*. It was, of course, a very bold decision, but even so, the Deputy Commissioner Montague Butler did not appear to be anxious enough to incarcerate me immediately. But he did send for my husband the next day and warned him, 'You have many enemies, so has your wife. You have engaged Sufi Ambaprasad for your journal, but do be careful how you use him. Do see that I may not have any cause to move against a lady like your wife.'

When Ambaprasad was told of the Deputy Commissioner's comments, all he said was, 'I am made of steel. Even if you smear by body with honey, any one wishing to lick me will finally get to the taste of steel!' Rumour had it that during the reign of O'Dyer Sufi Ambaprasad fled India in the guise of a Muslim and reached Turkey. By then *Hindustan* had been banned by O'Dyer. It was also reported that O'Dyer ignored Montague Butler and sidelined him to minor posts regardless of his seniority. After this the administration changed and Montague Butler was made the Governor of the Central Provinces at Nagpur. His son, R.A. Butler, was for a while Under Secretary of State of the British Government, and he came out to India as a member of the Franchise Commission when I had the opportunity of meeting him at Calcutta.

During my many visits to my *mejo-mama* I had been to a number of district towns of Bombay Presidency, such as, Solapur, Sitara, Poona, Pandarpur, Mahabaleshwar, etc., but never to the city of Bombay. In those provincial towns I came in touch with many accomplished musicians of Maharashtra, but they were all men; I did not meet a single woman. I spent much time listening to them singing Marathi or classical Hindustani songs. Like the cat which had smelt fish and was on the prowl, I too hankered after any singers with a reputation of talent and possessing a great voice. I listened to them keenly, learnt from them, made copious notes. I was never satisfied until I had filled my treasury of music collections. At Sitara I was introduced to a Sub-judge, by name Sohoni, who turned out to be a fine singer, and from him, I harvested some songs relating to Holi and an amusing song of a fight between black and white. I did not waste any time in indulging in my own music in case I missed out something for my collection.

Later, I did have about three weeks in Bombay city, when I was the guest of a very affluent Gujarati family, who had a seaside mansion named 'Darya Mahal'. My hosts were so very keen on listening to me that I hardly had any respite there from singing. The head of the family was Narayanji Dwarkadas, his elder brother was Gordhandas Tejpal, who had changed his name when adopted by another wealthy family. They had once gone on a pilgrimage to Puri. With them were their wives and some of their sisters. On that occasion they spent some days visiting Calcutta. They had earlier spoken to Charu Mitra, a resident of Allahabad, who happened to be friend of our father. My father, in turn, had asked me to take the Bombay ladies around Calcutta, and we did the usual round of the Alipore Zoo, the Botanical Gardens, the Indian Museum, etc., and in the process, became close friends. Some of the sisters of the family were married into families who were devotees of Krishna, and some others into families who worshipped Shiva. In those days there was a great divide between these two communities.

Nandibai, a sister of Narayanji, was married into a *vaishnavite* family and was an accomplished singer. She had a large stock of songs. All of them were keen on music and even though I sang in Bengali, they could still appreciate my songs because of some affinity with the Gujarati and Hindi languages. They asked me to sing some of their favourite songs as I in turn asked Nandibai to sing the songs I liked. Besides being a good singer Nandibai was also a composer of songs, and her fondness for me made her write a song on me. My friendship with this family firmly endured despite vicissitudes in their fortune. Many of them are now impoverished, and some of them no longer with us. Whenever I happen to visit Bombay I seek them out and make a point of calling on them.

98   *The Many Worlds of Sarala Devi*

When a National Congress conference was held at Poona, my father, *mejo-mama* and some other relations of ours attended the session. Narayanji treated them in a princely fashion as his guests. Having just gone to Mysore to take up my appointment there I could not travel to Poona, but the report that I had of the magnanimous hospitality extended to our family members was most gratifying.

I came to know another Bombay family who also much admired my music. It was a Muslim family — a different social circle. Akbar Hydari, married to a niece of Justice Badruddin Tayebji, was posted at Calcutta as a very senior person in the Accounts Department. He later became the Prime Minister of Hyderabad State. His wife Amina was with him in Calcutta. I have a close Parsee friend in Burjorjee Padshah, a right hand man of Jamshetjee Tata. With an introduction letter from this Parsee friend the Hydaris called on me, and ever since, we became close friends. He was good enough to ask the Maulavi, who came with them as tutor to their children, to teach me twice a week to read the Rubayiat of Omar Khayyam in the original Pharsi language. It was a long standing desire of mine to learn how to read and write Pharsi.

With *mejo-mama* we once stayed at Watson Hotel in Bombay city for a week. The owner of the hotel, a Muslim gentleman, came to see us regularly to ensure that we were looked after and were comfortable. During our stay he wrote a four-line verse in Urdu on a card and gifted it to me. I, of course, had no knowledge of Urdu, and so the gentleman read it to me and explained it. This made me appreciate the delicacy of Urdu verse. The Urdu calligraphy was pretty as a picture but totally illegible to me. I decided somehow to learn to read and write Urdu language, but back at our Kashiabagan home in Calcutta, where could I find anyone sufficiently knowledgeable in Urdu to teach me? In my desperation I caught hold of a Muslim postman and tipped him to teach me the alphabet. After my initiation I ventured into reading children's books in Urdu, when I discovered that unlike Bengali books for children which tended to be serious and prosaic, the Urdu books for children were full of humour. I wonder if these books are still in print.

Even today I can recall two amusing tales from those Urdu books. A patient asks his hakim (an Islamic medicine man), '*Hakim saab*, what is the right time for one to have one's meals?' And the hakim replies, 'For a poor man whenever he has access to any food, for the rich when he is hungry!' Another story goes like this: 'A tightfisted man wished to arrange for a religious dance featuring

Radha, but such dances, he was told, lasted the whole night, and for which he needed to provide three maunds (one maund roughly equivalent to forty kilograms) of oil for the lamps. That decided him: no way would such a vast quantity of oil be provided, and so nor would Radha dance.' It was embarrassing for me to read such stories sitting with the postman, because I could hardly break into laughter at the cost of losing my dignity in presence of a lowly placed person. I had, therefore, to preserve my gravity until he left, and then go into splits.

My maternal grandfather, according to the system of education that prevailed when he was young, was well-versed in the Pharsi language. Hafez was his favourite poet, and he always had a collection of his verses handy. He often recited from this book and explained the philosophical essence of the poems.

Meanwhile, a poem 'Ahitagnika' that I had written was printed in the magazine *Bharati*. I had also written 'Sunasefer Bilap' based on a hymn of the Upanishadas. These were read to my grandfather who was very pleased, and told me, 'Look, here are a few lines from Hafez. Can you set it to music and sing to me?' With much humility I accepted this assignment, and after a week I sent him a message that I had composed the music he had asked for and would be happy to sing it for him whenever it suited him.

Cousin Dipu-*dada* was asked to fix a venue where I would sing. Many of our relations were present on the occasion, and grandfather with ear trumpets, sat half reclined in an easy chair. I sang the Hafez song, set to music by myself, accompanied by a violin that I played. Grandfather apparently listened with deep concentration and with enjoyment.

A few days later Dipu-*dada* called on me. 'Come with me to the Hamiltons', he told me. 'Grandfather has asked me to buy you some jewellery within a thousand rupees. He did not wish you to know this in advance as he intended it to be a surprise gift. But I could not take the risk of buying something so expensive in case you did not like it. Much better for you to choose what takes your fancy, but please tell no one.' At Hamiltons, we found nothing suitable within the budget amount, and so we went to another jeweller. There I selected a set comprising a diamond and ruby necklace and a pair of matching bracelets. I was sent for a few days later, when at a gathering of family members grandfather handed over his gift to me with these words, 'You are blessed like the divine Saraswati, and even though it is not good enough for you, please accept this

100 *The Many Worlds of Sarala Devi*

modest offering.' Emotionally overwhelmed by these kind words I accepted his generous gift with due humility. The notation for this Hafez song, incidentally, is included in my book of notations.

I sang that song for Mr Siwani when he was President of the Indian National Congress and had come to tea at our home. He was astonished that a Bengali girl could render Hafez with such flawless diction. This song also created some sort of a wave in the Muslim community of Bombay. Though immensely popular it was but one song among the many that I had to sing for them. In spite of our taste for Sanskrit hymns, we nevertheless were keen to explore other types of music from various sources. It was the same with my Muslim friends. However rooted they were in Urdu language songs, they were ever eager for songs in other languages. I had to sing endlessly at their requests in Bengali and Hindi. There was a particularly favourite song that I had to sing repeatedly. It was 'Namo Hindustan' ('Hail Hindustan'), and they all joined in the singing.

Badruddin Tayebjis were six brothers and four sisters, and with the children of the brothers and the sisters and their own ten children it was a large extended family. In order to maintain a sense of family unity Tayebji had introduced a custom of holding a weekly dinner by turns, at different houses where the whole clan gathered. Being friendly with them I was included in these family dinners. Though a house guest of the Hydaris in Bombay, I became the focus of friendly rivalry amongst the many families about who could get me to their homes. A cousin of Mrs Hydari was the begum of the Nawab of Zanzira Island. Her name was Nazli Begum and her younger sister was Atia Bibi. Amina could not ignore Nazli Begum's request and allowed me to visit Zanzira Island for a few days. After they got to know me, the Tayebji family seriously took up the cultivation of music. Atia Bibi engaged the services of an Ustad (a master) for lessons in vocal music, and in the process initiated the patronage of classical music. A renowned member of the Congress, Abbas Tayebji was not only a nephew of Tayebji but also happened to be his son-in-law. His daughter developed into a fine singer with a sweet voice and many in the Congress had heard her. Her rendition of Mirabai's *bhajans* was particularly charming.

During my stay in Punjab, women there had just about started taking some interest in music. It was only in Madras and Mysore that I found the culture of music flourishing amongst the women.

North India had nothing in comparison. Ever since I started singing the 'Vande Mataram' at various gatherings, the popularity of the song soared and was picked up my many women throughout India. Talking about 'Vande Mataram' reminds me of a visit to Lahore of a well-known and senior English barrister in connection with some legal issue. Being invited to tea at our home he expressed an interest in listening to the song which he knew had been proscribed by the Bengal Government. I sang the song in accompaniment of the piano. When I finished, he said. 'By Jove! I may not have understood the words of the song, but the way you sang it convinced me what a tumultuous effect this song can have.' He then turned to my husband and told him, 'If I were anybody in the Bengal Government, I would have passed an order of expulsion on her so that she could never return to Bengal and start an agitation among the people there.'

Well, I do not think I was the only one who could galvanize people; there were many others. Bengal was then fortunately inundated by a plethora of competent women singers. Mrs Saviour, who headed the Vivekananda Asram in the Almora Hills, once told me, 'If nothing else, you will be able to stir up the nation just by going around the country singing this national song in the towns and villages.' Her remark struck a chord in me, and I often thought of forming a minstrel troupe and wandering round the country singing our national song to inspire our people. The country did not have to wait for this; on its own the country found its inspiration.

My arrival in the world of music was marked by my songs earning popularity with the people, bringing joy to them. I attribute this to beginner's luck, and not to any particular musical accomplishment of mine. I can hardly compete with the skill of the modern women singers. What I had to give to the country I did, and it is now the turn of the new generation of girls to pick up the baton.

Twelve

I have talked earlier about my many school friends who often visited us and stayed on for a few days, but we were never allowed to stay away from home. The only exception was the home of my friend Khusi whose father was Durgamohun Das. They lived on the second floor of a large house on Rawdon Street, regarded those days as a European locality. Khusi's eldest sister Sarala Ray occupied the middle floor of the same house with her husband P.K. Ray and her three children. Khusi's second elder sister Abala was then already married to Jagadish Bose and lived elsewhere.

Khusi had lost her mother many years ago. Her two brothers Satish and Jyotish, who later became well known as S.R.Das and J.R. Das, were very young then. It was said that Durgamohun Das took such excellent care of his motherless children that even mothers could not have done as much. Once when young Jyotish was ill, the doctor attending to him decreed that the boy was not to have any sweets. Durgamohun then himself refrained from eating sweets so that his son was not tempted. There were many such instances of his care for his children. No wonder then that the children grew up very devoted to their father. An instance of their concern for the elderly widowed father was the successful effort of his elder daughter to get him married to the widowed mother of Atul Prasad Sen, to look after him, to take care of him and be a companion at his advanced age. In turn, Durgamohun also took care of Atul Prasad and his three sisters, as if they were his own children.

A European lifestyle considerably dominated Khusi's home, particularly that of Mrs P.K. Ray's. Her three daughters went to the Loreto Convent School as did my Pratibha-*didi*, her two sisters as well as Bibi, but the ambience of our home did not allow any scope for European manners and custom. It was at Khusi's home that I first heard Bengali girls talking to each other in English. This had some kind of a glamour value and the little girls conversing in English, in a way, sounded attractive. But this charm was merely a veneer, generated by the trend of going against our own culture. Later when these children grow up and need to follow our cultural modes, they falter. In the so-called Anglo-Bengali society, girls who are taught in the English medium only with no grounding in Bengali language develop a quaint accent when they later start speaking in Bengali. This is neither like the distortions of English women trying to speak in Bengali, nor is it the natural way of speaking Bengali.

Khusi and Abala-*didi*, on the other hand, were products of a Bengali language school. In her later life Abala-*didi* left a mark demonstrating her abiding love for her country. In contrast, there is a curious story that was once doing the rounds about Sarala-*didi*. Apparently once when she was travelling in her car laden with purchases of foreign goods from the emporium of Whiteway & Laidlaw, she was stopped in front of the Presidency College by some *swadeshi* inspired students. They told her, 'Ma, please jettison those foreign goods, or else you will have to drive over our bodies.' There is no record how the story ended, but we saw no evidence of any slackening in her preference for foreign goods. The creation of 'The Gokhale Memorial School' is her great achievement, as to some extent, the 'Brahmo Girls School' is the creation of Abala-*didi*. The difference in the style and outlook of these two institutions reflects the cultural and intellectual divide between the two sisters.

Khusi, by inclination, was not a particularly energetic person, but after coming in contact with our family, she gradually turned into a *swadeshi* in her thoughts and attitude. She also helped out in one my mother's programmes of her Sakhi Samiti. One of the aims of this Samiti was to provide scholarships to train women teachers who after qualification would be assigned to teach other women in their homes. This was a time-consuming plan as until the training was completed no teachers could be sent out. Meanwhile requests

104   *The Many Worlds of Sarala Devi*

were pouring in for teachers. Khusi by then was married and lived on Beadon Street, very much a Bengali locality. She had no children then, and volunteered her service. 'I have enough time on my hand and am prepared to go out and teach. The money I will earn from the students will go to the fund of the Sakhi Samiti,' is what she told mother.

This activity continued as long as Khusi could do it but not thereafter, because none of the scholarship holders ever returned to discharge their obligations. The award of this scholarship, on the other hand, improved the prospects of the girls' marriage. Either the scholarship awardees or their guardians had to execute a bond that at the end of their training the girls would have to serve Sakhi Samiti for a specified period, or else they would be liable to refund the money spent on their training. But this liability remained a paper promise as none of the girls ever offered their services to the Samiti, nor did their guardians or husbands come forward to pay the compensation as agreed, save for one person. Sakhi Samiti could sue them but chose not to. The violators of the agreement continued to live with their transgressions, and the idea of educating women at home was abandoned. Much later I took up this task again when I founded the Bharat Stree Mahamandal.

Khusi was very close to the women of a Bengali family. They were the wife, daughters and a daughter-in-law of Justice Chandra Madhav Ghose, who lived in the European quarter of the town. His younger daughter Nalini, married to Jagadish Roy, was particularly fond of Khusi. Once when I was at Khusi's place she suggested that I should go with her to meet these friends of hers. I was in two minds because I never went anywhere without telling my mother, but Khusi assured me, 'Come along, I will clear it with your mother, she would take no offence.'

And so I did and had a wonderful time. The eldest daughter of Justice Ghose—she was Didimoni to everyone—was an adorable character. She had been widowed at an early age, was childless, and a zamindar of Taki. Post widowhood she came to reside with her parents, where she was coached in English by an English governess. She knew her Bengali very well, of course. She had a very high regard for the culture of our family, our standard of education, our proficiency in art and literature and our talent for music. She was most grateful to Khusi for introducing someone like me from an illustrious family, particularly a daughter of Swarnakumari Devi, to them. Our ties became so close that Khusi appeared to take a back seat, but in reality that was not so. I just happened to be another dear friend in addition to Khusi.

Soon followed my singing sessions, as elsewhere, the only difference was that in other places my audience included appreciative men, but in this house only women were my audience – women with whom I soon formed a cultural bond. Nalini's children were treated by Didimoni as her own. Nalini's two sons were Rabi and Chhabi, her two daughters Bina and Bibha. Chhabi's official name was Ashok, who later became well known as Sir A.K.Roy. He was adopted by Didimoni as her son, and most people knew her to be his mother. For all the children in the family Didimoni was the universal Mamoni.

When Bina reached school-going age she was sent to Loreto Convent. For her comely looks nature was responsible, but for her trim and elegant dresses, credit must go to Didimoni. Despite being surrounded by Anglo-Indian schoolmates and taught at home by an Anglo-Indian governess, there was no trace of any anglicized attitude in Bina. And this was all due to the masterly supervision at home by Didimoni.

There are certain chemical elements which easily dissolve and blend with other elements. Perhaps there were some such elements in my make up that I found it easy to mix with people who were unlike me, and form a bond with them. One such person was Mrs P.K. Ray. Though we had no common ground on national issues, she had certain attributes that drew me to her. She was a very cheerful sort of person, with an abundant sense of fun and humour, extremely sociable, mixed well with people, and was peerless when looking after others. The depth of her character was not always evident, but behind her cheerful countenance dwelt a very earnest and serious personality. Though not well versed in Bengali, she was a keen follower of weighty English literature, such as, the works of the American philosopher Emerson. On occasions she would discuss such literature with me. What most impressed me about her was that she was an embodiment of two streams of culture – English as well as Indian. At her Ballygunge home she would often have friends for lunch, and then for games of tennis in the afternoon. If the cook happened to be sick, that would not worry her as she would do the cooking herself turning out a wide variety of Bengali dishes, as well as some snacks for the afternoon tea. After a change of clothes she would come down to the tennis court, play a set or two, and then entertain the guests, tempting them to taste her food.

106   *The Many Worlds of Sarala Devi*

She was also an excellent nurse to sick persons. Her foreign guests were extremely comfortable at her home. She had once a Norwegian theist as her guest, who was not well off. She persuaded me to engage him to teach me French. The poor man soon had an attack of cholera, and despite Sarala Ray's intense care the man could not be saved. Ramaswami Iyenger from Mysore stayed as her guest, and it was Sarala who fixed his marriage with a sister of Atul Prasad. Gokhale was another eminent person who accepted her hospitality. In fact, whenever he visited Calcutta he invariably stayed with them. A testimony to their abiding friendship is the founding of The Gokhale Memorial School.

During one Puja holidays Dr P.K. Ray and Mrs Ray decided to travel to Mysore via Madras, assiduously persuaded by Ramaswami Iyenger. Sarala-*didi* asked me to join them. I hesitated wondering if mother would agree. Sarala-*didi* assured me not to worry as she would fix it with mother. Those days one had to travel to Madras by sea. Until then I had not set my eyes on a sea, let alone sailing on it. I did not wish to miss such a wonderful opportunity, particularly under the care of the Rays. My parents gave their consent, and this was the very first occasion that I stepped into a large sea-faring vessel.

Earlier on some occasions I had lived in *natun-mama's* houseboat 'Sarojini', moored on the Ganges. Leaving terra firma I had had a taste of life in a boat, and it was an unforgettable experience. When in the dead of night our boat would get rocked by a passing steamer or a large boat, the boatmen, awakened from their sleep, would start talking cacophonously across the boats, my sleep would also get disturbed and I would realize that I was not in my bedroom at my home, but in a strange and unknown surrounding. The early morning mist would cover the river surface with a film, and as the mist would clear, the sun would become visible long after the actual sunrise. One felt far more intimate with this sun than our familiar sun that we saw every day from our home. And looking out of the boat window is great fun, watching the water creatures frolicking around. This is not our familiar world on land; it is another world altogether.

We set sail on a large boat of the British Steam Navigation Co., for Madras. My immediate reaction was as if I had stepped into a piece of England. The lifestyle on the boat was absolutely English. Early in the morning stewards brought in tea and biscuits, then after a leisurely soak lying in long bathtubs in the common bathrooms, we dressed up for the day. To the dining room for breakfast at nine in the morning, where places were fixed for each passenger. Ours was a table for three. After an English breakfast passengers went up on to the deck, resting on reserved chairs or reading a book half reclined. Some chose to walk around the deck, a few engaged in talking to each others, some others just watching the passing sea. A few English and Armenian barristers whom we had known were also our shipmates. Around one o'clock in the afternoon, we were back in the dining room again for lunch, which was a larger meal than breakfast. Then followed rest and siesta in the cabins, then the afternoon tea and snacks, and up once again on to the deck to go for more walking or engaging in games provided for exercise to work up an appetite for the dinner. For dinner it was obligatory to change into evening clothes. Women had to wear silk and not cotton. That was the established etiquette, and the more one abided by the etiquette, the more one was known as a civilized creature. We reached Madras on the fourth day, and of these four days I stayed up on my feet for a day and half only. For the rest of the journey I fell victim to sea sickness, remaining confined to my cabin, with no desire at all to eat. The kindly stewards would try and cajole me to have some food. I suspect it is this abundance of food that tempts European men and women to travel by sea. The outlay by the steamer companies on catering for food must be far in excess of the fuel cost for the engines. The cost of the journey includes food whether one eats or does not, and there is no rebate if one chooses not to eat.

We sighted the coast of Madras on the fourth day. Here the ship did not berth at the dockside, but anchored on the sea some distance away from the shore, from where one was ferried across the short distance to the port on a country boat of the catamaran type. This was a rather tricky business; passengers hung on to a rope and were then hauled down with the help of the *khalasis* and then jumped on to the boat, trying to keep their balance. This was the only way to reach port. The sea around the Madras coast is choppy, which apparently can be tamed by catamarans only. Although I described this trip as tricky, there has been no report, to my knowledge, of any accidents or tragic consequences.

At the port waiting to receive us was Mr Rajani Ray, who was then the Accountant General of Madras. He was a close friend of the Das family, and his wife Bidhumukhi Devi was distantly related to me through my cousin Sushila-*didi*. They were hosts for our stay

108   *The Many Worlds of Sarala Devi*

in Madras of about ten days. Each day Rajani-*babu* would invite some of his Madrasi friends to meet us. Almost all of them were educated Christians or members of the Brahmo Samaj. We never got to meet any high caste Hindus as they were very orthodox. While in Madras I once heard a man singing somewhere close by, and as is my nature I immediately ran down and caught hold of the singer, a Madrasi. From him I picked up a couple of songs. The words were harsh and jarring to our ears, but the melody was lovely. At a dinner party I sang my just learnt Madrasi songs for Rajani-*babu*'s guests. As Christians they were normally used to western style music, and so were rather surprised and amused to hear me singing local songs. Some of them confirmed that I had quite faithfully reproduced the nuances of Madrasi music. Thus was initiated my collection of South Indian music.

Rajani-*babu*'s daughters could also sing, particularly his elder daughter Sukumari had a fine voice, but they were not crazy about music as I was. Otherwise during their stay in Madras they could have collected some local songs and gifted them to Bengal, which they did not. Perhaps, in the manner of Bengalis, they were indifferent to music other than their own. Bengalis sadly find nothing attractive about the music of other parts of the country; on the contrary they tend to make fun of it.

From Madras we travelled to Mysore where we were received by Dr Ramaswami Iyenger's uncle, Durbar Buxi. He had made all arrangements for our visit, and we were State guests there. Stepping into Mysore I felt I have arrived at a land of music. Music seemed to be floating in the air all the time. This music was nothing like the North Indian music; it had its own distinctive South Indian flavour. I went to the Maharani Girls' School, where I was charmed by the singing of the granddaughter of the Dewan. She rendered classical compositions of the most celebrated Telegu poet and composer Thyagarajan. I persuaded this girl to teach me some of the songs. Returning home I gifted them to Rabi-*mama* who later adopted these songs to write and compose Brahmosangits and thus expanded the orbit of Bengali music. Many of my maternal uncles in their travels collected devotional music from Gujarat and songs of Sikh gurus from Punjab, and wedded these melodies to Bengali music. There is a Bengali saying which avers that 'Men take to maternal uncles'. In my case it was a woman following the maternal uncles. Yes, I did indeed walk the path chalked out by my music-loving maternal uncles.

Thirteen

When after her marriage *Didi* left to set up her own home and my elder brother went away to England, I was the only child left at home. That provided me with the scope to get closer to mother. Until he left for England my brother was still at home, but being a man his was an outgoing life. To accommodate his fancy an Arab pony was bought for him. After a horse ride in the morning he would either visit our cousin Suren or get him and some others to our home in the evening. Sometimes they would hunt for jackals hidden in their burrows. That apparently seemed to be his main occupation; studies were secondary. About then, a children's magazine *Sakha* announced a poetry competition, and encouraged by mother I put down my name for it. Eventually I was adjudged the winner, and the prize was an English language book called *Classical Dictionary* that retold ancient Greek and Roman mythological tales. This was my first public exposure as a writer, although I had made some earlier forays in writing.

Our family often travelled to Santiniketan where my maternal grandfather had a house. Santiniketan those days was really an abode of peace for people of all ages. Shorn of work-related hustles and clamour of people, peace reigned supreme there. Arranged around the cornice of the portico of the Santiniketan house was a variety of large seashells. I had never seen such seashells before, and they held some sort of mystery for me. If you put one close to your ear you could almost hear the roaring sea surf, as if the sea

110   *The Many Worlds of Sarala Devi*

had secreted its turbulent heart inside it. The very conception of a sea was clothed in mystery for us until we became familiar with the term when it was announced that grandfather would be travelling to China by sea. May be these shells were collected during that visit.

Equally mystifying was the Khowai Hills of Bolpur and the mini streamlets that gurgled through their sandy surface. This could possibly be my initiation into the science of geology in the natural surroundings of Bolpur. Each branch of science helps to expand the horizon of human knowledge and ideas, but perhaps none of them can be so extensive in reach and thus help in broadening the mind as the knowledge of geology and astronomy. Geology takes us on a time travel exposing for us the various layers that formed and shaped our earth over millions of years, and astronomy opens up for us the space above, the limitless space that we call the sky. Whenever we look up at the sky, all we see is an endless blank space, a firmament not fixed to anything, a sight that brings home the concept of the infinity.

But does a boundless infinity produce any sense of fulfillment or comfort? I think not! Limitlessness becomes incomprehensible, that is why, probably, landscape painters put something identifiable amidst a large space – it could be the figure of a bird or animal, may even be a human figure. Yes, empty space can lead to monotony and lassitude. It is in a way possible to continue to live without any real knowledge of what constitutes life in scientific terms, but one must have some perception of what being alive means. If we can ever divine in our heart from this infinite expanse the image of our creator who is the source of all life in the mortal world, that is finite and bounded, then we can at least derive a measure of gratification by moving away from the eternal emptiness. I had that experience once when I visited the Kulu hills in the Himalayas with my five-year-old son. There were the two of us under the infinite expanse of space, with my living God occupying the entire sky above. And what was the image of my living God? Not dormant, but wide awake and alert. He was not formless; He saw everything; He heard everything; He moved along freely all over through the earth and the space untrammeled. His vision was a thousand times as powerful than the eyes of human beings; His sense of hearing a thousand times more acute than human ears; and with those eyes He keeps watching us all the time, and with those ears He keeps listening to all what we say. He is loving, not non-existent or dead,

Sukhendu Ray 111

not impaired of sight or hearing. He has a mind of his own. He is wise, omnipotent, omnipresent, omniscient. I once recounted this experience of mine to an English lady friend, which made such a deep impression on her that she apparently retold this tale over and over again to many others.

We were a large party visiting Bolpur, a mixture of people of all ages that included my contemporaries, my seniors, and juniors. Among the visiting party were *natun-mami*, Saroja-*didi*, Mohini-*babu*, and poet and solicitor Akshoy Chaudhury with his wife, who was a friend of my mother.

From the banks of the small streams we often picked up attractive pebbles, and one of the wise men in the group told us, 'These pebbles were once fruit or flower trees, now ossified being submerged under water for centuries. They are known as fossils.' With this knowledge we marked that spot, dug a hole and buried some amlaki fruits. Each time we went back we dug up the spot to see the extent of petrifaction, until some one warned us, 'You idiots, how can you expect a fossil so soon? Let them lie underground for at least fifty years when you may find your amlaki fruits turning into stone.' For the time being we abandoned any hope of returning fifty years later to look for our fossilized amlakis. Fifty years are long over, and no one gave any thought to our amlakis. Meanwhile, the river with its sand bank shifted its course much further away.

Anyway to return to our Bolpur visit, after our morning excursions we returned home to demolish piles of *luchis* and vegetable preparations, winding up our repast with the famed *patkhir* of Bolpur, followed by rest. In this context I remember my father's efforts to reform low caste people and employ them in domestic service, even as cooks. Twenty years later I found in Punjab the movement of the Arysamaj to re-admit low castes with great sanctimony. I found my father achieve this with no fuss at all when he engaged the son of a watchman who belonged to the lowly *dom* community as his bearer, and trained him to be an efficient worker. He served us at the table, and if needed, even cooked for us, with no disagreement from any quarter.

It was at Santiniketan that the writing bug seized me. The children's magazine *Sakha* (a friend) turned out to be truly a friend! During the afternoon, I used to read avidly all that was printed in that magazine, and that triggered my yearning to write. I started to write secretly and in a couple of days wrote a short story. Saroja-*didi* found me out. She appropriated my notebook, and made fun

112 *The Many Worlds of Sarala Devi*

of me. 'Look here, our Sarala is going to be a writer. She has composed a story. Is it going to be printed in a journal?'

Taunts of seniors can be very tragic for the youngsters. Saroja-*didi*'s derision effectively stopped my urge to write. Much later encouraged by my mother I sent in a poem for a poetry competition to *Sakha*, but that did not restore my incentive to write again. Those days I was far more interested in reading, particularly Bengali literature. I got hold of old copies of *Bharati* and delved deeply into them. *Natun-mama* was a frequent contributor to this magazine; his forte was classy humorous pieces, like Ramiad, a parody of Iliad, which tickled me no end. In fact, there was usually a witty sketch in each issue of *Bharati*. I wrote one anonymously which mother accepted for publication. Many readers attributed this piece to some well known author, which convinced me that perhaps I may have a gift for writing.

The comic songs of D.L. Roy reached us much later, but for a long time, they remained entertainment items only for singing sessions. Before I left for my job in Mysore I collected much of his music, and based on them, I sent an article to *Bharati*, titled 'Bengali Humorous Songs and Their Writer'. An upshot of this article was the soaring popularity of D.L. Roy's music and his songs soon gained the reputation of the highest literary merit. Till his dying day D.L. Roy never forgot my friendly action.

After *Sakha* some of my writings were published in the magazine *Balak*. Girindramohini at that time was a good friend of my mother. Gobindo Datta of the Akrur Datta family, and a relation of Girindramohini, was a keen follower of literature. My writings in *Balak* so impressed him that he wrote to Rabi-*mama* whom he knew, making a prediction that 'One day this young writer will find her place in Bengali literature as a mature writer'. Rabi-*mama* told me about this letter, with a smile, and I am not sure to this day whether his smile was of approbation or dismissive. I was, after all, no more that twelve years of age then.

Meanwhile, the time was drawing near for me to appear for the 'Test' examination to qualify to sit for the final Entrance examination. Mother, out of the blue, abruptly commented, 'I have a hunch that you will come first in the Test.' I found this ridiculous considering that Hemaprabha was also taking the Test. Strangely enough, my mother's words proved to be right. Not only did I top the Test, I was also the only successful candidate from our school at the final Entrance Examination, winning a scholarship in the process. Poor Hemaprabha, having scored low marks in one of the subjects, failed the Entrance. This affected her health so badly that for two years, she had to suspend her studies. The examiner for the History paper of the Entrance Exams was Mr N. Ghose, a barrister. He was well known as a 'note book' writer for English text books as well as the editor of the weekly, *Indian Nation*. Our History paper that year included a question on Clive's conquest of Bengal based on Macaulay's book, 'Lord Clive', which was the prescribed book for history. The question carried a lot of marks. The answer I wrote was entirely my own comments protesting against the views of Macaulay condemning the character of the Bengalis. We came to know later through sources that Mr Ghose, the examiner, instead of rejecting my answer as was expected, had actually awarded me very high marks. He was clearly impressed with my answer and had apparently made some enquiries to discover my identity. I believe that year I had scored the highest marks in the history paper.

Already a sense of pride for the achievement of the Bengalis had taken root in my mind. This consciousness fully unfolded ten years later or so when I started a nationwide movement in retaliation to a short story by Kipling, in which he had slandered the Bengalis venomously. I shall refer to that later in my story. It was then that I conceived of commemorating Bengali heroes like Pratapiditya as my tribute to our people.

My *didi*'s husband Phani-*dada* was a professor at Rajshahi College the year I passed my Entrance examination. *Didi* had arranged for mother's visit to them. Father was then away for the Congress session at Allahabad. When I went to see my mother off at the railway station, the very thought of parting from her so overcame me that I broke down. Mother was disturbed and quickly arranged for a ticket for me to travel with her. My requirements for clothes and other things were dispatched by a later train. This was my very first trip to the interior of Bengal. Come to think of it, I won the day ridiculously through my tears!

But in truth I was not that easily moved to tears; on the contrary I was more inclined to laughter and smiles. For no reason at all I would break into giggles. Sitting in a classroom when the professor was lecturing, suddenly espying a crow cawing perched on the veranda cornice would provoke me to chortles. It could be my cheerful nature as well as my skill as a raconteur that earned me much popularity in school, among both seniors and juniors.

114   *The Many Worlds of Sarala Devi*

Sir Taraknath Palit's son, the civilian Loken Palit, was the Assistant Magistrate at Rajshahi. Both our families have been longstanding friends. Loken Palit spent most of his free time with us when we were at Rajshahi. He had inherited his father's gift of being a good talker and kept us regaled with stories of his time at Cambridge University. The intimate style in which he spoke about his friends there made them come alive to us. Loken was an 'intellectual' with a deep knowledge of English literature, particularly poetry. It was a delight to talk to him and discuss all manners of literary topics. He once remarked to us, 'At Cambridge I was so close to my English and Scottish friends that it never occurred to me that we were different. But then I heard them sing a song:

Rule Britannia! Britannia rules the waves!
Britons never shall be slaves.

Then it dawned on me how far away I am from them, and it left a deep scar in my heart.'

Loken became our constant companion, be it in discussions on literature or politics, or at meals, or in our recreations. He once set an essay contest between *Didi* and myself, the theme was 'Love and Friendship'. I can recall one sentence of the essay I wrote — 'Friendship is love without wings'. I must have picked this up from some English writing, because I could hardly have any original thoughts on the theme at that point of time. I used to be an eager reader of writers like George Elliot then. Anyway, Loken announced that I was the winner and gave me the prize. *Didi* was very annoyed, accused Loken of favouritism, a proof of which was that he had already inscribed my name on the prize. The prize was a 'spectroscope', comprising a hundred sketches. Each picture was split into two, which when put together made the actual picture emerge clearly.

Loken was challenged to explain himself. He blandly declared that he knew I would produce a better composition. This, of course, did not abate my sister's pique, but as was my nature I burst into splits of laughter seeing them at loggerheads. I have always been like that; even adverse comments about me provoked me to amusement.

We used to go out in the evenings for walks. Rajshahi town at one end was fringed by a forest, and we thought of visiting it. We were warned that the forest was still infested with tigers, and that we needed to be extremely careful. We should all be together, create

Sukhendu Ray 115

a great deal of din, and must clap our hands loudly. We must remember to get back before it got dark. Being town bred we took in the story of the tigers with a grain of salt, not quite believing it. Once again the thought that a caged tiger in a zoo would confront us out in the open struck me as most amusing! I blurted out like a naïve idiot, 'What if I feel like laughing out at the sight of a tiger!' *Didi* commented, 'Great, just like a babe, laughs at everything'. Loken's comment was, 'I doubt if she really will start laughing if she confronts a real tiger out there.'

A heart unburdened of cares and anxieties leads to a fearless mind. The world around you then appears to be cheerful, and life, a load of fun. Not being conscious of horrors that fear can generate makes one intrepid. Even when I suffered from horrific thoughts, my innate nature tended to disregard them and laugh them away. During the dark days of my political life, Mahatma Gandhi told me, 'Your laughter is a national asset! Keep laughing!' It is not that I never shed tears in my life. Of course I did, but privately in my home, not in the presence of other people. In a Buddhist Jataka tale Bodhisatta tells someone, 'The tears I shed in my many lives, if collected, will form an ocean.' I suppose it is so for all human beings.

Fourteen

Our Kashiabagan home was the meeting point of our many relations — near and distant. Almost everyone from Jorasanko visited us regularly. The four brothers of Mohini-*babu* became as close as our own family. The second brother Ramani eventually married Usha-*didi,* younger sister of Saroja-*didi.* Ramani-*babu* immediately became a part of our family, and during the absence of Mohini-*babu* in England, it was Ramani-*babu* who took care of their large family. My father helped him to find a job in the Municipality of Calcutta. As a student and until his marriage, the fourth brother Rajani was also a regular visitor to our home. He was a meritorious student, and retold to us many tales from the books that he had read. I believe it was from him that I heard the story of Ivanhoe. He also taught us how to swim.

Rajani was more friendly to *Didi* as I was then rather young. His marriage with Sunayani, a younger sister of Gagan-*dada,* was fixed when he was still a student, and this restricted his visits to us, which was unfortunate. On the night of his wedding we watched from the veranda of Jorasanko the arrival of the groom in a procession with music and illumination. The groom travelled in a landau with an ornamental umbrella above his head. He was looking very handsome; he happened to be the fairest of his brothers. The minute he entered house No. 6/1 he disappeared from our life. There was no social contact between our home and of Gagan-*dada*'s. They were closer to the families of Pathuriaghata, Koilaghata and Madan-

babu, though our kinship was closer. Still, a day came when Dipu-*dada*'s son Dinu got married to a daughter of Sunayani and Rajani. She was the first wife of Dinu, and after her premature death, Dinu married for the second time into the family of Madan-*babu*, with whom our family had no contact for years. Time separates families; time again brings them back together. That is how it goes. As a matter of fact, much later, Pratima, daughter of Binayini, the eldest of Gagan-*dada*'s sisters, was married to Rathi, Rabindranath's son, Rathindranath.

After his marriage Rajani made his home with his in-laws, and that was the end of our contact with him. All his other brothers maintained their normal relationship with us. Mohini-*babu* was wise and erudite. Ramani-*babu* possessed great common sense, and was also an academic. He used then to teach at Vidyasagar College. Sajani, the youngest of the lot, was somewhat childish and a little crazy. I believe towards the end of his life he had lost his mental balance. Jogini, the other brother, was peculiar. There were times when he went completely silent like a clam. Some of our cousins made fun of him and ragged him, 'I say bird, perched in your cage, with your eyes shut, what thoughts do assail you?' But nothing riled him, and he remained quite impervious. He was adept in games of dice, and was unbeatable in debates and games of cards. My mother eventually helped him to qualify as a barrister from England. He had perhaps some sort of an expectation in life, but appeared to have realized in England that he was not going to achieve it. He did enroll to practise at Calcutta High Court, but his livelihood apparently came from his winnings from the game of bridge. In England he had married an English woman and had a daughter by her, but when he returned home, he left both of them behind. Being dutiful he remitted money for their maintenance, but reticent by nature, he never told anyone at home about his foreign wife and child. It became public knowledge much later when after the death this English wife, a grown-up young girl turned up in Calcutta and went straight to Mohini-*babu*'s home. She was Jogini's daughter, a nice young person, and she later qualified as a medical doctor.

There was another regular visitor to our home. He was Abinash Chakravarty, a son of the poet Biharilal Chakravarty, on whom the poet doted and wrote a poem on him, 'My Dear Son', and the son became well known overnight. He was a simple and unpretentious person, very fond of music. I was once playing on the piano that

118   *The Many Worlds of Sarala Devi*

classical composition of Beethoven, 'The Moonlight Sonata'. He apparently listened to it from an adjoinong room, and when I finished playing he came to me and said enthusiastically, 'How lovely!' The next day he came armed with a poem that he had composed for me, calling it, 'For my dear sister, the beautiful Sarala'. His visits became infrequent and finally ceased altogether. I believe that the poor man later lost his mind.

A new family was introduced to Kashiabagan—that of Ashu Chaudhury and his brothers. They came with a different sort of background, of the glamour of modernism. They were originally from Pabna, but they seemed to be influenced by the culture of Krishnanagar. Their Bengali diction had a touch of the diction of the brothers Monomohan and Lalmohan Ghose, and they, like these two brothers, were supremely eloquent. Their outlook was shaped by new and radical ideas. Ashu-*babu* was the most impressive of the brothers; he had such an attractive quality that drew everyone to him. His third brother Kumud was also to some extent gifted like him.

Loken, needless to say, as a dear old friend, came to see us whenever he was on leave. He and Ashu-*babu* had been good friends when they were in England, and through us, Loken got to know the younger brothers of Ashu-*babu*. Coincidentally, around the same time, I appeared to develop a gift for writing.

After my early writings came out in the children's magazine *Balak*, I contributed anonymously a humorous piece to *Bharati*, calling it, 'Premik Sabha' ('An Association of Lovers'), and like Byron, I found that overnight I became well known as a writer. Praises poured forth, and topping them all was an unexpected felicitation from Rabi-*mama*. 'This piece of writing was objectively assessed because you did not put down your name. The effort truly was nothing like a novice's, but that of a mature and well established writer.' This tribute took my breath away, and I accepted it with a combined feeling of exultation and humility. Sadly, there were some unpleasant offshoots: resentment of some writers with a feeling of inferiority; some other writers outraged through frustration. Anyway, this storm in a tea cup fortunately soon died down.

My pen flourished, and I started writing critical essays on Sanskrit poetic literature. The first to come out was 'Rati Bilap' based on Kumarasambhava of Kalidas. On reading it Hiren Datta sent his comments, 'There is a freshness of approach in this essay.' A couple of years before his death, when I was reading to him my article, 'Neeler Uposh', he, while complimenting me on the essence of what I wanted to say and my language, said to me, 'Have you given any thought to publishing a book containing all your writings? You are depriving the world of Bengali literature by not doing so. Your "Rati Bilap", I recall, created a sensation, but none of these pieces have come out in any book. There is still time to do that.'

My next essay was 'Malabika-Agnimitra'. I had sent this piece to Bankim-*babu*, and the priceless letter that he wrote me about it was sadly lost in fire during the political turmoil in Punjab. I also lost at the same time the complimentary letter I had received from Rabi-*mama* for the same essay along with at least fifty other letters that I had received from him since my younger days—all consigned to flames.

This was followed by 'Malati-Madhav', a part of my texts for my college syllabus. I also started on 'Mrichhakatik', but never did finish it. I had planned to publish my various compositions in a book which I had tentatively named 'Kabimandir'. As I was then moving to Lahore I had asked Dinesh Sen to oversee the printing, but he gave up after a few pages were done. I could not trace those printed pages afterwards, though I had paid the printers their dues in advance. I realized that it was a fruitless exercise to get any book published when you were away. Later when I returned home, I made some renewed effort to get the book printed, but with the ruinous world war then raging, printing paper was a scarcity. I was advised to abandon my plan.

My mother and I travelled to Solapur where my *mejo-mama* was at that time. The Gaekwad of Baroda came to grace the festival of Dussera during the Durga Pujas, that was organized by the Marathi Club. The Prince had a most royal manner and charmed us by the courtesy he showed mother and me. What struck me was the way the occasion was celebrated. It comprised demonstration of various martial arts with swords and rods, and physical exercises; also speeches on Marathi valour. No dances or music were performed by professional women, nor was there any orgy of drinking, which we find in Calcutta.

From there we proceeded to Poona to attend a fancy dress ball of the Bombay Presidency civilians. We—my mother, *mejo-mama* and I—happened to be the only Indians present at the ball, the rest of the gathering consisting entirely of European men and women. My mother, I remember, went dressed as a female ascetic, and I, as the goddess Saraswati. Mother always did look great in that garb

120   *The Many Worlds of Sarala Devi*

of an ascetic. Once she had a role of an ascetic when we staged Basanta Utsav, in which *natun-mami* acted as the neglected heroine, who with the blessing of the ascetic, won back her lost love.

The fancy dress ball for which we visited Poona failed to leave any permanent impression in my memory — transient like the drop of water on a lotus petal, as the saying goes. I recalled Loken's observation about the unbridgeable gulf between us and the English people. Anyway, what impressed me most when travelling through the town of Poona was when we stopped at the memorial tower erected to honour the glory of the Peshawas. The manner in which Dussera was celebrated in Solapur and the pride in the Peshwa glory enshrined in the memorial tower sowed a seed in my mind from which was born idea of marking the achievement of Bengali heroes. I had then penned an article for the *Bharati*, 'Bengalis and Marathis', drawing attention to the difference in the attitudes of these two communities. I wished to transform the character of the Bengali people through changes in the pattern of their festivals.

Participation in dances by girls has now become fairly common, whether in homes, at schools or at ceremonial gatherings. In our days even to take two steps in time with music was considered a social gaffe. I did something daring once by inducing some girls to dance to a song of Rabindranath. Another move of mine perhaps was even more daring!

Altogether, I spent ten years of my life in Bethune School which I entered at the age of seven years and left at the age of seventeen after I had earned my B.A. degree. My connection with the school however continued. Each year for the annual prize distribution ceremony the then lady superintendent Chandramukhi Basu and later Kumudini Khastagir invited me to coach the students for their musical presentation. One year I taught them a song I had composed. The song was actually written on the occasion to felicitate Jagadish Chandra Bose by *natun-mama's* music society. The notation of this song can be found in my musical scores for one hundred songs. During the rehearsal of this song Bipin Pal wrote in his journal, 'My daughters were practising a new song, the words of which struck me as extraordinary. Till now all our patriotic songs were full of anguish and dejection, always lamenting our lost glory. The tenor of this song is quite the opposite. Standing firmly in the present it sends out vigorously a bright message of a glorious future.'

Sukhendu Ray 121

Attending the prize day function was Sir Gurudas Bannerjee who was a member of the school committee. He appeared to be restless when this song was presented, and the following day told Chandramukhi Basu that it was not an appropriate song for the school. He particularly disapproved of the last lines of the song as they alluded to our country being in bondage.

During my student days the system of boys and girls studying together was unknown. When I commenced my F.A. course I was keen like Sudhi-*dada* to take up Physics as a subject, but disappointingly it was not offered at Bethune School. I made fruitless appeals to the Education Department to grant me the scope to read Physics but with no results. Finally it was arranged that I could attend the evening lectures at Dr Mahendrala Sarkar's Science Association. Dr Sarkar was a family friend. These evening lectures were filled with F.A. students from various colleges, all men, the only woman being me. Outside the lecture hall I was made to wait in the room occupied by Dr Sarkar and Father Lafont. With me were Sudhi-*dada* and my elder brother. Just before the lectures commenced I proceeded to the hall escorted by my *dada*s. The boys sniggered, 'The bodyguards!' Three chairs were placed in the front for us, while the boys occupied the benches behind us.

Thus progressed my lessons in Physics. I could have taken up Botany at Bethune School as this subject did not need any apparatus, but my heart was in Physics. I was helped out by Jogesh-*babu*, the second brother of Ashu Chaudhury. He had not yet travelled to England and was then a professor at the Metropolitan College. My perseverance paid off, and in due course I passed my examination and was awarded a silver medal. Since then I came to know Father Lafont quite well. He was just not a teacher of St Xavier's College, but was a popular sociable person. He was invited to dinners, to evening parties and to various other functions. He was a person of great charm, excellent in conversation and extremely courteous.

When I was an undergraduate student, two girls arrived from Lucknow's Miss Thoburn's School and became my classmates. Both were Indian Christians—one a Bengali girl Sarat Chakravarty, and the other, a North Indian girl called Ethel Rafael. Sarat was a committed Christian, full of missionary zeal. On her own, she admitted that she would go to any length to get Hindu girls converted to Christianity, even to the extent of enticing them away, secreting them in her own home, and putting their relatives on a

122 *The Many Worlds of Sarala Devi*

false trail. Ethel was a person of an altogether different hue. Also an orthodox Christian but she would never stoop to deception. Not pretty, there was some sort of a wistfulness in her eyes that made one warm up to to her. That was also Rabi-*mama*'s impression when he met her once our home.

At Bethune College, Ethel was passing through some sort of an internal conflict. Customarily, particularly in Punjab and North India, Indian Christian converts renounce their family names and adopt western names. That accounted for why Ethel was Ethel Rafael, though originally as a Rajput, her family name was Singh. Coming in contact with us she started developing a strong nationalistic inclination. On her next visit home during the summer vacation she officially changed her name by legal process to Leela Singh and it is as Leela Singh that she graduated from Calcutta University. Also as Leela Singh, she gave up the western mode of dress and took to wearing saris, and thus clad, she visited the USA as a representative of the Indian Christian women. Nationalistic spirit completely pervaded her.

These days Indian converts to Christianity retain their original family names. I recall those times when it was not so and how it had led to a dilemma in Lahore. Some converts to Christianity, to secure advantages, used their adopted western names to be entitled to the pay scale applicable to expatriate European employees. When the provincial Government woke up to this deception, it immediately ruled that such converts must add their Indian surname to their names to ensure that they were in fact 'natives'. Their pay scale was reduced. Leela Singh by voluntarily regaining her family name was able to maintain her self respect.

For a period of three years after my graduation I worked for the magazine *Bharati*. The thought of marriage was farthest from my mind then; clearly I had dedicated my heart and soul to myself. I was also toying with the idea of earning a post-graduate degree in Sanskrit, but privately studying at home. When Mahesh Nayaratna heard of my plan he warned me. 'Let me see how you acquire your Master's degree not attending the Sanskrit College!' My teacher Professor Shitalchandra Vedantabagish was equally confident of my success. He started me with the text of Sankhyakarika, and was delighted with some of my questions to him. Only one other student, he told me, had raised similar points with him. He was Hiren Datta, truly brilliant, sparkling like diamond.

Sukhendu Ray 123

In the end I never did complete my Master's, effectively succumbing to Mahesh Nayaratna's dire warning. The truth was that I had been restless for sometime; I wanted to get away from the cage called home, be on my own, travel to some faraway place, be able to earn my living independently as my brother did. I continued to pester my father until he gave in, albeit most grudgingly. It now remained for me to obtain my grandfather's consent. He was not known to oppose independent wishes of his children, so it was even more unlikely that he would do so for his grandchildren. The old man did not stop *mejo-mama* when he proposed take his wife to England with him. Nor did he demur when upon their return from England *mejo-mami* accompanied her husband to receptions at the Government House. On the other hand, so the story goes, the old retainers of the family were shocked that a wife of the family, namely, *mejo-mami* walking out through the gate to get into a carriage. When the women of this family went for a dip in the Ganges the palanquin that carried them was itself immersed in the river with the passengers sitting inside. That was the custom then. Even for visiting a neighbour one had to ride in a palanquin. And yet, when *mejo-mami*, in breach of all those old family taboos, travelled to England following the wishes of her husband, grandfather was no obstacle. I was, therefore, confident that grandfather would not stop me. Nevertheless, I had to tell him and ask for his blessings. He willingly gave his consent, and later told my *baro-mashi*, 'If Sarala takes a vow never to marry, then, before I die, I would like to get her married to a sword.'

This strange romantic pronouncement got me thinking. Am I prepared to take the extreme position that I shall never get married? During the period when the wave of theosophy ran through our home, a Mataji from Kashi visited us. I recall a remark of my mother's then. 'Perhaps I will not get Sarala married. Let her emulate Mataji, and dedicate herself to the service of humanity like her.' Parents' observations leave deep impression on the children, and may be because of this, I grew up with the idea of remaining unmarried. Mother, however, changed her mind later and was keen to see me married and settle down. But I was unwilling and rejected whatever names she dangled before me for a husband. At the same time, my rebellious nature bristled at grandfather's suggestion and refused to accept it. Indeed, why should I take such a thoughtless vow? And I decided against it. I think no woman can take celibacy as the

124   *The Many Worlds of Sarala Devi*

ultimate goal of her life. It is fine so long as a woman can keep going following her own dictates, but a day might come when she would look forward to someone by her side to lead her by the hand. I was not inclined to put up a permanent barrier against such a consummation.

It is possible that behind my father's reluctant permission to allow me to leave home was the belief that I would never find a suitable occupation. But I did. Earlier, when I had visited Mysore in the company of Sarala Ray, though I had missed the opportunity of meeting the Maharaja who was then away in Ooty, I did get to know many high-ranking officers of the State including the Dewan. All of them had high regard for Maharshi Debendranath, and as his granddaughter, I received considerate treatment from them. Narsingh Iyer (Durbar Buxi), the maternal uncle of Dr Ramaswami Iyenger, was a great favourite of the Maharaja and a very influential person in the State. He was the founder of the Maharani Girls' School, and was for all purposes, the all-in-all of the School. I sent him a cable. 'Want to serve the school. Wire if opening.' I had an immediate reply from him, 'Always opening for you. Start as soon as you like.'

Later he told me that my cable so pleased him that he went and reported to the Maharaja, 'A girl from an A1 family has on her own offered to serve the School. Most propitious.' [Translator's note: The quoted sentence is repeated verbatim from the original book].

Mother escorted me to Sitara where *mejo-mama* was then stationed, from where we travelled to Mysore escorted by *mejo-mama*. He had no inhibition concerning women working for a living, since he was in favour of social reform in all spheres. Nor did he think that a granddaughter of Maharshi going out to work lowered the standing of the family. He left after he was satisfied that all arrangements for my stay there were in place.

It just happened that Kumudini Khastagir was at that point of time, the Assistant Superintendent of the Mysore Girls' School. She had to resign her job there as for personal reasons she had to return to Calcutta. In the event, there was no need to find a vacancy for me. In any case the school authorities had planned to install me as the Lady Superintendent when the current but unpopular incumbent left in a year upon expiry of her contract.

This was a new turn in my life; I stepped into another world where I would be living all by myself, bereft of my family.

Fifteen

My stay in Mysore revealed to me an altogether new and unique image of India. It was not the India that we know now; it was the India that was depicted in our classical Sanskrit dramas and literature. In a painting that I had then done I tried to catch an impression of this India. I titled it, 'The Ancient and the Modern'; it was printed in *Bharati*.

I applied to the music teacher of the school to learn how to play the vina. The opportunity was too tempting to miss! The first day I went to see him I found him sitting at one end of a large reed mat with a space for me, and in between rested two rudra-vinas. He picked up one of them and – being unfamiliar with either Hindi or English language – greeted and spoke to me in Sanskrit! It shook me, I rubbed my eyes. Had a time machine taken me back five hundred years? The young girls around me, with their hair freshly washed, perfumed and adorned with flowers – had they emerged from a scene in Kalidasa's 'Meghadootam'?

Speaking of Kalidasa, there are Bengalis who pretend to claim that Kalidasa was a Bengali, but from the prevalent culture and manners of South India I do not think there is any substance in their claim. Bengalis tend to be obnoxiously vainglorious. Why must we argue that Kalidasa and Bhavabhuti were ancestors of Bengalis and not of any other Indians? Since we have our own poet like Jayadeva, famed throughout India, why must we hanker after poets who really belong to other parts of India and insist on claiming

126   *The Many Worlds of Sarala Devi*

them as our own? It is much like the assertion of Prasannakumar Tagore that the poet Bhattanarayan of the Shandilya community was the ancestor of only the Tagore clan, and of none of the others even though they happened to belong to the Shandilya lineage. I hope we do not live to see the day when Bengalis will not be happy to have just Rabindranath as their poet and stake a claim to Shakespeare and Goethe as well!

Everywhere in Mysore I saw the past come alive. Impressed by my appreciation of Mysore culture, Darbar Buxi undertook to show me around the State. He was a committed reformer. He first took me to a place where past traditions were firmly entrenched. This was the Sanskrit College, for men only, and a clearance had to be obtained from the Maharaja to allow me to visit it. Presenting me to the deeply orthodox scholars Mr Buxi asked me to recite some verses from the Upanishadas. The South Indian brahmins were shaken by this proposal — a proposal from none other than another Brahmin, Darbar Buxi (Narsingh Iyer), ruffled them. But he was the right hand man of the Maharaja, and no one dared to raise a protest. They had no option but to listen to a woman reciting Sanskrit verses, that too from a holy text. I recited some verses from the collection of my grandfather which he had compiled for his book on the Brahmo religion. Fortunately my Sanskrit diction was impeccable, and not faulty like that of most Bengali scholars. My acquired skill in Sanskrit enunciation had a strong grounding.

When my older male cousins went through their group initiation into the rites of the sacred thread, they were coached by Guru Hemchandra for a length of period, both before and after the ceremony, to commit to memory the relevant Sanskrit mantras, and also to learn to enunciate correctly. I asked my grandfather's indulgence to permit me to learn the same lessons. After the boys' training was over, he assigned Bolu-*dada*, the only son of my *natun-mama*, and who was the best among the boys during the training, to teach me these mantras accurately. The way the acharyas of the Adi Brahmo Samaj spoke Sanskrit was in no way inferior to the way Sanskrit pandits of Benares and South India did, unlike Bengali scholars in general. Grandfather paid them handsomely for their services.

To listen to the recital from the Upanishadas by a modern girl may have hurt the orthodox sentiments of the Mysore pandits, but it did not jar on their ears as they could not fault my enunciation. I cannot now recall from which Veda I had recited, but the pandits

Sukhendu Ray 127

there had a brief discussion about it in Sanskrit. I had to be wary about Sanskrit grammar as I had to speak also in Sanskrit. A delighted Darbar Buxi then took me to the class teaching Sankhya. To try me out the Professor there invited me to ask the students a question. I hesitated initially, but pressed by Mr Buxi, raised a point from Sakhyakarika at which the Professor cried out, 'Excellent! Excellent!' The students fumbled for an answer. This appreciation made Mr Buxi very proud of me, and thus ended our expedition for that day.

At Mysore it struck me rather strongly that the educational institutions in Bengal neglected to teach students to speak in Sanskrit and that it was a grave mistake. We began our Sanskrit studies with Vidyasagar's book of grammar, *Upakramanika*. All that we did was to learn by rote declamations of nouns and verbs. There was no effort to teach students to form a sentence using a noun, an adjective and a verb. On the other hand, in Mysore, the first text for teaching Sanskrit was by the Maharastrian scholar, Bhandarkar, which from the very beginning, taught some elementary conversation in Sanskrit. Somewhat like the book by Alenyorf (?), popular in Europe. This book is famed for teaching English people how to speak in French, German and Italian. It starts with the introduction of some familiar phrases by way of teaching by direct method before leading on to the intricacies of grammar. I believed this method should be tried out in Bengal's academic institutions.

And the second fault is the use of Bengali script instead of the Devanagari script in all prescribed books by the University of Calcutta. As a result, let alone the students, even teachers of Sanskrit are not familiar with Devanagari script. And then they fumble when trying to read Sanskrit in original texts. Bengalis can neither read nor write in Devanagari. I could read, but I learnt to write much later after persuasion by Mahatma Gandhi. Along with spinning the charkha, I had to devote some time each day to learning to write Devanagari.

The third, the most serious fault, is enunciation. I have known some teachers to speak fluent grammatical Sanskrit, but with atrocious and painful pronunciation. They just do not know the distinction between vowels — long and short — and many consonants which are wrongly pronounced. This is, however, not the place to talk about such failings, for which we have become the laughing stock of India. The only other person that I knew who was a stickler for correct Sanskrit enunciation was Hem, a daughter of Shivnath

128   *The Many Worlds of Sarala Devi*

Shastri. She had traveled to North India and Punjab and come into contact with women in those places, and was alert enough to ensure teaching Sanskrit with the correct enunciation. I had to take a great deal of trouble to correct the Bengali way of speaking Sanskrit. I repeatedly warned the teachers at Bharati Stree Siksha Sadan on this point.

Coming back to Mysore, the house the State had provided for my stay was pretty decent—small, double-storied. The sitting and dining rooms were on the ground floor with two bedrooms on the upper floor plus a bathroom and a veranda. All the rooms were tastefully wall-papered. Near my home was 'Agrahar', meaning a tax-free gift of land by the Maharaja to the Brahmins. The rulers of Mysore are Khatriyas by caste, but a majority of their subjects are Shiva-devotee Lingayat brahmins and Jains. There is a marked difference in the style of wearing saris by the women of these two classes, and in the sectarian symbolic marks painted on their foreheads. These distinctive practices spell out the class to which women belong.

The school sat twice each day—once in the morning and then again in the afternoon. Most of the students were married, some already mothers. They came in the morning still wearing their overnight cotton saris, went back home at the end of the morning sitting to do their household chores. Later in the afternoon, they returned fresh after a bath, in attractive Mysore silk saris. Regardless of the kind of saris they wore, they wore it with a natural grace. Nearly everyone fastened a belt with tinkling bells over their saris; some wore belts made of gold. Otherwise, they did not put on many ornaments except for diamond or pearl pieces for the ears and the nose, and a couple of bangles. Married women must wear glass bangles which are the symbol of marriage, like the bangle wrought from steel for Bengali married women. Widows are prohibited from using glass bangles, but gold bangles are allowed.

On religious occasions it is obligatory for the women to visit temples and offer pujas. Women on the streets are a very common sight, and men do not leer at them nor do boys make rude remarks. Like all Hindus in the country they also have 'thirteen festivals in a period of twelve months'. Depending on the community some may have even more. What did strike me was how remarkably these festivals knitted India together!

The celebration of Bhratri-dwitiya—the occasion when sisters pray for brothers to wish them well and for their prosperity—is as keenly observed in Mysore as in Bengal. Special foods are cooked in each home, brothers and sisters exchange greetings and gifts, sons and daughters in the family are drawn close together for the occasion. Following the new-age practices in emulation of the Christian world, many of our traditional family get-togethers are becoming rarer. Even in our days I had sadly observed how this loving celebration was reduced to a soulless ritual when brothers just called on sisters, carrying calculated gifts, but had no time to consume the food the sisters had prepared for them. What a great pity! The only occasion, when in spite of accumulated differences, brothers and sisters still come together is losing its charm.

In Bengal on the occasion of 'Brothers' Day', customarily it is the sisters who offer gifts to the brothers, but it is just the reverse in the rest of India. Here, brothers carry gifts for the sisters, and the sisters apply a 'tilak' (a ritual mark) on the forehead of the brothers, tie a ceremonial red thread round the latter's wrists, and feed them with home-made delicacies. If the brother is away, then the symbolic tilak and thread are sent by post, in the fashion of Christmas or New Year greeting cards. Have the applicable inheritance laws anything to do with the different practices in Bengal and the rest of India? The system of Dayabhaga operates in Bengal, whilst elsewhere in India it is the Mitakshara system. It is my impression that on the whole, outside Bengal, parents and brothers appear to treat daughters and sisters more generously. Parents and brothers seem to think no matter how much they give to the girls, it is not enough! In places where the system of dowry for a daughter's wedding is unknown, the groom's family makes no demand. Nevertheless, parents provide for the daughter as much as they can afford. And whenever a married daughter comes home, she returns loaded with gifts. This giving of gifts in certain societies is so excessive that many Rajput families are scared of married daughters visiting them for fear of getting financially crippled. The daughters can also be thoughtful and understanding, and many on their own, do not visit their parents to spare them the embarrassment. Adulation of unmarried girls is proverbial in Hindu families. Note the custom of Kumari Puja (ritual worship of a girl child) during the Durga Pujas. It has also been known that in some homes, girls are not allowed to touch the feet of elders, as it is considered inappropriate for girls. Despite all these differences in the customs round the country, it is undeniable that festivals are a unifying thread that knits the Hindu India together.

130 *The Many Worlds of Sarala Devi*

During the Diwali celebrations in Mysore I discovered another thread of unity. Unlike in Bengal, Diwali is just not an occasion for illumination and setting off fireworks. For many, it is the beginning of a new year when traders and businessmen inaugurate new books of accounts. It is also an occasion when friends and relatives get together forgetting past differences and greet one another warmly. Almost as we Bengalis do for our Bejoya Dashami Day. But for me the most moving event of Diwali festival is to mark this day as Luxmi Puja—homage to the goddess of wealth and prosperity. Gambling on the occasion is permitted as it is considered auspicious. Each home, be it a mansion or a humble hut, is given a thorough cleaning and is decorated with designs and motifs using rice powder and paints. The home is then ready to welcome goddess Luxmi! This is known as 'Diwali Safai', equivalent to 'the spring cleaning' of the West. In this context I recall a tale I was told: A poor Brahmin couple had done their Diwali cleaning with much care and devotion and, forgoing their sleep, waited the whole night for Luxmi's visit. Every home had similarly kept this sleepless vigil for Luxmi. Meanwhile, goddess Luxmi went round peeping through the windows of the houses, but did not find any that interested her. Then she spotted the local magistrate's home, where she found the dining room marvelously set up. The table was covered with a snow-white cloth, had shining glasses and sparkling cutlery, all brightly lit up, and was gorgeously decorated with fruits and flowers. Luxmi was so entranced that she entered that home and settled down. And the poor Brahmin couple spent their sleepless night waiting desolately for the missing Luxmi!

I had observed in Punjab that, during Diwali, Luxmi Puja was performed by the head of the family and his wife without the help of any priest. Where women are themselves the priests, the rituals naturally are simplified and have a feminine touch. Their mantras spoken in vernacular are just a version of the unintelligible Sanskrit mantras recited by the priests. I once had the opportunity of watching a couple performing Luxmi Puja at their home. They sat on the floor facing a clay image of the goddess, along with the idols of many other gods and goddesses. Five earthenware oil lamps had been lit. On a silver plate were placed a number of shiny rupee coins, and on another plate, there were some flowers, a pot of water, a sheaf of paddy, some sweets, etc.

Sukhendu Ray 131

The wife picked up a flower and said, 'Luxmi is here. Bathe her, greet her. Yes, the goddess is present, no further waiting for her, we can see her! Welcome her!' Then she said, 'She has been bathed. Hail her!'

Meanwhile, the children of the family, after they had finished putting up the illuminations on the roof, came down and sat with the parents. Then all of them together sprinkled holy water on Luxmi, and bowed their heads before Luxmi's image.

The wife then said, 'Luxmi is here. Offer her flowers, greet her!' They all showered flowers on the image. 'Luxmi is here. Greet her with incense and light!' This was done. 'Luxmi is here. Offer her food'.

The plate containing food offerings was dedicated to her. The husband then recited a Sanskrit verse, probably without understanding what it meant. Then they all sang in chorus a devotional song, which ended the ritual. The wife sat quietly for a while meditating, and then requested me to say something. I knew a mantra which I recited in Sanskrit and explained its meaning. 'She is the Mother of the three worlds; she provides sustenance for us; gives us strength. The intense yearning of my heart has brought her amongst us. Let her manifest herself through harvest, in wealth; let her materialize in gold and silver and in food.' They were so pleased with this mantra that they wrote it down, and I gather that ever since, it has become a part of their puja every year.

The husband who had been earlier a member of the Arya Samaj was converted back to the traditional Hindu beliefs. The wife's comment was, 'Paying homage to Luxmi and Shakti is a must for each family, or else how can a home survive?' Confessed the husband, 'I have lost all faith in the tenets of the Arya Samaj and the Brahmo Samaj. Their doctrine is a negation of everything as it provides nothing positive on which people can lean on for support.'

Mysore was excessively dominated by Brahmins, and it was inconceivable that any devotional activities could be conducted without an intermediary priest. I have seen no evidence there of women performing pujas by themselves. As a matter of fact, the offerings that women carried to temples were passed on through priests.

On festive occasions a few of the older students and some teachers visited me carrying gifts, usually items of foods specially

132 *The Many Worlds of Sarala Devi*

prepared for the festival. Occasionally, some of them would get together and sing and play the vina for me. I recall one particular song which was not in Telegu (sic) but in Hindi. The song consisted of just a few words, but it was presented in such a variety of melodies and beats that it seemed to be a long piece.

A couple of girls could play the violin. I had myself once taken lessons in violin at Loreto from an Italian professor — that was after my graduation. Indira had also taken some lessons from him although she had earlier been taught by a European teacher at Solapur. Playing the violin in the western style and the style in which it was played in Mysore was vastly different. One can spend a lifetime in mastering the art of violin in the West. Unless the violin becomes a part of your life, no manner of running the bow on its four strings can extract the true muse, however correctly you play the notes. It is not easy to capture the soul of the music even you play the melody well, but not so in the fashion this instrument is played in Mysore. The difference lay essentially in the manner the four strings of the instrument were tuned in Mysore, which made it comparatively facile to get to the heart of the music. Our ragas become lively by the 'fingerings' of the violin in Mysore, but western music, if played in this way, falls flat. The violin is known in Mysore as a fiddle, perhaps a legacy from the Portuguese. Most likely that the Portuguese introduced the violin to the people of South India, who then innovated their own style of tuning the strings in the fashion of the vina. The way the girls played the violin conveyed a feeling of sadness. The rudravina here is vigorous, but the violin, melancholic.

In which language did I converse with the girls? In English. I knew no Telegu (sic), and they could not speak Hindi. I was amazed by their command over spoken English. I was told that everyone in Madras Presidency knew how to speak in English, but that was not really true. They speak in a corrupt version, known as pidgin English. Here, in Mysore, they spoke in refined English. Even so, there were some hilarious situations, such as, when I was once asked by one of my girl students, 'Tell me please, the uncle who came to reach me, is he a matricide or a patricide?'

Sixteen

My loss in abandoning midstream the pursuit of a Master's degree in Sanskrit when I opted to travel to Mysore was to some extent compensated here. The incumbent Principal of the Sanskrit College, who had two Master's degrees, took personal interest in tutoring me, and with his help, I had access to Sanskrit books on a variety of subjects. Mahadev Shastri, M.A., the curator of Mysore's Oriental library, also extended a helping hand. This Oriental library is a huge institution, famed throughout India. One of its principal objects is to retrieve through arduous researches ancient Sanskrit manuscripts, to restore them and to print them. The prefaces of many of these books carry the imprint of the vast scholarship of Mahadev Shastri. Sets of such books were gifted by Mahadev Shastri to those whom he considered erudite enough and interested enough to deserve these books. I was fortunate enough to receive a gift of such books. He himself often called on me and talked with me.

I had another regular visitor, Ramachandra Rao, a high placed officer of the Mysore Civil Service. A man of considerable intellectual calibre, extremely sociable, alert and well informed on political situation, he was also a fearless critic, yet very good humoured. Among my other acquaintances was a Mr Iyenger, a former principal of the Sanskrit College, and a Mr Iyer, a former curator of the Oriental Library. Along with Ramachandra Rao they were apparently descendants of Maharastrian Brahmins, who had

134 *The Many Worlds of Sarala Devi*

migrated to South India with the brothers of Shivaji and who now regarded themselves as South Indians. They became members of my circle of friends. Dr Ramaswami Iyenger whom I had known earlier was, of course, one of them, but he was never too keen to get into intellectual discussions. He was a very helpful kind of person. Whenever he came to see me, he always carried flowers or something else that pleased me greatly. I imagine he picked up this pleasant gesture while staying with Mrs P.K. Ray in Calcutta.

My special friend at Mysore, however, was Mrs Bhaba, the wife of the Director of Public Instruction, and their daughter. They were Parsees. The daughter was exquisitely beautiful and very well educated. At Bombay, Poona and Satara we got to know many Parsee families and got on fairly well with them. *Mejo-mami* and my mother had many Parsee ladies among their acquaintances. I became very close to the Bhabas. I was rather intrigued by the beautiful Meherbai, the daughter. Such a lovely rose blossoming, away from their normal habitat, unknown in a corner of Mysore city with hardly any Parsee population. Would ever somebody come to court her, a Dushyant in search for his Shakuntala? Yes, he did; Prince Charming did appear and he took her away!

Sir Jamsetjee Tata's eldest son was a big fish amongst the Parsees in Bombay, and the wives of many millionaire Parsee families were keen to land him for their unmarried daughters. He continued to elude them. He was getting on in age, and the hopeful would-be mothers-in-law were getting impatient. But destiny played out its own game. On a visit to Mysore on some Tata business project, Dorabji happened to meet Meherbai, and was immediately smitten. This was no catch by an angling mother; he succumbed to Cupid's arrows. The age gulf between the two was initially a source of hesitation for the parents of the girl, but the course of true love is never frustrated by such minor concerns. Soon after they were engaged to be married, and when this news spread, the disgruntled mothers in Bombay roundly condemned Dorabji's choice of an unknown and unheard of girl from a faraway place like Mysore. This, of course, did not stop the union, and on an auspicious day, they became man and wife. They returned to Bombay, and fairly soon, Dorabji received a knighthood. The new Lady Dorabji Tata was accepted as a leading light of the Parsee community.

I had already left Mysore by the time Meherbai got engaged to be married. I got to know all about it from her letter. She wrote me a twenty-page missive starting with the arrival of Dorabji Tata at

Mysore, their romantic attachment to each other leading to their engagement. This was the first gushing emotional outflow from a teenage girl deep in the flush of love. It was likely that she had no friend of her age to whom she could open her heart out freely and joyfully. She had to share her ecstasy with someone in whom she could confide both her bliss and her apprehensions.

Many years later I met her again in Bombay when she as Lady Tata was a prominent dignitary of the Bombay society. She was a member of the Swadeshi Exhibition Committee, amongst her many other commitments, and that was how I came to meet her. She was no longer the young Miss Bhaba of Mysore that I knew. Sadly, both Dorabji and Meherbai have passed away. They were childless. Dorabji's younger brother Ratan also died childless when he was killed during the 1914 war, a victim of German torpedo attack. No direct descendant of Jamshetjee Tata is now left to carry on his name. Only his noble achievements keep his memory alive.

At Mysore I also became friendly with another family — they were Muslim and residents of Bangalore. The husband Mr Sujatali, who was from U.P., was a Deputy Collector. His wife was a Bengali, whose brothers were all well placed government employees. She came to meet me all the way from Bangalore when she came to know of me. She promptly extended an invitation to visit them and be their guest. She made all the necessary transport arrangements for my visit. Not just once, I visited them a number of times. Her nostalgia for her home in Bengal was at the root of our friendship.

I recall other instances of similar nostalgic sentiments. Much later when I was invited to visit the Aligarh Muslim University, I noticed a young man following me when I was taken round the campus. Later he introduced himself. He was a Bengali Muslim, a student at the University, and he could not resist the temptation of meeting me when he discovered that I was a Bengali. Then there was another occasion, and this was in Burma. I was visiting the town of Pegu, not far from Rangoon, to see the famous statue of the reclining Buddha. It was past midday when we came out, and made for the Railway restaurant for lunch. My Gujarati companion went inside to order some food and came out disheartened. All the food cooked that day had been sold out, and there was no way to get any so late. When I observed two of the waiters talking in Bengali, I asked them in Bengali, 'Are you from Bengal?' They replied, 'Yes, from Dacca. Are you also a Bengali? Why did you come so late? No food is now left. But please do wait, let us see if we can fix something

136 *The Many Worlds of Sarala Devi*

for you.' After an hour they produced a meal of rice, lentil, fish and a vegetable curry. The boys from Bengal looked after their Bengali guest superbly. They were not inclined to accept payment, but eventually relented to avoid getting into trouble with their employers, the Railway Company.

Though Sujatalis had to an extent adopted a western life style, what particularly drew me to them was that the women in that home adhered to the traditional dress mode. Many years later at Bombay, I had a similar experience when I got to know the Tayebji family. The Hindu world of Mysore was for me a revelation: absolutely unfamiliar, belonging to the past, in an ancient world of poetry and paintings, of which I was an enchanted spectator. I was not, however, intellectually involved in it. The only touch of a modern world there came from the Parsee and Muslim family, with whom I could relate with no inhibitions. It came home to me pretty forcefully that divergent religious faiths are not necessarily a barrier for people to come together. It is the affinity of the mind that brings people together, when no particular spiritual persuasion can raise an admonishing finger.

After some months stay there, my interest in Mysore started flagging, and I grew restless, homesick, and nostalgic for the lively atmosphere of home; of the family gathering on the first day of Baisakh for the New Year day celebration, of the 'Brothers' Day' jubilation, I desolately looked back on the life of Calcutta. Navaratri festival in Mysore recalled to me the magic of Durga Puja, the pageantry of the immersion ceremony. I can now appreciate why my friend Khusi persuaded her husband, a successful medical practitioner in Bombay, to abandon his career there and return to Calcutta, to start their life afresh.

Then I had the shock of my life. On the other side of the road, facing my house, a contractor was building a large house. A smaller house that he had earlier built was now occupied. The only son of the contractor was wayward and profligate with his father's money. The parents could not control him, whilst the son's unhappy wife continued to reside with them. The unruly son was hardly ever at home, and no one knew where he was or what he did. One night when I was asleep and my South Indian maid was sleeping in the landing, I was suddenly awakened by the shrieks of the maidservant. She said that someone had walked over her and gone into my dressing room. There was a police post across the road, and I shouted for help. Two policemen came rushing and I repeated what the maidservant had told me. Just then a man went running past and broke his leg trying to escape by jumping out of a window. He was immediately caught by the police. He turned out to be the contractor's son.

By then two security guards assigned to me by the State had woken up as had my Bengali servant Bipin. I sent one of them to Narsingh Iyer's home and the other to Mr Bhaba. Both came round immediately, and with Mr Bhaba came with his daughter Meherbai. The Bhabas took me to their home where I spent the rest of the night. The contractor's son was duly tried and sentenced to jail for six months. But that was not the end of the story, because through a network of agencies, this report reached the Calcutta Press, and the Bangabasi made a longish comment which in essence said, 'What was the need for a Bengali girl to leave home for employment in a far-away place and live on her own? This young lady did not really need a job to earn a living, so why put oneself to such risk? It is nothing but aping the Western custom.'

There was a grain of truth in this observation. A steady diet of foreign literature had ingrained in my mind certain fanciful and impulsive ideas. Though I had equal opportunity in education at par with my brother, my motivation to go away and earn my living was really not to flaunt my spirit of equality with him. It might have been so subconsciously, but the reality was my wish to be different. If you work for a cause you stand on firm foundation, and that is the test of your determination. But my mission driven by fanciful impulse lacked this foundation and was moored in sand, which shifts and shakes your purpose. After a brief period of dalliance the fancies take a back seat, and this is precisely what happened to me.

Then I had a spot of bother. I went down with a bout of malaria, and was in the care of the European Civil Surgeon, who prescribed some allopathic medicines. Till then I never had any allopathic medicines, and did not even know how they tasted. My father was a staunch believer in the homeopathic system, and whenever we were unwell, major or minor, it was either Dr Mahendra Sarkar or Dr Solzar who took care of us. And my introduction to allopathic treatment was at the ripe age of twenty years!

A cable was shot off to mother who happened to be at Satara then. She rushed to look after me. When I got better the Civil Surgeon told my mother to take me away for while as the Mysore season was still insalubrious for malaria. On a three months' leave,

138 *The Many Worlds of Sarala Devi*

I went off to Satara with mother, then returned to resume my job only to resign after another three months when my contract for one year was over. I returned home to Calcutta, and wherever I went, whomsoever I met, I was teased, 'So, have you had enough of your job? End of wish to be a free bird?' Yes, that was the end of my hunger to have gainful employment, but not my desire to be free and live a life of my own. By then my personal aim to be independent had found a wider field and that was to fight for the freedom of my country. Earlier fanciful wishes had now decidedly metamorphosed into a cause.

Seventeen

The magazine *Bharati* was founded by my *baro-mama* more than twenty years ago, and later sustained by Rabi-*mama*, who once wrote in its pages:

Tell me, Bharati [Saraswati], why has thy vina gone mute?
Why has thy muse ceased to resonate
Through the air and space of Bharat?

I took up this challenge when upon my return from the South I started writing for *Bharati* and converted it into a combative organ. I urged Bengalis to cultivate and develop an intrepid character, unafraid to face death. My very first piece published in *Bharati* did just that. Bengalis are prone to be over-protective to save their skin. My message was loud and clear — go ahead and learn to court danger, do not shy away from death, certainly not cravenly yield when death stares at you. Defy it, boldly dare it — in all aspects of life; when engaged in sports; at recreation; at hunting trips and treks; when taking care of distressed people during epidemics of plague; rescuing victims from burning houses; saving drowning persons — all at the sacrifice of your life. Teach yourself geography, not by pouring over atlases but by travelling through the world; sail across the seven seas; climb the Everest peak. In the ancient days our holy men roamed through inaccessible regions, carrying nothing more than a drinking vessel and a blanket. In modern times European explorers undertake arduous journeys, albeit better

140   *The Many Worlds of Sarala Devi*

equipped. What is, however, common to them is a strong and fit body. A sturdy body and a robust health—these are mankind's supreme blessings. Bengalis can be equally blessed if they go for regular and vigorous physical training as others elsewhere in the country do. That was the second sharp note of my vina to warn our people.

My cousin Aru-*dada* was conversant with the Urdu language and equally fluent in Hindi. When he read Urdu he was most meticulous about correct pronunciation. As a young man he kept himself in good shape through physical culture and exercises. He occasionally travelled to Bombay to visit *mejo-mama*, and used to recount his experience during the return railway journey to Calcutta. He noted that the porters at railway stations in western India and Bihar were heftily built, and their voices rang out masterfully when they announced the names of the railway stations: 'Al–la–ha–bad', 'Bux-ar', 'P-a-t-n-a', etc. Such stentorian announcements often alarmed the sleeping passengers as if they had been raided by bandits. The scene changed as soon as the train crossed over to Bengal. The announcers' voices faded to feeble and feebler, and they looked so emaciated that a little shove could probably topple them over. The truth of Aru-*dada*'s observation was confirmed by many others who had travelled away from Bengal. Porters in Bengal and porters elsewhere were both men, and yet what a difference between their physical conditions! I decided that my first mission would be to shape Bengali weaklings into sturdy men, like their compatriots in Punjab, Maharastra, etc. And that was not all. I must equally do something to get Bengali men to shed their faint-hearted mentality. Particularly galling was to note the morbid fear of our men when confronting a white-skinned European. We must eradicate this reprehensible vulnerability from the minds of our countrymen.

I devised a plan of action, which had to be combative—a sort of British boxing versus Indian fisticuffs! I started my campaign by an announcement in the pages of our journal *Bharati:* inviting reports of humiliation suffered at the hands of white civilians or military personnel—be it in railways, on steamers or anywhere—personally or by members of their families, where the victims immediately retaliated instead of taking recourse to the courts of law to seek redress. An amazing crop of reports was received and printed in *Bharati.* The latent fire in our readers was now fanned into a blazing flame. One had no idea which way the wind was

Sukhendu Ray 141

blowing. The literary field (of *Bharati*) that was once smooth like the manicured grass lawn and the sanctuary of Saraswati, the Goddess of the muses, was all of a sudden, transformed into the dancing arena of the violent Shiva, and consciously or otherwise, Shiva's frenzied rhythm caught the imagination of many adherents. A fallout of all this was that a vast number of young people and groups of students from schools and colleges sought to see me, many of whom became celebrities in their later lives. I had visits from older men as well. From amongst the young people I formed a select group. I initiated the indoctrination of this group by making them salute a map of India and then taking a pledge that with all their heart, body and soul they would serve the motherland. I tied a *rakhi*, a symbolic thread, round their wrists binding them to their oath of dedication and sacrifice. It is said that the Mughal Emperor Humayun once promised to protect a Rajput princess, at any cost, by accepting a *rakhi* from her. Similarly my *rakhi* was an acceptance of commitments by the young men of my group to face any hardship in the cause of service to the motherland. Though in no way a secret society, I still cautioned the members not to talk openly too much about their mission, as I strongly believed that a resolution if nursed close to one's heart gained in motivation.

Despite this restraint the report about my activities somehow reached the ears of Maharaja Jagadinranath Ray of Natore. His bonhomie attracted many people to him. Ashu Chaudhury, who was very fond of me and also held me in much respect, warned me, 'Be careful Sarala. At Natore House gatherings people have apparently been talking about you: Sarala Devi is trying to create a dauntless band of young men by tying red threads to their wrists. Reportedly the police force is on alert.' A few years later when Bengal was partitioned, this custom of tying *rakhi* spread throughout the country under the leadership of Rabindranath. Natore was also converted.

Manilal Ganguly was one of the young men who often came to see me. He was a nephew of Satish Mukherjee, then the editor of the journal *Dawn*. Satish-*babu* and I often got together. Manilal was keen on literature and ran a literary society in Bhowanipore. He once invited me to chair the annual function of his society. In my life I had been intrepid enough to travel all by myself to many distant places away from home. Even so, the thought of presiding over a literary event, consisting of men only, that too in the heart of Calcutta, appeared daunting. I hesitated, but when Manilal continued to press I gave him an alternative proposal, which was

142 *The Many Worlds of Sarala Devi*

to convert their literary event to commemorate the legendary Bengali hero Pratapaditya, and to shift the date of the meeting to the first day of Baisakh to mark the anniversary of his coronation. There should be no speeches, I suggested, but instead, we should arrange for a display of martial arts to celebrate the occasion. I advised him to comb through Calcutta to locate young men who were skilled in boxing, wrestling, displays with swords and rod, etc. I also asked him to do some homework to collect material about Pratapaditya's life and achievements, and to write up a brief sketch which would be presented at the ceremony in place of the society's annual report.

Manilal readily agreed. He succeeded in ferreting out Hardayal, a Rajput boy but now almost a Bengali, who was skilled in the display of sword fights. Boys from Masjidbari Guha family were to take part in wrestling, and for boxing, a team came from Sailen Bose's gymnasium. Some other boys were located for demonstrations with rods and poles. The meeting was conducted as I had planned. At Manilal's request I inaugurated the celebrations to create an ambience for the occasion. Manilal then read his short report on Pratapaditya, which was followed by displays of various martial arts. The event concluded with me distributing prizes and medals to the participants.

Almost all the Calcutta Press was present in a body at the function. Reported the *Sanjivani*, 'It was, indeed, most gratifying to find a lady presiding over a gathering of young men in the very heart of Calcutta.' *Bangabasi* was even more enthusiastic. It gushed, 'What a wonderful sight it was! A meeting with no speeches, no table thumping, only evocative of a past hero of Bengal, demonstration of martial arts by youths of Bengal, and their leader is just a young Bengali lass — a Brahmin lady from whose tender hands the boys received their prizes.' Bipin Pal, on the other hand, made a tongue-in-cheek comment in *Young India*, 'As necessity is the mother of invention, Sarala Devi is the mother of Pratapaditya to meet the necessity of a hero in Bengal.'

Bipin Pal's sarcastic remarks did not dissuade our people, and gradually, Pratapaditya became firmly entrenched in the heart of Bengalis. The first manifestation of this fascination was a new play written by Professor Khirode Vidyabinode and its successful run at the Star Theatre. In competition, a second play, also on Pratapaditya, by Amar Datta opened at the Minerva Theatre.

Nevertheless, a nasty shock awaited me, a blow from an unexpected quarter. It was none other than my uncle Rabindranath, not directly, but through his emissary Dinesh Sen.

'Your uncle is most cross with you', Dinesh Sen informed me. 'But why?' I asked.

'You disregarded the heinous character of Pratapaditya as portrayed by your uncle in his book *Bouthakuranir Haat*, and instead turned him into a hero for veneration by our people. According to your uncle, a character like Pratapaditya can never deserve to be glorified into an object of hero-worship.'

I told Dinesh-*babu*, 'Please tell my uncle that I never attempted to present Pratapaditya as morally ideal; neither have I condoned his evil deeds like assassinating his uncle. But no one can deny that he was politically a great man; he was, so to say, a Shivaji of Bengal, who stood up alone against the might of the Moghul Emperor to defend Bengal's independence. He even dared to mint coins in his own name. I have only tried to re-establish him as that super personality whose bravery is worthy of our admiration, and that is all. If I have made any historical blunders, I will be open to correction if he tells me where I have gone wrong.'

Nothing more was heard about this episode, but the hero-worship continued unabated in Bengal. Soon thereafter I undertook to publish a selection of booklets for a general series titled 'Heroes of Bengal'. I followed it up with a celebration in honour of Udayaditya, son of Pratapaditya. *Bengalee*, then a major English language publication, edited by Surendranath Bannerjee, began to take a keen interest in the many activities I promoted. After I announced my plan for Udayaditya festival, *Bengalee* reported, 'Sarala Devi regularly keeps springing surprises on us, so much so, that we get breathless in trying to keep pace with her. Each morning as we get up we ask ourselves, what next?'

I have noticed that we Bengalis get emotionally excited by the various tales of the young Rajput boys like Badal, glorify their exploits, compose adulatory verses on them, yet at the same time know nothing of a Bengali hero, who laid down his life fighting the Mughals in the cause of defending Bengal's freedom. I was determined that the heroic tale of Udayaditya must be revived and implanted in the hearts of Bengali youths. Srish Chandra Sen, a highly educated young man, came forward offering to organize a festival to commemorate Udayaditya.

144 *The Many Worlds of Sarala Devi*

Narendranath Sen, an elderly gentleman, was at that point of time the editor of *Indian Mirror* as well as one of the trustees who managed the Albert Hall. I sent advance money to him to hire the Albert Hall for the Udayaditya Festival. Sadly, we could not find any portrait of Udayaditya, but there had to be something on the stage to represent him. It struck me then that what could be more fitting to represent a Khatriya warrior other than a sword? A sword would be placed at the centre of the stage where visitors would pay homage with flowers. We were fortunate in locating a non-Bengali zamindar who kindly lent us a magnificent sword with precious stone decorations on the hilt. Khirode Vidyabinode was to preside over the function. Handbills announcing the occasion had been generously distributed, the meeting was to start at four in the afternoon, and organizers were already at the venue from ten in the morning. Suddenly at around noon, Srish-*babu* came running to tell me that Naren Sen had a sent a message that this meeting could not be permitted as he understood that the boys would pay homage to a sword. This would be a highly seditious and treasonous activity, which he was unable to allow.

I told Srish-*babu*, 'Please go ahead and fix an alternative venue whatever it may cost. Meanwhile, I shall write to Naren Sen to see if I can change his mind.'

I wrote to Naren Sen, 'I believe you are a devout Hindu, so you must be well aware of Hindu practices which allow worship of three articles symbolizing deities — a Ghat (a vessel), a Pat (a pictorial image), and a Kharga (a battle axe). If at this stage you stop this event there will be a great deal of furore and you will attract strong condemnation in the press throughout India. It will be said that a band of Bengali youths was planning to offer symbolic homage to a Kharga, but a senior Bengali Hindu leader threw a spanner in the works. This very devoted subject of the Raj, smelling sedition, was so panicky that he had to suppress the meeting. It may have escaped you that you may find yourself involved in litigation. You were well aware of the purpose of our function and knowingly rented us the Albert Hall having taken in advance the full amount of your charge. And in any event you did not care to refund us the money when you decided to cancel our show. If you still insist on preventing this festival, the boys can sue you for damages, and you will be held liable in the eye of the law. Perhaps you may re-think and permit us to go ahead with our celebration.'

Sukhendu Ray 145

The old man sent in a reply. 'So be it. Let the boys go ahead, but you will be held responsible for consequences.' He washed his hands off any possible liabilities, and shoved them onto the shoulders of a young girl, who in terms of age, could well be like his daughter.

Very soon a message reached me that Srish-*babu* had found an alternative venue but at twice the cost of hiring the Albert Hall. This other venue was the Alfred Theatre, not too far away from the Albert Hall. I immediately paid the money asked for. Our boys took care to tell the Marwari owner of the theatre that we proposed to offer homage to a sword at the function. The Marwari gentleman was totally unconcerned. So long as he got his money, it was immaterial to him what we did. 'You may sing, you may dance, do a *puja*—all that is your affair,' he said. He was promptly paid his dues.

When I informed Srish-*babu* that Naren Sen had withdrawn his objection with a rider, the boys were reluctant to go back to Albert Hall. We had to station volunteers at the Albert Hall to direct persons who came to attend the meeting to the new venue.

Although I did not attend the Udayaditya celebrations, the meeting started with a message from me which the President read out. Khirode-*babu* then addressed the meeting, which terminated with homage to the sword. In his address Khirode-*babu* narrated a tale from the ancient Matsya Purana. A holy man found a tiny fish in a well and threw it in a pond, and in time this tiny fish grew to the size of the pond. The holy man then threw the fish into the sea where the fish expanded to an endless gigantic size. Taking a cue from this tale Khirode-*babu* pointed to the future. He said, 'This rather small but visionary celebration will one day spread wide amongst the Bengalis to shape them into enormously valiant people.' Whether his reading of the future was correct or not, whether my vision, my ideas, made any impact, only our countrymen can tell.

The year's stay in the south away from home and coming in contact with many people there helped in expanding the horizon of my love for the country. The peerless Sankaracharya unified India from the North to the South, from the East to the West, by establishing four religious Dhams (centres) or holy places, and it is this very India that pervaded my thoughts. I was totally focused those days on Bengal which lies in the eastern frontier of our country. My concern then was to make Bengal prominent enough

146 *The Many Worlds of Sarala Devi*

so that it could stand with its head held high with the other areas of the country. But again it would be unpatriotic to ignore other areas. So, when the Congress session that year was held in Calcutta, with Vacha as the President, and where I had to sing, I composed a special song for the occasion that gave vent to my deep felt patriotic thoughts.

Sing, Hindustan, sing!
Sing the tale of our glorious past!

This fresh approach in the theme of the song touched all hearts, and an appreciative Rabindranath came forward to conduct the song.

At that session of the Congress three hundred volunteer helpers were engaged to man both outside and inside the venue. The evening when Surendranath Bannerjee was scheduled to speak, the volunteers outside the venue, in their eagerness to listen to the distinguished speaker, broke their order and discipline, and surged into the hall to occupy seats earmarked for delegates. Bhupen Bose took them to task for their disorderly conduct at which the volunteers rebelled and refused to report for duty for the next day's session. I still do not know why Bhupen Bose approached me with the request to reason with the boys. Frankly I had no clue how to bring the boys round. Anyway, I had an idea, and suggested to them, 'Please, will you all join me in chorus in the opening song when we meet tomorrow? Wherever you are, inside or outside, let us sing in unison, all together. But before that you will need to learn the song, so come with me now and I will teach you.' And I taught them until all of them learnt the song well enough. It was almost ten in the evening when we finished. The music drowned out their earlier resentment and on the following day, we had no problem. When the opening song commenced, voices rang out from every corner in unison.

Sing all together, in all voices
In all languages
Sing in praise of Hindustan!
Say Hara, Hara, Hara – Hail Hindustan!
Say Satshri Akal – Hail Hindustan!
Say Allahu Akbar – Hail Hindustan!
Sing all together – we salute thee Hindustan!

The song created an unprecedented stir amongst those present. The experience of that occasion set me thinking. Each year during the annual session of the Indian National Congress a corps of volunteers is raised. The volunteers receive training by way of paramilitary exercises. After the Congress session is over, this voluntary body is disbanded, the members of the corps disperse, no longer subject to discipline and regulations. In the process, all the rigorous training and efforts to build this corps are wasted. It occurred to me that a preferred alternative would be to form a permanent body of volunteers who would receive regular training at least once a week for a whole year. The idea, I believed, was well worth a try. The Captain of that year's corps was a grandson of Pandit Chandrakanta of Bethune College. He agreed with me that my scheme of raising a permanent body of corps was a sound one. At the end of the Congress session I invited all volunteer workers to my home for dinner, when the foundation was laid to create a permanent corps of volunteers.

About then I happened to read a short story by Rudyard Kipling about the Pathan revolt in the western frontier of India. A Bengali I.C.S. Deputy Commissioner was in charge of that district, When the Pathan rebels began their assault and rampage, killing people, the Bengali Deputy Commissioner, according to the story, went missing, abandoning his post and responsibilities. When the Pathan agents eventually caught him, they beheaded him and setting up his head on a spike, went round the city shouting, 'the Bengali fox'. My blood boiled when I read this shameful story humiliating the Bengalis. I wanted revenge, but what could I do? I wrote a letter to Kipling, which in essence was a challenge to him. 'I dare you to come and fight with any of our men to avenge the vilification of our people. I will give you five years to get ready with whatever weapon you chose. In five years time our challenger will give you fight with your chosen weapon.'

But that put me in a fix. I wrote that letter but had no idea where to send it. Meanwhile, I had to visit Cuttack, where I got to know Madhusudan Das, a well known patriot of Orissa. He was almost a Bengali, and I casually spoke to him of my proposed letter to Kipling. I had the letter with me, and I read it to him. Being a wise man he gave me sound advice. 'When you are prepared to give Kipling five years time, so why not wait for five years and use this time to build up a body of Bengali youths training them to acquire

148   *The Many Worlds of Sarala Devi*

skills in the use of a number of weapons. Let these boys earn a reputation, and then throw a challenge to Kipling.' I found his suggestion very sensible and logical.

Returning to Calcutta my search for an expert coach to train our boys in the art of wielding swords, clubs, etc., eventually led me to Professor Murtaza, a Muslim gentleman. I engaged him on terms of a generous remuneration to train our boys at a club that I had founded at our home. This club was later shifted to No. 26 Ballygunge Circular Road to which we had moved. It was a big house with a sizeable lawn in front and a water tank at the back. Behind the tank was a sort of square plot which was used by the boys to practise with their weapons and equipments. I personally funded the expenses of the club which included not only Professor Murtaza's remuneration, but also the cost of equipment, such as, boxing gloves, clubs, swords and daggers, shields, rods and poles. I made it a point to be present when the training sessions were on, sitting at a table and marking attendance of the trainees. In time the reputation of the club spread, and boys from other areas travelled long distances to join the club. Similar clubs sprang up in many other locations. Pulin Das, the leader of the Anushilan Samiti, arrived from Dacca. Many of such clubs received assistance from me, either in cash or in equipment, as did the Anushilan Samiti, and all of them by turns borrowed the services of Professor Murtaza.

Eighteen

A s I grew up I discovered that the greatest slur on Bengalis was their cowardliness, and I was determined to erase this stigma. Possession of a weapon does not necessarily rid one of pusillanimity, but with appropriate skill in the use of a weapon, one knows where to hit an adversary, not to kill him, but just to stun him. One can then be charged with injuring a person, and not accused of murder. Dogs have teeth, cats have talons, even insects have a sting, and they all retaliate when attacked. Only Bengalis do not; when repeatedly hit they do not return even a single blow. Why are they such poor specimens of humanity? Why are they so weak?

And I spotted the weakness; lack of co-ordination between the body and the mind. Many Bengalis in the past were accomplished in the martial art of the *lathis* (a bamboo or wooden pole), but their inactivity over generations had rendered them sluggish and placid. Unless this defect is remedied, unless their mind is re-activated to prod the slothful Bengalis to action, they will not pick up their weapon and jump into a fray even though they may be well trained in wielding *lathis*. And why? Because they are not ready to face combat lacking the needed strength of mind. There are all manners of observations. One of them says that the source of power is in one's arms; another says that the spirit of the mind is the real power. From all this the message was clear: that the mind and the body were dependant on each other to stimulate any action. It was not a

150   *The Many Worlds of Sarala Devi*

mere whim that induced me to undertake my mission of creating a strong Bengali nation.

I made a study of this issue and did considerable research to decide on my course of action. In my search I came across this passage in the work of a British educationist:

Physical weakness is a crime against yourself and those who depend on you. Weaklings are despised and a weakling nation is doomed. The decline of ancient Greece and Rome which rapidly fell from the pinnacle of supreme civilization was due to physical neglect and abuse of the inflexible laws of the Nature. A physically weak nation is drained out mentally, its feet are on downward path and it will end upon the scrap heap if it does not act before it is too late. To change from a weakling to a perfect man build yourself up, clear your befuddled brain and develop your muscles. The one great test of manliness is courage, both mental and physical. Your mind is alone the maker of your physical future and your physical strength insures a high moral standard.

There is also an adage in English which says, 'The battles of England are fought and won in the fields of Eton' (Attributed to the Duke of Wellington, but not in these exact words).

Games of football or cricket are played with a certain degree of physical aggression, and it is this experience that makes them combative at wars to engage the enemy. The time I am talking about, Mohun Bagan as a football team was still in the future, and only the Hindu College boys occasionally played football against a team of Anglo-Indians from Calcutta Medical College, which often turned violent and led to bloodshed. Hindu College boys were regularly thrashed in these matches. My club boys once told me that in a game played the previous day, the Hindu college boys had won with unbiased umpiring decisions that went in their favour. In spite of that some Anglo-Indian boys were ruffled by the result and in a mad fury, assaulted the Hindu College boys, who ran away to save their skin. No doubt they were following the old maxim, 'He who escapes survives!' Apparently not a single Hindu boy dared face the Anglo-Indians. When I asked the boy who gave me this report, 'But what were you all doing, and how many of you were there?' he answered, 'But what could we have done, we were no more that a dozen of us?' So they ran away!

I was disgusted and was very contemptuous of the boys, and told them so. 'All the training you received in martial arts has gone waste. Do not report for any further training.' And then I wrote a

Sukhendu Ray   151

series of scathing articles in *Bharati* on the pusillanimity of Bengali youths. I cited the instance that even after wining their game they chose to turn tail rather than face the aggression of their opponents, the Anglo-Indian boys. I quoted an episode from the Mahabharata, when Krishna's son Aniruddha got hurt in his battle against King Samba and rendered unconscious, his charioteer drove away removing him from the battlefield. On regaining his consciousness he berated his charioteer. 'What have you done? By your act you have now erased my name forever from the roster of brave men. What will the elders of my Jadu clan say? What will be their reaction when they learn that I had run away from the battlefield? Will not the women of the clan detest me as a blot on the escutcheon? Turn back, charioteer, and return me to the battlefield, turn, turn, I say!'

I later told the boys, 'Remember always that you are children of India, heirs to that boy hero Aniruddha, you are of the same blood. Do not sully your heritage, do not run away from the battlefield. You may think that out of your generosity you have forgiven the assaulters, but let me tell you that to forgive is not for the weakling. Before you earn the majesty to forgive, you need to be strong and powerful, and then from your position of strength, by all means, show mercy to the offenders, absolve them of their misdeeds. Otherwise to overlook wrongdoings is nothing short of a demonstration of cowardice.' A couple of months later Saila of Chorbagan Basu family along with a few other boys came to see me. Greeting me after touching my feet, they said, 'We are off now, we shall be back in six months.'

'What do you mean? Where are you off to?'

'Tomorrow we play another football match against the Anglo-Indians, and we promise you we shall not run away scared of thrashings by them. We shall give them as good as we get, we shall take them on and give them the hiding of their life. And for that we may be sentenced to a jail term, but for such offence the penalty is a maximum of six months. We should be back then.'

They left and were back the next day with their heads held high. It was the turn of the Anglo-Indians to turn tail, and none of our boys went to jail.

The then editor of the *Statesman* was a Mr Ratcliffe. We often met at dinners and other parties. He was well aware of my ideas and activities, and we often talked about that openly. The year Mohun Bagan football team had its historic triumph by lifting the IFA shield, the first Indian football team to do so after beating a

152 *The Many Worlds of Sarala Devi*

team consisting entirely of white soldiers, Mr Ratcliffe was already back in England, in Manchester, and I had made my home in Punjab. As editor of the *Manchester Guardian* he commented on this unprecedented victory of a Bengali football team against white army men, 'I know who will me most elated by this victory. She is Sarala Devi, a daughter of Bengal.'

Many young men regularly called on me. It was often alleged that some of them could be secret agents of the police, but that never deterred me. After all, I had nothing to hide. Two young men, Kedar Chakravarty and Brojen Ganguly, both from Mymensingh, approached me with a proposal for assistance. Along with some other young men they had formed an association, named, Suhrid Samiti, and their avowed purpose was that instead of looking for government employment they would be self-employed as farmers by taking lease of a large plot of land. For this they needed a capital sum of five hundred rupees. They had already approached many leaders in the country including Surendranath Bannerjee, but no one was willing to come forward to help them by way of a loan. Meanwhile, they had a promise of the required land, kind courtesy Brojendrakishore Raychaudhuri, the eminent zamindar of Gouripore in Mymensingh. He was willing to lease the young men a thousand bighas of land in Assam, provided the men did the farmwork themselves. They needed money to buy farm equipment, cattle, seed, etc., without which it would be pointless to take possession of the land.

I was well aware that in my mission for the upliftment of our young people I may have to lay out money with no expectation of ever getting it back; a kind of a bad debt to be written off. Must Bengali youths always look for a paid job? Was there no other scope for their employment? Could they not go in for self employment? That had been a general lament aired from various forums and in the press. Here was a bunch of young people, who enthused by such comments, wished to be self employed, but then if we did not help them, were we not proving untrue to our ideals? I decided to lend them this money with no expectation whatever of being repaid. It could be that the men were dishonest; equally they could be sincere and in spite of their genuine efforts, might not succeed in their venture. My money could go down the drain, but we had to be prepared to suffer such losses. I agreed to lend them the money, but I told them that before I did so I wanted a written confirmation

Sukhendu Ray 153

from Brojendrokishore Raychaudhri that he had indeed agreed to lease them the land.

A week later the men returned empty handed. Brojen-*babu* was now unwilling to lease them the land but would do so to me when he came to know that I was with them. Brojen-*babu* saw me along with his secretary Monomohan Bhattacharya, and the deal was done. The lease now was in my name, the farm equipment, cattle, etc. were also bought in my name. They would now run the show on their own, and when they repaid the loan, everything would revert to them. And that is how I came to be close to the Suhrid Samiti.

For sometime I had been cogitating over the idea of a designated National Fesival for Bengal, to be observed on a specified day each year. The Muslims have their Muharram which they celebrate with great gusto taking out processions and with vigorous demonstrations of their martial skills with swords, rods, etc. Hindus outside Bengal have also similar festivals, such as, Ramlila, Dussera, when they present spectacles of martial arts. I was keen to launch a similar occasion for Bengal, but which was it to be? That was my dilemma. Immersion of images was not really a part of the Dussera celebrations, as it is for our Bejoya Dashami, and Bengalis are too preoccupied that day to be diverted to any other programme. According to the Mahabharata, it was a day in the autumn that the Pandavas collected their secreted weapons from a Shami tree and went forth to give battle to their enemies. To my mind the national festival that I was contemplating had to be situated during our main autumn festivities, otherwise Bengalis would not be able to create a linkage of unity with other Hindus elsewhere in the country. As I was racking my brain for an answer to my query, I found it almost by serendipity. I was leafing through a Bengali almanac to find the dates of the forthcoming Durga Puja when I discovered that the second day of the Puja, commonly known as Ashtami, had also been celebrated in the past as Birashtami— paying homage to the brave and the valiant. I did not have to seek any further; my problem was resolved! It remained for me to resurrect a long lost tradition of the Bengalis.

I planned to re-introduce the celebration of Birashtami starting with Bengali mothers. It was necessary to indoctrinate them with the ideals of motherhood that produced and nurtured brave and heroic sons. The idea was to mould the otherwise timid mothers to be stout hearted, to be able to tell their sons unequivocally to be

154   *The Many Worlds of Sarala Devi*

daring, encourage them to go for adventurous activities and games. There had been, I believe, an ancient tradition when mothers and sons, as part of religious rituals, worked hand in hand to lead the country to a glorious summit. How is it, I wondered, that the same country had now sunk so low? It broke my heart when I contemplated this decline. When in certain instances I tied the *rakhi* on some boys, they addressed me as 'Mother', which puzzled me, until I found out that it was once customary for mothers to invest their sons with *rakhi* on the day of the Birashtami. I immediately decided to go round the many clubs and by the symbolic *rakhi*, initiate young prople to learn the intricacies of martial arts and later engage in public displays of their acquired skills. I accepted the Birashtami mission as the command of my 'motherland' and it became almost a religious obsession with me, or else why should the existence of Birashtami Day be revealed to me by such a miraculous chance?

My plan to launch the Birashtami festival was kicked off by a public announcement that it would be held on the day of the Ashtami on the grounds of No. 26 Ballygunge Circular Road. The programme would include competitive demonstrations of martial arts by young men. Invitations were sent out to known clubs to attend the festival and to participate in the competition. A married daughter of the dowager Begum of Murshidabad was a good friend of mine. She along with her mother and aunts sat on a dais screened by a lace curtain. I had earlier persuaded her to distribute the prizes which she did by extending her arm through the curtain, remaining otherwise invisible. The prizes consisted of boxing gloves, knives, swords, etc. Each participant also received a medal specially struck for the occasion.

We also set up a code of how to conduct the Birashtami festival. Participants were to stand in a circle around a flower bedecked sword, sing hymns of praise recalling past heroes, and as the name of each hero came up in the song, flowers were to be offered in his memory. The hymn was specially composed by Asutosh Ghose, a reputed nationalist from Kidderpore. The hymn could also be accompanied by other patriotic songs. This ceremony hugely excited the watching crowds.

Since then the observation of Birashtami gained rapid currency in Bengal. Those who could not travel to Calcutta celebrated the day in their own localities. Where facilities were not available for martial arts, my recommendation was to organize a swimming contest instead. The basic idea was to participate in some form of physical activities.

The Gaekwad of Baroda and his wife, after a holiday in Darjeeling, halted in Calcutta on their way back home, and I promptly took the opportunity of their presence to invite them to tea at our home. Upon their arrival, the boys of our club offered them a guard of honour, and after tea there were displays of martial arts. I told the Maharaja that during a visit to Solapur about eight years ago, I had witnessed similar displays by the boys of a Maharashtrian club, at which the Maharaja had presided. That display, I told him, had made a deep impression on me, and was the inspiration behind the present show.

In our home we had a magnificent painting of Goddess Kali which I had commissioned a Japanese artist to do for me. In the room, among other paintings, were portraits of my parents as well as a portrait of myself, in which the artist had painted me with my luxuriant tresses totally loose and flowing down. This portrait of mine had appeared in many publications, and was probably included in Jogen Gupta's book, 'Women Poets of Bengal'.When I drew the attention of the Maharaja to the painting of the Kali, he looked at my portrait and said with a mischievous grin, 'Which Kali? This or that?'

Nineteen

Natun-mama ran an organization, Sangitsamaj, which was actually a centre for the rich and famous to put up amateur musical and theatrical shows. There is an amusing incidence connected with this organization. The Samiti once staged Balmiki Pratibha in which Jogen Mallik played the role of Balmiki. When he was due to sing the song asking Luxmi to go away and not to visit his poor cottage, he suddenly stopped singing and declared, 'No, I cannot continue. How can I turn Luxmi away? On the other hand I will always entreat her to come back for ever and ever to the cursed and poor hut of mine.' And then without another word he left the stage!

The Maharaja of Baroda was invited by the Sangitsamaj, but instead of putting up any stage show to mark his presence, the highbrows and the elites arranged for a display of skills in arms and weapons. It looked they felt, as if, to demonstrate the softer aspects of the Bengali character would be unsuitable for such an august visitor. A sign of the changing pattern of the Bengali character!

Around that time, many stories and rumours started flying about me, not necessarily complimentary. I digested them without making any comment. I had been variously described as the 'Joan of Arc' of Bengal, as well as 'Devi Chaudhurani' (based on the famous character of a valiant Bengali woman, created by Bankimchandra). Once, apparently, the Railway Police discovered an unaddressed parcel packed with guns, and the needle of suspicion pointed to

Sukhendu Ray 157

me as the importer. But nothing happened as no one ever came to our home to investigate.

Chittaranjan Das warned me. 'Take care. Do not venture out alone in the evening even to walk to your friends' homes. The police believe that you are committing excesses, and they would like to nab you but so far they have not found any plausible excuses. What they are apparently planning to do is to let off some of their hired goons when you are out alone in the evening, and then they will catch you on the plea that the ruffians are your creation.'

The Russo-Japanese war had by now broken out. I wanted to seize this opportunity to raise the level of humanitarianism among the Bengalis by forming a body composed of Bangalis in the model of the Red Cross Society to go out and render aid to the wounded Japanese fighters. I put out an advertisement inviting volunteers and financial contributions. I estimated that the the total cost of this project would be about ten thousand rupees. I humbly welcomed all potential contributors. I received applications from more then three hundred volunteers, and the first contribution that reached me was an unexpected cheque for one thousand rupees from the Maharaja of Mayurbhanj, Sriram Chandra Bhanja. Maharaja Suryakanta Acharya of Mymensingh and many other friends wrote back that they were willing to contribute if I let them know what my needs were. What this revealed clearly to me was that our country did not lack in compassionate human souls; all that was needed was for someone to fire them up.

My idea of forming a Bengali Volunteers Group came to the notice of our British rulers, because very soon I received a letter from a Colonel Yates [presumably the famed Col. F. Yates-Brown of the Bengal Lancers], an English military officer, who wrote to me asking why I was proposing to send out to Manchuria, a separate Bengali Ambulance Corps? And why should I not attach it to the Corps the Government of India was sending out at the initiative of Lord Curzon? In any case, he asked, were the members of the proposed corps trained under St John Ambulance Association? If not, then my efforts would be futile, he warned me. Perhaps the British Government did not take kindly to an independent initiative of Bengalis; it could also be that this letter was written with the tacit approval of the Government. Anyway, it taught me a good lesson by making me aware of the magnitude of the task. The idea to form a Bengali equivalent of the Red Cross Society and to send

158   *The Many Worlds of Sarala Devi*

volunteers to the battle area was nothing but an emotional upsurge, with no conception of what the project involved. No one apparently gave it any critical thought, and none cautioned me about what was needed to be done. Only my lively keenness fired others up. It did not occur to me that just to be brave enough to face the dangers of a war was not acceptable. That the volunteers needed to be trained adequately to provide first aid to the injured and the dying had absolutely escaped my calculations. I was rightly alerted to this need by Colonel Yates' letter.

But how to go about it—that was my worry? Will St John Ambulance accept Bengali trainees? This Association was a part of the British Red Cross Society, and my impression was that none other than British and Anglo-Indian trainees were admitted. I wrote to the Director of St John Ambulance asking for a meeting, and he paid me a courtesy visit. When I explained to him my concern, he confirmed that presently all his trainees were of British and Anglo-Indian descent. The question of training Bengalis had not come up so far as no Bengalis had ever applied for such training. He was willing to offer training to Bengalis provided I requested him in writing. A binding condition was that the selected candidates for training must be located in Calcutta for at least three months before they could be considered fit to be sent out.

While these discussions were on, a news report published an anouncement of the Japanese Government. 'Many nations through the kindness of their hearts have offered to send their respective Red Cross reliefs, but the Japanese Government, while very grateful for such offers, regret their inability to avail of such help.' I suppose their political sagacity must have led to this decision.

Our attitude towards Japan those days and our present attitude are poles apart. A victorious Asian nation fighting the forces of a mighty western power brought glory to all Asian countries. Their cry, 'Asia is one', became a strong unifying message to the nations of Asia. But who could have known then that some years down the line that unifying message would be revealed with a latent message, which was to bring Asian nations under the suzerainty of Japan through their military prowess? For the last few years Japan has been waging a relentless war to subdue China, and its intentions in countries like Siam, Burma, Malaya Islands, Korea, the Phillipines, are quite evident now. Japan, being a small country at the eastern fringe of the world, has grown arrogant enough to assume that they are equal to any other imperial power. There is a parallel between

Sukhendu Ray 159

England and Japan. England has spread its wings around the world with the 'avowed' mission of carrying 'the white man's burden' entirely for the good of the 'inferior' nations, planted their standards in those countries of their 'thoughtful humanitarian pursuits'. Japan, apparently an apt pupil of England, has now assumed 'the yellow man's burden' on its shoulders, spreading its grasping arms to other Asian nations for the benefit of those countries. Why should, then, any Asian nation be reluctant to get out of the shackles of England and exchange them for the stranglehold of the Japanese? After all, the latter is fashioned by Asians, home made. But no one appears to be prepared to embrace this alternative.

After the Great War was over India received several visitors from Japan, many of whom we came to know well. Two of them were artists, Yokoyana and Hishida, well-known names in their own country, who upon return from India, became celebrities. Both of them, on being commissioned by us, did several paintings on Indian themes. Japanese artists normally do not paint on canvases like European artists. Instead their preferred material is silk. This lends a particular delicacy to their paintings. The magic of their brushwork gives life to dainty colours which is appreciated by lovers of art. At my request, Yokoyana painted an image of Kali, and Hishida, a Saraswati. These two paintings still adorn my room and charm all visitors. I preserved these paintings carefully through the four years of the Second World War, regardless of the risk of destruction by enemy bombings. Photographs of both these paintings were printed in the magazine *Prabasi* as *Bharati* was not an illustrated journal. The painting of Kali is not like the usual familiar image. There was a fresh approach in the conception of this painting, which I explained in *Prabasi*.

Suren got them to do some paintings on the theme of the Gita, and reproduction of one of the paintings was included in his book, Sankhipta Mahabharata [abridged Mahabharata]. This painting depicts both Krishna and Arjuna sitting on a chariot drawn by two white horses. Krishna's image, glowingly incandescent, was a masterly portrayal. Gagan-*dada* and Aban-*dada* had a few paintings executed by them on Rashlila and similar themes. I recall a Rashlila painting especially — supernatural moonlight, fine textured clothings of the *gopis*, and their ethereal dancing poses. These were large paintings. When I was away in Punjab, an emissary of the Japanese Government convinced Suren and Gagan-*dada* that these valuable paintings by Japanese artists ought to be back in their country, and

160　*The Many Worlds of Sarala Devi*

acquired them by paying high prices. Since I was away in Punjab, my two paintings are fortunately still in India.

Contemporaneous with the visit of these artists we had another visitor from Japan, known as Prince Hito, a scion of the royal family of Japan. He had renounced the world, had become a *sanyasi,* and was going round India visiting places of pilgrimage. In looks he resembled a person of Tripura's princely family, very comely, with graceful features. Everyone was attracted by his simplicity and his polite manners. He wandered like a wayfarer who had apparently lost his way. If anybody was ill-mannered enough to jokingly question him about female Japanese dancers, he would merely stare at him with blank eyes.

Yet another visitor from Japan was Okakura. He was a friend of Mrs Olebull (?), an American lady, who was a disciple of Swami Vivekananda. It was with her contribution that the foundation of Belur Math was laid. Okakura had spent some time in America and had a good command of the English language. A distinguished art critic, a highly placed government officer, he was truly an image of a Japanese 'samurai' – in his looks, in his manners, in his dresses. A person of all-round accomplishments, supremely nationalistic, a firm believer in Asian unity, he was eager to knit every part of Asia – from Siam to Java, from India to Persia – instilling a sense of Asian patriotism. One of his most celebrated books was written when he was in Calcutta under the guidance of Mrs Olebull and a Miss Mcleod, and helped out in typing by Sister Nivedita. The book begins with the sentence – 'Asia is one', and ends with the sentence – 'Victory from within or Death from without'. The essential ideas propounded in this book and its message spread through word of mouth from Bengal to Punjab. His thoughts were reflected in the writings of Lajpat Rai and similar other nationalistic leaders.

Many Japanese visitors put up with Suren as his guests, and so did Okakura. Okakura came to know another Bengali family, that of Hem Mallik, an uncle of Subodh Mallik of Creek Row, and who was the head of that family. When Okakura returned to Japan, a son of Hem Mallik accompanied him.

After the end of the Russo-Japan war, trade relations between Japan and India prospered. Many young men from Bengal went to Japan to learn the technology of manufacture of many products. Ramanath Ray of Sylhet, a well-regarded person, had just returned from Japan after receiving training. He came to see me carrying with him samples of diverse items manufactured by small industries.

These articles were most attractive, though not expensive to make in Japan, yet marked with the imprint of Japanese artistry. Ramanath planned to set up small industries in the manner of Japanese enterprises, but sadly his untimely death put an end to his dreams. Among other students visiting Japan was Satyasundar Deb, a grandson of Umesh Datta of the Brahmo Samaj. Partly helped by me in winning a scholarship, he went to learn how to manufacture ceramics. On his return he set up Bengal Potteries, which did well, and Bengalis were happy to drink their tea out of cups and saucers made in the country. As far as I know this business passed through many vicissitudes and change of ownerships, and finally failed when managed by the Maharaja of Kashimbazar. Now converted into a joint stock company, it is presently being run by a family of Punjabi owners. Satyasundar Deb had also set up his Behar Pottery at Rupnarayanpur, and his son Saral Deb, the Bengal Porcelain Company, both of which I am told are doing well.

Twenty

Acommon feature among the many Japanese visitors was that they carried from home almost everything that they might need, even note papers for writing letters home. I asked one of them, 'Why do you cram your bags with so much stuff?', and the reply was, 'This is done by our women, because they believe you cannot get your needs in India, not even writing paper. This explains the note papers we pack so that we can write home.' Pathetic! These are the people that the poet Hemchandra had once dubbed as 'uncivilized Japan'! And the same people have now such a dismal perception of India as a poorly endowed country where nothing is available, whose people cannot make anything that are commonly needed — not even a piece of paper to write letters!

In a way there is a grain of truth in this. Yes, we have everything, but mainly acquired through shiploads of imports. And we appear to be happy and complacent with no sense of shame. It gave me a severe jolt. I decided to use our indigenously made yellow paper manufactured from cotton pulp for the cover of the *Bharati* magazine. Unfortunately, I cannot use this paper for the inside pages, which would otherwise effectively close down the publication. At that point of time paper made by Titagarh Mills run with foreign capital was not so easily available. My use of Indian cotton pulp yellow paper for the cover of *Bharati* was at first taken as another example of my crazy ideas, but I noticed that this practice gradually caught on.

This led me to found a shop with my own funds dealing only with Indian-made products, located on Cornwallis Street, and I named it 'Luxmir Bhandar'. This outlet catered only to the needs of women. It stocked dress materials collected from the various regions of Bengal. We appointed a Brahmo widow as a paid sales person. Jogesh Chaudhury, a brother of Asutosh Chaudhury, was a dedicated swadeshi as well as a man of refined tastes. By profession he was a barrister, and had his chambers near the High Court. We once went to have tea at his chambers, and we were agreeably struck by the décor of his office, all done up with Indian fabrics and furniture. The curtains were made from Indian cotton prints which came from many areas of India, and none of the furniture pieces came from the famous House of Lazarus which dealt exclusively with imported items. All the furniture was locally fabricated, attractively designed, and we were quite impressed. Subsequently, with the help of Jogesh-*babu*, we formed a limited liability company and set up a shop calling it, 'Swadeshi Store', at Bowbazar. Efforts, of both Jogesh-*babu* and mine, to promote swadeshi goods date back long before the protest movement during the partition of Bengal.

Soon thereafter an exhibition of Indian-made goods was organized in Bombay coinciding with the annual session of the Indian National Congress to which I sent consignments of Bengal-made products from our shop Luxmir Bhandar. These products were highly appreciated, and I was awarded a medal. Later I turned that medal into a brooch and used it regularly. After a lapse of almost fifteen years when I first met Mahatma Gandhi, he noticed the brooch. When I told him what it was, he immediately realized that my swadeshi proclivity preceded his return to India. After that whenever I was with him at any meeting he would introduce me as a swadeshi. I still have that well designed medal-cum-brooch.

My clothes, made entirely from Indian materials, that I regularly wore even on special occasions like weddings or the Maghotsav festival, started getting noticed. Women came to realize that one could be equally fashionable or trendy with Indian-made clothes without a stitch of imported material. I recall that at one stage, my friends could not stand my Indian *nagra* shoes, being accustomed to foreign made high heel footwear. However the day came soon when those who were most hostile to my *nagras* rapidly coverted to swadeshi mode and they would have nothing other than *nagras* to adorn their feet!

I used to get a regular stream of visitors who came to talk to me about my martial arts club. Two gentlemen from Sylhet called on me one day to tell me about the tyrannical treatment of tea garden

164   *The Many Worlds of Sarala Devi*

workers by the European planters. They spoke of how unscrupulous Indian recruiting agencies employed by the European planters mislaid poor ignorant people with false promises and enticed them to sign on the dotted line to enroll for what was nothing but slavery. Some of our nationalist leaders including Dr Sundari Mohan Das were determined to put an end to this ignominious system. These gentlemen also produced a pamphlet condemning such exploitation: 'Is it Tea or Blood you are drinking?' Apparently Dr Sundari Mohan Das had suggested that they meet me.

My thoughts were already occupied with the dreams of attaining freedom from foreign domination, and now my eyes were opened to the myriad-headed viper that a subjugated nation is. To eradicate fear and cowardice is no doubt the first step towards freedom, but freedom is like a piece of diamond with many facets, each facet radiating prismatic light of many hues. Real freedom is the core of the diamond and its light, the guiding beacon. But what is freedom without self rule? A truly free nation must have its own system to frame its own laws. A country, whose trade and commerce, agriculture and industries, are shaped and controlled by foreign rulers and their laws, can never aspire to attain the glory of an independent nation. A nation whose people remain perennial hewers of wood and drawers of water, a nation which is exploited by a bloodsucking foreign country to build its own wealth, a nation whose peasants with their backbreaking toil produce golden harvests but cannot provide two meals to their families, because all they have is mortgaged to the hilt to money lenders from the day they start sowing and thus have them no surplus, any idea of freedom for such a country is inconceivable. A nation is like a human body, and if there is no co-ordination between the various limbs, that body will remain dysfunctional. Unity among the diverse elements of a nation is the supreme prerequisite in its fight for freedom.

These are the thoughts that flashed through my mind when I was told of the oppressed tea garden workers. I realized clearly enough that for those of us who live a comparatively comfortable and easy life, the desire for freedom is just an emotional luxury. What real ideas have we of the shackles of a slave? The workers of the indigo plantations in their time knew this devil well and so they rebelled. And presently the tea plantation workers are passing through the same sort of miserable existence. Behind this are the tyrannical exploiters supported first by weapons like fire-arms, and second, by the Indian Government laws that favour the ruling class

Sukhendu Ray   165

to the detriment of Indians. Until we have command over both the arms and the laws we shall always remain aliens in our own country. With no control over our own life we shall continue to be in the dark regardless of random flashes of lights.

It is the history of England that has taught us that a nation united can stand up against a tyrannical ruler. People of England came together to extract the Magna Carta from the despot King John. Only absolute unity foreswearing all differences can attain such a goal. Indian history teaches us that we had to wait for someone like Krishna to deliver us from the diabolical Kangsa and Jarasandha. Equally we find from the evidence of English history that one does not need divine intercession for liberation. Someone like Cromwell, bolstered by people power, exterminated the autocrat King Charles. Not divine intercession but divine inspiration — that is the lesson we learn from the history of England. The House of Commons and the House of Lords, the two arms of the British Parliamant, together constitute the people's power, and it is this people's power that forced the repeal of the infamous anti-people Corn Law.

Of essence, then, are an all-embracing unity and the determined efforts to achieve this unity. Common interest will beget a common goal; what harms you also harms me; when your home burns it can also scorch my home, it will then be in my interest to save your home. If you and I are partners in a gainful venture, it will be in our common interest to nurse this venture. If we go our separate ways we shall be destructively torn apart. Self interest is at the root of unity, and that is the strength of a country like England where motivated by common interest, they stood together. The foundation of unity springs from the perception of the mutuality of interest. The well being of a nation cannot be sustained purely by sentiment, nor can it find root in some vague emotional ideas.

Twenty One

This was the time when I was trying to run my life along many routes. Courage, strength, wisdom, unity, self-reliance and self-rule — these were the signposts that guided me. On the other hand I was deeply engrossed in literary activities, writing mainly for the *Bharati* magazine. I did write prolifically those days, but I was wise enough to refrain from filling the pages of *Bharati* with my output only. On the contrary my objective was to build a band of dedicated writers around *Bharati*, and I made a list of about forty writers who by then had gained some reputation, some were based in Calcutta, some others elsewhere. Each month, by turn, I would write to them soliciting their contributions, and remarkably, I was never let down. This speaks volumes for the chivalrous approach to literature that Bengali writers have.

But a similar sense of chivalry cannot be claimed in the field of politics. Politics is an arena where no man would be prepared to sacrifice his 'seat' in favour of a woman candidate. The men are all for themselves, and that is why starting from the All India Congress Committee to the Legislative Assemblies/Councils there are just limited reserved seats for women. Men would not interfere if women fight amongst themselves in clamouring for those reserved seats. It is not unknown that some men will band together behind a particular woman candidate, but for ulterior motives. If some woman candidate dare ask any of the sponsoring men to give up his seat in her favour, then woe betide her! The macho man registers a virulent protest and says, 'never!' There are no reserved seats for aldermen and councillors in the Municipal Corporation of Calcutta, and it is almost impossible for any woman to aspire to penetrate that protected bastion. Sadly, there is no respect for women, no consideration for ability, and the only operating concern is to preserve male domination. If for some reason a female is nominated to head a political organization, be sure to find some men appearing to be supporting her but entirely to serve their own interest behind her shield.

Fortunately rivalries or unethical competitions are rare in the field of literature unless, of course, literature is turned into a commercial commodity. It has been seen that where writers depend upon their pen for their livelihood, they harbour a sense of animosity towards similar other practitioners of literature. And there the gender of the writer is immaterial. The basic theme is who gets the lion's share of the spoils. Literature then ceases to be an intellectual pursuit and engenders selfishness, anxiety, hopes and disappointments. Fortunately, I was spared the need to live off my writing, and so was quite free from money worry.

In running and managing the *Bharati*, I discovered, to my surprise, that after all expenses of paper, printing, staff, etc., *Bharati* earned a surplus. This surplus normally goes to the proprietor, but the writers who sustain the distinctive achievement and promote its sales get nothing for their trouble. This was palpably unfair, I felt. The editor who works hard for the success of a magazine ought to be adequately compensated, but should the proprietor and editor happen to be the same person, must he then pocket the entire surplus earned? And yet, it is the writers who make a publication worthy and a profitable venture, and that being so, why should they be deprived of a share of the gains? This dichotomous thought of the conflict between capital and labour occurred to me spontaneously and not through skimming the pages of a tome on Capital & Labour. I decided then that I must reward our contributors.

It will come as a surprise to most to be told that there were those days many writers who considered that accepting payments for their contributions was dishonourable. Their motto was — I write for the pleasure of it, why should I then expect to be paid for that? That was undignified, they felt. As far as I was concerned I paid fairly well, those who did write for money; those unwilling to accept payment,

168   *The Many Worlds of Sarala Devi*

I would reward by sending them gifts, perhaps a gold fountain pen or a good book, on the occasions of New Year or the Pujas. An upshot of this innovation at *Bharati* was that other magazines were obliged to follow suit to retain the contributors in their stables. Undoubtedly it was the tribe of writers who benefited. Smart editors more solvent than I took to enhancing the remuneration of writers so that these writers understandably preferred writing for them, alas at my cost.

I take credit for another milestone in *Bharati*, and that was ensuring punctuality — in publishing and in delivery to subscribers. This was was absolutely unknown in the world of journals those days. The Baisakh issue came out in Asadh, the Aswin issue saw the light of the day in Agrahayan! I was determined to remedy this chaotic mismatch. And I succeeded. Irregular and untimely publication of issues was erased from the record of *Bharati*. Not depending on helpers to bring proofs to my office, I would go out in my carriage, often correcting proofs while travelling, and after I had gone through the final proofs, I would make the lives of the printers devil's hell till the job was properly completed. I often went over to the quarters of the bookbinders, which always reeked of raw leather, got a few copies of *Bharati* ready which I brought back, leaving the manager to ensure that the balance copies were all ready by the evening and delivered. Not merely ensuring that the magazine came out on the due date, I was equally firm that the subscribers must receive their copies when due. It was not unusual for a subscriber, on receiving his copy of *Bharati* to say, 'It must be the first of the month now that *Bharati* has arrived.' Publishers of contemporary periodicals were obliged soon to follow me, and the publication of issues on due dates became the rule and not the exception.

One of my editorial missions was to spot and build up a bank of promising young writers. I could easily fill up the pages of *Bharati* with contributions from established writers, but I was not too happy with that. Like many other journals, *Bharati* received a whole lot of unsolicited contributions, most of which, found unacceptable, were consigned to the waste paper basket. Soon I stumbled on to the realization that many of these rejected pieces contained some bright nuggets, which, if properly edited and reconstructed, may stand the test of acceptance. I immediately started experimenting with a number of the contributions that at first sight were deemed

Sukhendu Ray 169

unsuitable only to be rejected, conducting a sort of surgery by excising, amputating, resetting 'limbs', and in the process, bringing alive a dead piece by putting flesh and blood into it. On the basis of this experimentation, I found I have been able to recreate several bright pieces of compositions. One particular episode is worth recalling. A Bengali writer, resident of Behar, sent me a few pieces depicting life in Behar. I noticed that these pieces had meat but no merit. I had an inspiration; I decided to turn these contributions into a series. I named it 'Ram Anugrahanarain's Infancy'. This very name intrigued readers. The basic theme of this series was what Behari mothers did to raise their children. The birth of 'Ram Anugrahanarain's Infancy' was announced with a degree of hype, and apparently his deeds and misdeeds caught the imagination of the readers. After some trials and errors, the author seemed to get the hang of it, and his subsequent contributions gave me no problems. It was in this fashion that that I built up a number of promising new writers. We were not blessed those days with the plenitude, as we have now, of writers. That is why I found it gratifying that I was able to open up a few buds and unfold them into writers of gift. At *Bharati* I was not just a mechanical editor; my life was charged with human susceptibilities. I hardly knew our contributors personally, and our mutual connection was via exchange of letters. When I had to reject a contribution, I always sent a polite note. Even so, that often invited displeasures. One rejected writer wrote back, 'You are the past mistress in the art of denial.' Such uncalled-for incidents recurred many times over in my life.

During my editorship of *Bharati*, it was not an organ of just literature and fine arts; it was also the mouthpiece of nationalistic evangelism. Swami Vivekananda appeared on the scene just about when my nationalism was engaged in the eradication of all sort of assaults on our national dignity. On the occasion of the nation's felicitation to him at the Star Theatre and his speech in reply, I published a special article. On reading it Vivekananda wrote to me and I responded. The first few exchange of letters initiated our acquaintance. Sister Nivedita came to see me on his behalf and invited me to to visit the Belur Math. I seldom went out, keeping to my rooms engaged in my work. I was also not greatly inclined to go out as many modern women are. I was hesitant to start with for even today I am most reluctant to travel by public transport. I just cannot stand being jostled by other passengers.

170   *The Many Worlds of Sarala Devi*

At the same time it was difficult to refuse Sister Nivedita, and as I was not stout-hearted enough to venture out alone, I asked Suren to escort me, which he did. We travelled by our own private carriage to Baghbazar Ghat, where we were met by Sister Nivedita. We took a boat across the Ganges.

On the other side of the river Mrs Olebull, clad in a Japanese kimono, and Miss Mcleod sat waiting for us on cane chairs. Swami Vivekananda was there in his usual saffron robe of a monk but minus his headgear. He sat there radiating an uncommon aura. With them was Swami Swarupananda who later became the Director of the Mayavati Advaitashram. It was on a built-up area, considered safe from the risk of caving in, where we sat. Tea was served. I was still a little nervous, sceptical about the safety of the place, but it was altogether quite pleasant. A clear sky above, down below the flowing Ganges, on the other side was the Dakhsineswar Temple, the sanctum of Ramakrishna, and behind us the Belur Math. The Math then was a derelict structure, which has since been renovated and reconstructed into what is the present Belur Math. Vivekananda's bedroom is still reverently preserved there with all his memorabilia.

Talk there was mainly confined between the two American ladies and Sister Nivedita, with Swarupananda chipping in from to time. Vivekanada hardly spoke, neither did I. I repeated this visit a few more times, always with Suren. Swami Vivekananda gifted me some of his books including Rajyoga, which he inscribed inside, 'With love', in his own hand. I also gave him to read my 'Ahitagnika' and 'Khano Sesher Bilap', both printed in *Bharati*. He read them immediately, and I got to know later from Sister Nivedita of his comments. 'Sarala's education is perfect, and this is the kind of education that women in India need.'

Soon thereafter I was invited to accompany him on his trip to England, to represent the women of India and to spread the spiritual message of the Orient to the women of the Occident. In one of his letters to me before we met, his thoughts on this issue had been expressed very clearly. These letters now form part of his biographies. Sadly, I could not take up this priceless offer and missed a lifetime opportunity. To some extent my own indecisiveness, a sense of diffidence, and above all, my family's unwillingness to let me go, came as a hitch. Sister Nivedita accompanied him, and she became the conduit of his thoughts.

Sukhendu Ray 171

After his return I met Swami Vivekananda only twice. The last meeting is unforgettable. He overwhelmed me with the warmth of his reception, his regard and hospitality. He had arranged to surprise me with an international feast, and for that occasion, he had cooked every item himself. From Norway to France and America—he served a selection of cosmopolitan delicacies. His disciples went overboard in looking after me, and when at the end of the meal, one of the disciples brought a jug of water, I strongly protested. Who am I that they should humble themselves for my sake? I am a mere mortal woman; not the *devi* they perceive in me in their imagination.

Twenty Two

Many streams flow in and nourish a river, and in my life, Swami Vivekananda was one such stream that fortified my knowledge and resolve. His preachings in our country as well as abroad opened windows to let in his spiritual message of a new age. His was a many splendoured personality, and he presented diverse images to diverse people. Nationalists regarded him to be at the forefront of their movement, and people who believed in action considered him a great motivator of hard work for causes. But he had his detractors. Some of the monks in his Math are believed to have made whispered comments, 'We had an easy life during Paramhansa's regime. All that we did was to meditate with few responsibilities. And here is Swamiji, back from America, and all he wants from us is dedicated application to work and service. Can't even sit in peace for a moment. A difficult time for us.'

Vivekananda had studied deeply the psyche of the people of both East and West. He came to the conclusion that the balance between the three primal attributes of life — namely, *sattwa* (knowledge), *raja* (spirit) and *tama* (ignorance) — in human beings make individuals different from each other, and also determine collectively the character of a nation. India, according to him, lies presently buried deep beneath the debris of ignorance accumulated through untold generations. This petrified debris need to be chipped away, and people led to climb out on the path of action. It is in this process that

Sukhendu Ray 173

we shall regain our spiritual supremacy that we had lost ages ago. And to instill the spirit of action in his disciples he preached the message of Gita, urged them to follow 'the path of action (Karmayoga)', and took this message also to his brother monks. The objectives of Ramakrishna Mission, founded in the name of the Saint Ramakrishna, were to help the deprived, the distressed and desolate, and to work for their cause. The monks of the Mission are not like the received image of the saffron-clad *sadhu* who either remains engrossed in meditation or blissfully drawing on a clay pot stuffed with narcotics! Wherever Ramkrishna Missions operate, be it in India or abroad, they do so in the service of the poor and the disadvantaged. Their activities have no room for social or political movements or controversial agenda. Mahatma Gandhi's activities, on the other hand, are unequivocally in the political arena, and so his programme has to be belligerent, even though he has disarmed his movement by preaching 'non-violence'. Monks of the Ramakrishna Mission, imbibing the virtues of the Buddhist monks, take care of the helpless but do not engage in any social or political revolutions. On the contrary, the Mission had come to the rescue of many young people who were arrested and punished for their part in political revolutionary movements and later released. It did this by sheltering them in the Mission's ashrams and restoring their scarred body and soul back to health to lead them along the path of peace and tranquility.

Nationalist sentiments were deeply entrenched in Vivekananda's disciples, but these were the kind of sentiments that extend their arms to embrace all nationalities and encourage people, men and women, to enrich themselves by drinking deeply of their distinctive cultures. It could be that Vivekananda perceived in me a kernel of our national culture, and observed to Nivedita, 'Sarala's education is perfect'. Equally, he may have discerned in my writings that I identify myself as an Indian in every respect, not British or French. He may have spotted in my very first article on him in *Bharati* the latent seed of nationalism in me, which could be nurtured to grow into the Indian woman he has been searching for to travel abroad and propagate Indian culture.

When he met me later and was convinced of my eligibility, he was keen to take me with him abroad as his aide in his undertaking of carrying the message of Indian religion and philosophy. But in his eagerness he perhaps failed to detect my unpreparedness for

174   *The Many Worlds of Sarala Devi*

this solemn mission. He may have also argued that if someone like Nivedita, a woman from the West, who had no clue to Indian religion and culture, could be trained from scratch, so perhaps some one like me would be easier to bring up. If Nivedita can be tutored well enough to talk about the essence of Goddess Kali at a public lecture in the Albert Hall, surely then I can be tutored far more readily. Dr Mahendralal Sarkar of the Science Association was so unnerved by listening to Nivedita's talk that he apparently cried out, 'Goodness gracious! Till now we knew all about our traditional dark Kali, but now this white Kali preaching Hindu religion to us, we can no way get rid our country of idol worship.'

Swami Vivekananda knew very well, of course, that I was a granddaughter of Maharshi Debendranath, brought up in the Brahmo faith, nurtured under the influence of Brahmosamaj, and must be powerfully averse to any ideas of Kali and Durga. Yes, that could be true, but so what? Vivekananda, as Naren Datta, was for a while swayed by Brahmananda Keshubchandra; did that not make him a Brahmo albeit for a short duration? Is it also not a fact that coming in contact with Ramakrishna Paramhansa opened his eyes to the artificial barrier between formless God and idol worship? That might happen to me also. It is possible that Vivekananda was so certain of it that he proposed to take me with him, but I was not enthused enough due to my longstanding superstitious beliefs and the resulting timidity.

Vivekananda died plunging the entire nation into deep mourning, but his missionary work went on. Even to this day his preachings remain a source of inspiration for me. My keenness to find a route to spiritual awareness began slowly to dig a tunnel inside me as a tiny seed grows into a tree breaking through the cracks in a building. A quotation from one of his letters to me from Patanjali Yoga prompted me to read this book, which I did, armed with a translation in Bengali. From there I went on to study Rajayoga, and thereafter, I read many books on yoga in tandem with discussions with knowledgeable practitioners of yoga. My attention to Bhagavadagita was first drawn from a booklet that I received as a gift from Vivekananda. Before then I had not read even a single verse of the Gita, because in our family Krishna was not held in any esteem. This brought home to me that in spite of my Indian roots, my knowlege of our own spiritual culture was deplorably poor. The enlightening sparks from the many-faceted gem of our

Sukhendu Ray 175

inherited wisdom had passed me by, and viewed from that light, my education was hardly perfect.

I was troubled by such deprivation and was driven by a strong passion to remedy this loss. What is Hindutva, I asked myself? At one extreme is the meditation on Brahma, the Supreme Being, and at the other, the rituals of worship of deities as laid down by the ancient religious texts. I was most keen to comprehend how these two controversial tenets were conceived in the minds of our ancestor sages. And I concluded that neither of these tenets could be overlooked. After some familiarization of the Vedas, I started on the Puranas, and I was firmly convinced that the tales from the Puranas were in fact parables in which are deeply entrenched the essence of Brahma as revealed by the Vedas. Influenced by the Koran and the Bible, Rammohun Roy turned against the traditional idol worship, and instead preached the worship of the formless Brahma, but did it take roots? Come to think of it, how can one genuflect at the feet of a formless God? How can God lead you by the hand if He has no hands? How can He look at you with loving eyes if He has no eyes? Strictly speaking, it is not feasible to imagine a formless God; He has to be perceived in physical terms. I find nothing wrong in that, and I believe even Christians do that. But as soon as you depict His image in painting, carve in stone or model in clay, you are dubbed a heathen. This stigma of heathenism with which new-age Christian missionaries assaulted Hindus was unpardonable. Equally unacceptable was the trend of young Indians embracing Christianity, which went against our national sentiments. This precipitated the cult of the veneration of the formless Brahma, and the propagation of the new religion. The practice of idol worship must be eradicated from our country, or else the world will regard us as 'uncivilized, barbaric'. And thus was launched the era of Rammohun Roy's Brahmo faith.

Soon followed another era—side by side with the worship of a formless God, idol worship regained its lost shine as it was found to be logical. After all, this was the age of reason. Threre was a renewed interest, not just in the Upanishadas, but in many old Hindu religious texts. They were re-discovered as a store house of priceless wisdom, not to be jettisoned in the mid-seas. And slowly many followers of Brahmo Samaj began to call themselves Hindu again, and in coming back to their devotion, reinstated idol worship in their homes. A leading light of the Brahmo Samaj those days, Bejoy

176   *The Many Worlds of Sarala Devi*

Krishna Goswami, broke away from the Samaj, and many Brahmos followed him and became his disciples. And then appeared in our midst a dynamic personality — none other than Vivekananda. Who is a dynamic person? Someone, who is fired with vision, is endowed with mighty spirit, can break and build both. I must have received a spark from that fire which re-created me. My thirst for spiritual attainment took me far away from the path of my childhood indoctrination in Brahmo faith.

Twenty Three

When one talks about a 'foreigner' these days, one refers to someone from abroad, such as, Europe or America. In earlier times anyone outside Bengal was a 'foreigner'. In the eyes of a Bengali all non-Bengalis were aliens. Fortunately, owing to the activities of the Indian National Congress over the last half a century India is today regarded as a sub-continent, and people from one end of the country to the other now consider themselves to be of one nation. For a long time people from one district in Bengal regarded people from another as aliens. For example, residents of Varendra area and the residents of Rarh area looked upon each others as outlanders. So much so that though belonging to the same district a girl from one village would not be given in marriage to a groom in another village, again on the grounds that he belonged to another 'land'. Although such petty perceptions of difference may still linger among the lower echelons of the people, it is no longer a factor in the life of the educated layer of the society. Indeed, it will be quite offensive to call any Indian from outside Bengal a 'foreigner' these days.

In any case, this artificial barrier still stood very firm when I used to edit *Bharati*. I tried to breach this barrier by coaxing illustrious persons from other parts of India, whom I personally knew, to write for *Bharati* on themes of their special fields of experience. And this venture of mine procured an article written by Mahadev Govinda Ranade on the issue of converting back to Hinduism, persons who

178 *The Many Worlds of Sarala Devi*

had abandoned the faith as well as removing the stigma of untouchability from them. Naturally he wrote in English, and it was published in *Bharati* in Bengali in my translation. Another so called 'foreigner' was trapped into writing for *Bharati*—his name is Mohandas Karamchand Gandhi. He had not been anointed a Mahatma then, but was just about getting to be known for his activities in South Africa. He was visiting Calcutta from South Africa to attend the Congress Session. He came to our home for an evening reception. Nothing much to look at, but a charming smile lit up his face up. With so many guests present at the reception I saw him only very briefly, but at a later meeting, he told me that though he had no idea what I did, he looked upon me with some respect because of my father who was then the tireless General Secretary of the Congress. I was at that stage of my life hunting for big catches for my magazine. I found one in Gandhi who had made quite a stir in South Africa, and in my eyes was a 'lion'. Caging an article from a celebrity like him to enrich the pages of *Bharati* would be an achievement, and I regarded him from this practical need of mine.

Another contributor gave me an article written in English. No, we certainly cannot regard him as a foreigner, but to us he was almost one. He was the barrister Sir Syed Amir Ali, later a High Court judge. His son by his English wife is Justice Amir Ali, the second. He gave me his book, *Spirit of Islam*, as a gift. The complex issue of Hindu-Muslim unity was already much in my thoughts. I was once asked by Srish Sen to give a talk at a meeting of the Sadharan Brahmo Samaj, which I accepted provided I could speak on the question of Hindu Muslim unity. His committee agreed, and the venue selected was the Mitra Institution on Harrison Road. I have never felt comfortable addressing a public meeting, and I was also not keen to do so on this occasion. So I sent my written speech and requested Srish-*babu* to read it on my behalf. At the packed venue when many of the young people present came to know that I would not speak and that Srish-*babu* would read my speech, there was a near riot. Having already announced through handbills that I would be speaking, the crowd abused Srish-*babu*, calling him a cheat, a liar. The following day Srish-*babu* met me and made a forceful plea for me to speak personally at a re-convened meeting. Otherwise, there would be a severe loss of face for Srish-*babu*. I had no option but to yield. The subsequent meeting was convened at the Albert Hall, Jagadish Bose was to take the chair and Bipin Pal would be the other speaker. I went and gave my talk, the hall was overflowing with eager listeners, and among them were many Muslims.

The essence of my talk was that the conflict between communities in India was nothing new. It was part of India's history from time immemorial – since the days of conflicts between Aryans and non-Aryans. The original inhabitants resented the incoming hordes of migrants, and over time, these migrants assimilated with the original people and became one with them. And in turn they all resented the new migrants. This had a parallel with the British history. The original inhabitants of England were overrun by successive invasions by the Angles and the Saxons from Breton, and they all subsequently became one nation which we know as English or British. They now proudly sing in unison 'Britons never, never shall be slaves'.

Indian history has a backdrop of continuous clashes between communities and communities; Aryans, non-Aryans, Saks, the Huns, Pathans, Rajputs, the Moghuls. The lesson of all these conflicts was that common interest was at the root of unity, any one who opposes this unity becomes an adversary. The first disharmony was between the original non-Aryan Indians and the invading Aryans, and then they together fought the subsequent invaders from across the borders, the Saks and the Huns. Next to arrive were the followers of the new faith, founded by Muhammad. Clashes with them were more intense and deep rooted. These newcomers were unable to distinguish between the crude idol worship of the semitic Arabs and the conception of Indian sages of idol worship. They classed both of them as equally offensive, and during their invasions they ruthlessly destroyed temples and images of deities. They were not merely fortune seekers, they carried with them the standards of their religious faith whose only objective was to preach, propagate and convert locals to their religion. It was no longer a case of conflict of interest; it was inflicting a wound on the psyche of the Indians, hurting their pride and respect. And this assault continued unabated. There were serious repercussions, because the communities refused to mingle and break bread together. The other curious outcome was that the converts to this new faith, while continuing to speak their mother tongues, were given Arabic or Persian names. Thanks to mullahs, converted Indians of all castes and colours sported names, as if they had just arrived from Arab or Persia or Turkey.

This cult of names also affected the Brahmo Samaj. Arising from their intense aversion to idol worship they abandoned the traditional names usually derived from Hindu gods and goddesses,

180 *The Many Worlds of Sarala Devi*

and searched for fresh lyrical names from nature. The Indianness of both Christian converts and Islamic converts was lost under their new names, but shorn of that they were no different from the other Indians. Not just the names, new converts to Islam were thoroughly indoctrinated to adopt Arabic culture and customs which severely clashed with the time-tested Hindu system. The fundamentalism of both the communities only helped in widening the breach. The message in my speech was that unless we all shunned this fundamentalism we would be in deep trouble.

Mr Jinnah, the Jinnah, who has become a sworn enemy of our country and is ready to rend it asunder, forgets that he is a child of Hindustan, as is clear from his name. Jina or Jinnah is a Gujarati word meaning tiny and applied to a little boy, as is common for Bengalis to call a little boy Khoka. Apparently, before conversion to Islam a Hindu mother of a few generations earlier must have lovingly called her little son Jina, and that name stuck and became a family name. That same 'Jina' of Gujarati Hindu ancestry is up in arms against his own country. Does he not realize that by his action he is inviting obloquy on himself? What is driving him to to commit this disastrous act? What is his motivation? Leadership of a party, leadership of the nation? My ideals of Hindu Muslim unity do not allow for one community to coolly accept the wrongdoings of another. Gandhi's non-violent movement does not meekly accept wrong and discriminatory treatment by the British of its subjects. On the contrary, action programmes of the movement aim to protest against such injustices. His advice is not cravenly to yield to the misdeeds of the Government.

I recall once during a stage performance of the play 'Aurangzeb', a band of Muslim Bengali youths, helped by hired hooligans from outside, raided the Minerva Theatre, and Amar Datta, the actor, escaped for his life through the backdoor. *Bharati* magazine roundly condemned Amar Datta's cowardice.

On the occasion of the conference of Bengal Provincial Congress at Mymensingh, the Suhrid Samiti invited me to attend their annual festival. I have said earlier that once at their meeting I was welcomed by shouts of 'Vande mataram', later to be accepted as a national slogan. I was told that the celebrations this year included staging a play based on Bankimchandra's story 'Ananda Math'. Many eminent persons including Surendranath Bannerjee had arrived to attend the Provincial Conference, as did my father. He and I were guests of barrister Nripen Palit, a nephew of Sir Taraknath Palit.

Sukhendu Ray 181

At the opening of their function when displays of many martial arts were on, I was taken aside by Kedar Chakravarti of Suhrid Samiti and was told, 'I need your advice. We decided to stage Ananda Math for you specially. On our own we have eliminated anything in the story that might hurt Muslim sentiments. The organizers of the provincial Conference now tell us that after much persuasion a number of Muslim delegates have agreed to participate, and in fact Surendranath brought many of them with him. If we, the Hindu boys, persist in staging this play, then Muslim delegates will refuse to attend the conference. We have been asked to refrain from putting up this play so as not to disrupt the Conference. Please tell us what we ought to do.'

I suggested that they should invite the leaders and have a rehearsal of the play in their presence, and if they find anything objectionable, then delete it.

'We have already made this suggestion,' I was told, 'but Muslims would not accept deletions of just some portions of the play, because they take exception to the entire book. Rightly or wrongly, we have been asked to desist from our plan to produce this play in the face of Muslim opposition.'

I was stunned. 'Don't tell me that the followers of Surendranath, whose name is synonymous with "surrender not", have asked you to desist. I am not in favour of surrender, so my advice for you is to go ahead.'

The following day my host Nripen Palit told me, 'Some leading citizens of the town along with a number of political leaders led by Anath Guha are here in a deputation to see you.' This intrigued me. Why should elderly dignitaries of my father's generation arrive in a deputation to me, a much younger person? Of course, I met them, and my father was also present. As their spokesman Anath-*babu* said, 'We have come with a request.'

'A request? To me?' I was embarrassed.

'Please ask the boys of Suhrid Society not to go ahead with their plan to stage Ananda Math.'

'But the Suhrid Society boys are boys of your town; surely your words will be more effective than mine. I am just their guest for the day, so why do you not speak to them?'

Hemanta Basu, a barrister, son of Dr Dharmadas Basu and son-in-law of Rajani Ray, spoke somewhat heatedly. 'Do not try to be smart. You know well enough that the boys will pay no heed to us, and will only listen to you.'

182   *The Many Worlds of Sarala Devi*

'If that is so, then you need to tell me why must I stop the boys?'

'Because, Muslims regard this play offensive. If the boys still insist on going ahead, Muslims will desert us, will not attend the conference. After a great deal of effort Surendranath has succeeded in persuading the Muslim delegates. He has even paid for their railway fares, and all this labour will be lost.'

'Even if the play is presented after deleting the offending parts?'

'Yes, even then!'

'But is it fair?' I asked. 'Just so that Muslims can attend the conference must we yield to their perverse demands? There will be no end to it then. Why do you not ask them to attend a rehearsal, and then censor out objectionable contents. I am sure the boys will be agreeable.'

Hemanta Basu almost shouted, 'That won't do. The boys must abandon their plan to stage this play.'

'And if the boys do not agree?'

'There will be bloodshed then.'

'Oh, really? If your Muslim friends hold out such threats, then I will instruct the members of the Suhrid Samiti not to be scared, not to yield to injustice. If there is bloodshed, so be it. I will tell the boys—go ahead, fight for your rights, even if that means courting death.'

My refusal to concede to the request of senior citizens of the town and the local leading lights embarrassed my father. He commented, 'My daughter can be impetuous. Please don't take offence.'

Hemanta Basu left, fuming; the others, after polite greetings. Eventully, Barrister Hemanta Basu won the day and prevailed. He ran to the Chief of Police and persuaded him to ban the play on grounds of breach of peace. He was cock-a-hoop about his great achievement. Fortunately, Anath-*babu* became a friend and later extended his helping hand on many occasions.

Let me add here a word or two about my parents. Did they disapprove of the activities of my club teaching boys disciplines of martial arts at our home, or observing Birashtami festival with a spectacular show? Not at all; they never ever stopped me. Their tacit approval was my back-up strength, without which I could not have progressed even one step.

Twenty Four

The very first familiar association is the family, and then with the widening circles of friends, other associations develop. For many there is the fellowship of religion related affiliation which has a distinct identity. For us, in our young days, our association was confined within the bounds of Jorasanko. Our get-togethers, whatever the occasion, festive or mourning, were of family members only. After we shifted to Kashiabagan our social contacts expanded because of the Theosophical Society and mother's Sakhi Samiti, but these friendships were not deep, rather superficial.

Hindus on the other hand were not confined to the immediate family, but their association nevertheless was restricted to the community within which they could inter-marry. Friendships outside the community, regardless of affinity of minds, could never be very close. This may be due to the caste system that prevails among the Hindus.We got to know some orthodox Hindu families, and even though we visited their homes on their festive occasions, we still remained in the periphery. There was no such barrier when an 'Anglo-bengali' association found a footing and grew. We became part of this community, which certainly extended to our familial circle. This association was mainly the home ground of the followers of the Sadharan Brahmo Samaj, particularly those who were affluent and had been to England, with a handful of Christian members thrown in.

184   *The Many Worlds of Sarala Devi*

Brahmos had their own religious bodies to which all Brahmos could belong, regardless of their social status. Regrettably we had no dealings with them, but we did have some ideas of the deeply religious families in the homes of the children of Brahmananda Keshubchandra Sen. They were most enlightened, indeed, and Baidyas from Coolootola or Gorfa were not the only relations of his family as all devotees of the founder of Naba Bidhan Samaj were treated as equal members of his family. There was certainly a world of difference between the standing of the Maharani Suniti Devi of Coochbehar or Maharani Sucharu Devi of Mayurbhanj and the ordinary members of the Naba Bidhan Samaj, but these ladies with their natural courtesy and grace downplayed this difference.

Maharshi's home lacked this affinity of one extended family knit by religious bonds. One reason could be that the members of the Adi Brahmo Samaj outside of No. 6 Jorasanko House attended the temple of the Samaj, joined in prayers and meditation, and returned home after listening to a few Brahmo hymns. They hesitated to mingle with the members of Maharshi's family. It was also suspected that while the men of those families publicly worshipped the formless God, their ladies still continued privately to stick to the traditional Hindu customs.

All these accounts just go to explain why Maharshi's family had no distinct religious association.

We slowly assimilated with the Anglo-bengali group, particularly after we moved to Ballygunge Circular Road from Kashiabagan. Ballygunge those days was hardly populated, and with very few buildings. It consisted mainly of big gardens and large tracts of unused land. Much of this property belonged to Sir Taraknath Palit. He invited people to settle there, started cultivation on the unused land, and sold piecemeal his property to his many friends. No. 26 Ballygunge Circular Road to which we moved belonged to Jadu Mallik. We built our own home later at No. 3 Sunny Park. Ashu Chaudhury built his home at No. 6 Sunny Park; my *mejo-mama* bought an old house at No. 19 Store Road; K G Gupta constructed his house at No. 6 Store Road. After Indira's marriage she first made her home at No. 14 Ballygunge Circular Road, and later moved to her own place in Bright Street. My elder sister first built her home on Jhowtala Road, and then shifted to Hazra Road. In this way around the Ballygunge Maidan and nearabouts, a large settlement took shape consisting of our relations and friends.

Sukhendu Ray 185

Almost every member of the Anglo-bengali group came originally from East Bengal. Except for their traditional morning meal of rice they were in every other respect substantially anglicized. This prompted me to formulate an idea to instill some sense of Indian culture in them. I started with the bindi on the foreheads of women and tinting their feet with the red dye, *alta*. In addition I tried to reshape some of our Bengali festivities by giving them an anglicized touch to make them acceptable to my friends. The invitation to Saraswati Puja declared it as the Spring Festival, and also included an invitation to tea. By way of a footnote it said, 'For women, saffron coloured sari and/or blouse and for men some trace of saffron is desirable'. That was no problem for women. They came decked up in lovely saffron dyed saris and dresses. Many men chose to arrive clad in saffron coloured *kurtas*, and those who preferred trousers and jackets sported saffron coloured ties or saffron coloured handkerchiefs adorned their breast pockets. In the evening we had music after tea.

In my ongoing friendship with the Anglo-bengali group I discovered that many of the ladies from East Bengal were expert cooks of Bengali sweets. With the objective of getting this talent a national recognition I organized the celebration of 'Poush Parban' (a harvest festival). I invited some of the ladies to our home to cook the special sweets connected with this festival. The ladies assembled in the morning and started cooking and after a modest lunch, they resumed their labours until their task was completed. In the evening they freshened up, dressed up for the occasion and gathered on the lawn. By then members of their families and other guests had assembled there. Replete with the feast of the sweets prepared by the ladies, everyone had a good time.

Another occasion that I arranged to celebrate was the festival of Nabanna (the new rice crop). To the invitees I first served a traditional preparation with new rice, followed by tea and other eats.

I also founded a music club the aim of which was to propagate and cultivate both Indian and western music. Atulprasad and his sisters joined me in own compositions. The songs he sang for us are included in my book of notation.

Frequently our club would hold musical concerts which were well attended. The very last concert held was arranged by my *Didi* on the occasion of my birthday. The club continued till all the girls got married.

186 *The Many Worlds of Sarala Devi*

My talk on 'Hindu-Mussalman' came out in *Bharati*, and an English translation was printed in the *Hindustan Review* of Allahabad. An English version of another article that I wrote for *Bharati* called, 'Congress Republic', also found place in *Hindustan Review*. Both these articles drew considerable interest in North-west India. Lala Lajpat Rai, who had read these articles and who also had a report on my Birashtami festival from (now late) Jogesh Chaudhury, happened to be in Calcutta around the same time. He was keen to meet me, but unfortunately I was not at home when he called. We met the following day and had a long and fruitful talk. In answer to his query I unfolded my plan how to win our freedom. He appeared to share my ideas to a great extent and we both agreed that we must have, 'Victory from within or court death from without'.

Meanwhile, a man called Jatin Bannerjee came to see me carrying a letter of introduction from Aurobindo Ghose who was then in Baroda. Aurobindo's elder bother Monomohan Ghose, the well-known poet from Oxford, had by then become a close friend of mine. I had a number of letters from him full of poetic flavour. Both the brothers were by nature visionaries but in a different way. One was steeped in poetry, and the other was a man of action.

Jatin Bannerjee was earlier a private soldier in Baroda's armed forces. I gave him all the help that I could. Under Barin Ghose's leadership, a political party was founded that openly declared its intention to liberate India from the British. Jatin joined this party and rose to be one of the leaders. He lived in the premises from which the party operated. Jatin's job was to train new recruits in the party taking them through various physical exercises and drills, as well as teaching them how to ride on horseback. Horse riding was a speciality of Baroda, and I remember having seen Maharani Chinnabai trying to control a horse in the courtyard of the palace with the help of a Sikh *sardar*.

Jatin had my full support in his training methods, but I took strong exception when I learnt that Jatin's party had been asked to mount a robbery and brigandage. Apparently, so I was told, they had the support of Sister Nivedita. Sister Nivedita was known for her views that the order and peace brought in the country by the British through ruthlessly subduing violent elements had reduced our men to a body of docile creatures. A certain degree of unrest was necessary to rouse the men, hence she justified the practice of banditry.

Jatin usually faithfully reported to me the discussions at their party meetings. He told me one morning, 'Early tomorrow morning

Sukhendu Ray 187

some members of our party will raid the home of an old widow in Diamond Harbour. The idea is to kill her and rob her of her wealth which she keeps buried in her home.'

I was utterly horrified. 'How wonderful!' I said. 'What a great idea to rob a helpless old woman by killing her. How daring! And what are you planning to do with the looted money tainted with blood?'

'Use it for our cause, in the service of the country.'

'Do you really believe that your mother country will happily accept such dirty money? Will your mother country be able to withstand the shock of murder of one of her aged and innocent children?'

'Of course. It has been decreed by Tilak Maharaj.'

'I cannot believe this until and unless I have it directly from him. I will go and see him, and till I get back you must promise me that you will not go through this heinous plan of yours. Give me your pledge.'

'Yes, we promise.'

I arranged to travel to Poona immediately to meet Tilak. My friend Mr Hydari, Deputy Accountant General, was going to Bombay on leave, and on my suggestion readily agreed that I could travel with him. During the journey I told him that I proposed to get down at Poona to meet some friends and proceed to Bombay later.

Govind Karkare, a former professor at Poona Elphinstone College, an elderly and somewhat eccentric person, was an old family friend of ours. I had earlier cabled him, and he came to the railway station to meet me. Professor Karkare's home was inside the military cantonment, and on the way to Kharki one comes across the confluence of the two rivers, Mula and Mutha. Almost twenty-five years ago my *mejo-mama* had a bungalow near that confluence, where my elder brother Jyotsnanath was born. *Mejo-mama*'s son Suren was born a year later, and so we nicknamed them both 'Poona Brahmin'.

After I rested, bathed and fed at Govind Karkare's home, I told him that I wished to see N.C. Kelkar, the editor of *Mahratta*, whom I knew well. In the afternoon I set off in a Phaeton carriage provided by Govind Karkare. I told Kelkar when I met him, 'I need most urgently to see Tilak. Please, will you fix it for me? I suggest you invite both of us for lunch at your home as I do not wish to see him at his home.'

Tilak at that point of time was involved in some kind of (political) criminal case, and his house was under strict surveillance

188   *The Many Worlds of Sarala Devi*

by the police. Detectives were planted near his home, and it was not a safe place to talk to him there. Anyone who visited Tilak immediately became a suspect in the eyes of the police, and his movements were watched.

Kelkar did arrange for the proposed lunch where I met Tilak. Being occupied in preparing his own defence he hardly could spare any time. At Kelkar's home he came armed with many law books and documents. This was my first meeting with Tilak, who gave me the impression of being a strong and determined person. The tender sensitivity in Gokhale's look was absent in him. He stood there like a tower, fired with radiating power. Despite his preoccupations he still found time for me.

I told him of my misgivings and asked him, 'Do you really approve of young men commiting armed robberies?'

He denied this vigorously. 'No, not at all. Even disregarding the issue of morality from the religious point of view, merely speaking from the political angle I regard such deeds as futile and pointless. I say this from my experiences of the marauding activities of our local young men. They are bound to get caught. To collect money by killing our own people will alienate the people, who will furiously turn against the perpetrators of these criminal activities. I have no sympathy with misguided movements like this at all, and you are at liberty to take my name in dissuading your young men from such pursuits. Those who take my name to support their violent activities are preaching lies in my name.'

His views came as a great relief to me, and ever since Tilak became one of the most revered heroes of my life. He was truly a towering leader. With a lightened heart I turned to the food provided by our host. I ended this trip with a visit to Bombay for a few days.

No one will have the faintest idea of the courage that I mustered to face someone like Tilak, the lion in his den. Anyway, my mission was successful, my nerve paid off, and I returned home pretty pleased with myself. And to crown it all I was able to prevent the dastardly plans of Jatin Bannerjee and his party.

Twenty Five

No two lives are moulded in the same template. The weaving shuttles of the three women that the Creator proverbially charged to regulate the lives of the people continue to fashion the changing fabrics of life, and infusing degrees of diversities in the nature and pattern of each individual life. The innovative creations of the Original Artist of the infinite manifestations of human life can in no way be uniformly the same as are the products turned out by an automated machine. The external manifestations of the differences between one human and another are clearly etched in the lines of the palms and the feet, in the endless variations in the patterns of the fingertips. No two human beings are identitical in every respect, and no person is a clone of another. Each has his distinctive persona; where contrasts or distinctive features are conspicuous they get noticed, otherwise not. The warps and wefts of life begin in the mother's womb and end at death. The pattern of my life keeps taking shapes like a variety of floral designs, each passing day, each passing year. The arbitrator of my fate is the Creator at whose feet I sit. And his weaving shuttle suddenly took me away from my home in Bengal to the far away shores of the land of five rivers, Punjab.

I was on a visit to the Mayavati Ashram in the Himalayas, founded by Swami Vivekananda. There I feasted my eyes looking at the towering peaks of the Himalayas; there I set my eyes on a variation of my motherland, another India, crowned with the

190   *The Many Worlds of Sarala Devi*

dazzling white diadem of snow. What a glorious sight, how magnificently awe-inspiring! The mesmerizing vision of the coruscating peaks of Kedarnath and Badrinarayan! Beyond these snow-capped hills lie other countries, other civilizations; and on this side is our ancient and eternal India and her civilization, enshrined in the hymns of the Vedas which resonate through the sky and around the hills and dales of our country even today. Do not the rising clouds from the valleys still carry traces of the smoke from the sacred fires of our immortal saints?

At the ashram I engaged myself in taking lessons in Upanishadas from Swami Turiananda, an ashram brother of Swami Vivekananda. At the same time I was also initiated into the Bhagavadagita. On some nights I dreamt of Yagnavalkya or Rishi Narada giving me guidance.

Besides being a spiritual home, the ashram also had a material existence. Wherever there are human beings, they need wherewithal to sustain life. It had not occurred to me earlier that the mundane needs of life have to be procured, stored and preserved. I now realize why in those ancient times forest dwellers built their humble cottages not too far away from human habitations, which were usually flush with water resources as well as other material requirements. Here I observed Swami Swarupananda, head of the ashram, whom I had earlier met at Belur Math, engaged in editing the highly rated English language magazine *Prabuddha Bharat*; taking regular classes to teach Vedanta to the novices; and at the same time finding time to make all necessary arrangements for procuring various victuals, such as, rice, lentils, wheat, almonds, etc. He also took assiduous care to put the foodstuffs out in the sun to avoid them being infested by rodents, as well as to to get these ingredients properly cleaned and storing them in the pantry. No task was too small for him. And he was all attentive to the needs of the guests.

Slowly I came to comprehend the synthesis of the paths of knowledge and action in the work of the ashram. The domestic activities here have no element of selfishness that saddles the lives of ordinary people. The ashram residents are motivated solely by their sense of duties and service to others. Each resident of the ashram has his or her own earmarked sphere of responsibilities. During the winters, the roads of the ashram become snowbound, and it is then difficult to move around even within the ashram. That is why much before the advent of the cold weather, it is necessary to collect and store firewood. The location of the ashram is some distance away from the facilities of inhabited neighbourhoods, post

Sukhendu Ray 191

offices and other similar amenities. The inmate sanyasis could travel to Kedar and Badri via an alternative short-cut.

Even casual visitors like me who come here seeking diversion usually choose the right season to arrive, and arrangements have to be made to look after them. Some of them tend to overstay until the winter. Those who are able to pay are charged a fixed monthly sum for their stay. Mother Saviour, who is in chargeof administration, once told me that certain strict measures had to be adopted in view of the tendency of many guests, even if they could afford to pay, to stay on enjoying the free hospitality of the ashram. Before leaving they left not even a small contribution for its running. They treated the ashram as a free retreat and sanatorium. How long could the ashram sustain itself in these circumstances? Hence the decision to charge some compensations from visitors. The monks are in a sense the genuine 'guests' as they had renounced home and dedicated themselves to serve at the ashram. Nevertheless, the visiting guests, paying or otherwise, are always treated with considerable courtesy.

There are two houses on the hilltop—the house on the higher level is reserved for the resident monks, while the lower house is used by Colonel and Mrs Saviour as their home. Colonel Saviour has recently passed away, and Mrs Saviour stayed on as the 'mother figure' of the ashram. The ashram was established with their money and continues to be maintained by their funds.

An American monk and an American novice share quarters with the monks in the upper house. The American monk keeps himself immersed in the pursuit of spiritual attainment, whilst the American novice is put through the rigours of initiation step by step towards the final goal of spiritual attainment.

During my stay at the ashram, there arrived a lady visitor from America, dressed in a saffron robe and declaring herself to be a disciple of Swami Vivekananda. This American lady was much attached to her only son, and his ill treatment had broken her heart. Around then she met Vivekananda in the States when he addressed her as 'Mother', she was so touched that very soon she became a disciple of Swamiji and found much strength in following him. Finally she came to India and found the peace that had eluded her so long.

Contrasting saffron garbs of the monks against the expanse of greenery all round presented a most aesthetic picture that would tempt any sensitive artist to paint it.

Soon there arrived a young man from Mahratta, who was an expert in *hathayoga*. He demonstrated some *asanas* for me, but my real gain

192   *The Many Worlds of Sarala Devi*

was in picking up from him a number of Mahratta songs. Also at Mayavati I heard for the first time, and collected, bhajans of Mirabai. I had the good fortune of listening to and learning devotional songs of Ramprasad, songs in praise of the goddess Kali, from a couple of resident Bengali monks. Often during my evening walks with Mrs Saviour we were accompanied by some monks. When we found a suitable spot to sit down, the monks would sing and I would join them. The reflection of the setting sun across the hills created a magical spectacle, and I had a vision of an ecstatic Mother Goddess set against that panorama. A feeling of utter bliss engulfed me.

The Mahratti youth said that he was planning to travel to Tibet. En route he would depend on the help of local people, and many rest houses would provide him with shelter. I was awfully enthused by his grit and determination and tempted to follow him. Mrs Saviour strongly disapproved of my intention, and I suspect she probably wrote to my mother warning her of my wild desire.

It is likely that as a reaction to Mrs Saviour's letter I soon received a long screed from my *Didi* telling me that mother was in very poor health and that one did not know what turn it could take. She also added that it was my mother's devout wish that I should get married, and that I should not take her last wish lightly. My family knew well my views on marriage: I would never accept anyone as my husband unless I could personally approve of the individual concerned, regardless of his social status, be he in the top echelon of the civil service or a scion of a princely house. Apparently, my family had settled on a groom who, so my sister averred, could not but be acceptable to me. Marriage to him, I was told, would fully comply with my ideals. The person identified was a Brahmin, belonging to an illustrious family of Punjab. It is well known how my maternal grandfather had been keen to promote marriages within the Brahmin communities throughout India, as he believed that would lead to a significant avenue to achieve solidarity among the Brahmins in the country. We all know how upset he was when my elder brother contracted an inter-caste marriage with a daughter of the Coochbehar Raj family. Had he been alive he would have heartily approved of my proposed marriage connection.

By all accounts the groom was very eligible. He was a leading light of the Arya Samaj, to establish a link with which and the Adi Brahmo Samaj, grandfather had dispatched Bolu-*dada* as an emissary. My chosen husband, besides being a reputed orator, was a dedicated nationalist and, most importantly, handsome.

Sukhendu Ray 193

Truthfully, there was no reason for me to object to this choice. I knew, of course, that he was married earlier and was now a widower. My sister was keen that I should not reject this proposal out of hand before I met my intended. 'Come and see for yourself', she wrote, 'before making up your mind either way. Do not thoughtlessly turn down this proposal which will hasten our mother's end.' A time-tested ruse of raising the spectre of threat to parents' lives to get around recalcitrant children to agree to marry! This ploy was used to trap me, and I had no option but to answer my sister's summons to go down, thus terminating my sojourn in the Himalayas.

Mother was then in Baidyanath trying to recuperate, and so I had to go there instead of Calcutta. On the way I needed to change trains at Lucknow station. I sent a message to Atulprasad that I would have a wait at Lucknow for a few hours. He came himself to meet me and that was not all, he told me that the resident Bengalis of Lucknow had convened a meeting to mark my visit and that I could only leave after I had accepted a Scroll of Honour from them. This meant a couple of days halt in Lucknow. I had to concede and accepted Atulprasad's hospitality. I felt gratified to be so honoured by the Bengalis of Lucknow, more so, as a receiver of so much affection from them. Would they but have known that I was soon to be an exile from home!

Atulprasad's home was the meeting place of Congressmen. I knew a Mr Gangaprasad Varma in Lucknow, a very renowned personality. When we met at Atulprasad's home, I drew him aside and told him. 'I need to speak to you in confidence, and I need your advice.' I told him then about my would-be husband and asked him if he knew anything about him, and what his views were on my proposed marriage to him.

He confirmed that he knew my future husband very well, and observed that I could not have found a more fitting life companion. He also added, 'Our countrymen may not be too pleased at your marriage, because the country would in that process lose a dedicated soul in the service of the nation. That would be their apprehension.'

Even before I reached Baidyanath, my sister had conspiratorially fixed all arrangemrnts for my wedding. She had practically tied me up hand and feet making it impossible for me to do anything else. The moment I arrived at the Baidyanath railway station, I discovered that I did so already as a confirmed bride. I was whisked away in a palanquin, my feet hardly touching the ground. I discovered that the date of the wedding had been fixed, invitations sent out, and the

194   *The Many Worlds of Sarala Devi*

groom's party had reached and settled in another house. All this was accomplished keeping me absolutely in the dark, in case I did anything rash to upset my parents. I was utterly bewildered.

The next day was set down for the traditional pre-nuptial ritual of anointing the bride with turmeric paste, for which all the required paraphernalia had been procured by my sister with the help of Sankar Pandit of Bhowanipore, who had been designated as our contact person with the groom's party. Morning saw the arrival of a host of relations, including Rabi-*mama,* from several parts of the country — from Bolpur, Ranchi, Calcutta and Madhupur. The house teemed with friends and relations. The sehnai played wedding music throughout the day. In the evening the bride, me, had a brief glimpse of the groom. No denying he had eye-dazzling looks, regardless of what the heart might feel. The wedding was to take place in the evening the next day. The die was cast; no turning back now.

Before the marriage ceremony I was asked if the rituals were conducted according to the Arya Samaj rites, which embraced all the Vedic mantras used by the Adi Brahmo Samaj, but also included offerings to the sacred fire as in Hindu weddings, would I find that objectionable? 'Not at all', I confirmed. 'In fact, I am fully in agreement with it.'

Many of our friends happened to be in Baidyanath then as health seekers, all of whom came to my wedding. The wedding was concluded in due course; a pre-destined bond, dictated by the karma of our past lives. We went back to Calcutta a few days later, where my parents had a dinner to celebrate our marriage, to which were invited their many friends. From the groom's side came well-known persons belonging to the Arya Samaj, which included Deepchand Poddar, Sir Chhajuram, Rai Bahadur Balaram, the Chief Manager of A B Railways, etc. The Birashtami celebrations were due then, and for the occasion, the boys of the Club had already made all the preparations. Immediately thereafter we had to leave for Lahore. At the railway station many friends belonging to the Arya Samaj came to see us off carrying traditional gifts of fruits, flowers and sweets. All along the route, at all major stops — Patna, Allahabad, Saharanpur, Ambala, Jullunder, Amritsar — we were greeted in an equally lavish fashion. A massive crowd awaited our arrival at Lahore station. Sir Muhammad Shafi managed to steer through this multitude and was the first person to reach me. He warmly welcomed me with a garland of flowers, and it was in his car that we drove to my new house.

Twenty Six

Soon after my arrival in Lahore many ladies came to see me, carrying according to their custom, pieces of sugar candy, almonds, the traditional neckchain for married women, plus a few rupees. Almost none of them were any relations of my in-laws; they were the wives, mothers or sisters of the members of the Arya Samaj or relations of important persons. Other than them the first visitor to arrive was Lala Lalchand, a partner of the well known Gulab Singh Press, founded by his father. They were two brothers, Mohanlal and Lalchand. Both had two wives each and both were childless, which was a cause for much distress to their mother. Lalchand's first wife was orthodox and kept herself engaged in religious activities, His second wife, on the other hand, was thoroughly modern, adopting the lifestyle of her husband, who had been to England. She could converse in English and accompanied her husband even to ball dances.

Lalchand was very sociable. When he decided to shift to Calcutta to open a branch of his press, he carried a letter of introduction from me to my father to seek his help as a newcomer to Calcutta. Surprisingly, the wife who accompanied him to Calcutta was not the second wife whom I got to know. He had, meanwhile, unknown to anyone, married for the third time, and all his children are from this wife. His conduct towards his first two wives remained faultless, and they lived their own lives with dignity, though without the husband. His elder brother also took a third wife, a woman of Brahmo Samaj, and finally had a son with her.

196   *The Many Worlds of Sarala Devi*

For the first time I had direct introduction to Hindu male polygamy. Once earlier I had met a Hindu gentleman who had two wives. He was Mr Sohoni, a sub-judge and a good singer. I never met his wives, and the report was that the two were not on good terms with each other. I believe Mr Sohoni's second marriage was in pursuit of a son and heir but his wish remained unfulfilled.

Though polygamy for Hindu males is legally valid, in practice, educated persons rarely take another wife. Exceptions are made in special circumstances, such as, when the existing wife fails to produce a son. It is possible to adopt a boy from another family, but the preference is for having an heir born from one's wife. It is not unknown for a childless first wife herself persuading the husband to have a second marriage and be prepared to share the husband with the second wife. This is traditional Hindu culture passed down through generations. A Hindu wife perceives it as a personal obligation to ensure the continuation of the husband's lineage. This apparent self effacement is also an instrument to preserving one's self respect in the face of the husband's attachment to the new wife. Not everybody is capable of such self sacrifice, but if a wife does, should she be then faulted?

This provokes a thought. If an entire group of people indulge in polygamy, will it be right to condemn them? Certain reformation measures in the law governing the Hindus are currently under consideration, and in the process along with the elimination of many iniquitous practices, some sensible traditions are also going to be sacrificed. When a garden, however well maintained, has undesirable weeds and other growths, it becomes necessary to uproot them, but sadly in this exercise, many healthy plants are also weeded out.

Living with one lawful wife is, no doubt, the most honourable thing to do, but behind many monogamous marriages in the western world is the ugly practice of keeping mistresses. In the East, legally married multiple wives live honourably. In some princely families, in addition to validly wed wives who had taken seven steps round the sacrificial fire, even the women who had walked only three steps are entitled to maintenance by husbands. In the West, unlawful wives get no recognition and live a life without any honour, and their maintenance as well as their children's is dependant on the capricious whims of the men. In spite of the legal validity of polygamy in our country, as I have already said, such instances are rare amongst the educated classes. This custom still prevails amongst the princely classes, and if the custom is abolished there will be some difficulty for them. 'Where will we marry our daughters, then?' is what they would be asking.

The early lady callers from the Arya Samaj who came to see me were variously introduced as a *chachi*, a *tayee* or a *bhabi*. I had no clue then if they were really related to the family or these were courtesy labels. In time I came to know who were relatives and who were not. I disovered that, as in Scotland, they have 'clans' in Punjab as well. This is totally alien to us in Bengal. The Brahmin 'clan' to which my husband's family belonged is known as Mahial Brahmins, and they are, in turn, sub-divided into six sub-classes. They are — Datta, Bali, Chhibbar, Mohal, Lou and Bhimbal. Marriages are restricted within the members of these classes only. The daughters will not be given in marriage to men from other Brahmin classes, although there is no bar for men to fetch a wife from other Brahmin groups. The Brahmins of my husband's clan can carry arms, and when attacked by enemies are able to defend themselves. They are mainly agriculturists, governed by the Land Alienation Act. In British India they guard the borders, a frontier force called 'King's Own Guides' is formed entirely by the members of this Brahmin group. When Alexander reached the borders of Punjab, it was their ancestors, Raja Jaipal and Raja Anangapal, who gave him battle.

My husband's ancestral home and the land of his birth is Kanjrur. This village nestles at the foothills of the Himalayas, and is part of the Gurudaspur district. The full name of the village is Kanjrur-e-Datta, meaning Kanjrur of the Dattas. Hearsay has it that an ancestor and his family were massacred mercilessly while trying to prevent the abduction of a pretty Rajput girl whom the Nawab of Lahore coveted. Shortly thereafter the Nawab suffered from an ear affliction which no physicians could cure. Then an astrologer told him, 'In a battle you had slain countless numbers of Brahmins, and that is why you are cursed with this punishment. Unless you atone for this sin, you will never be cured.'

'What atonement do I have to make?' asked the Nawab.

'If there is any survivor of the Datta family, go and search him out. His spit will cure you, there is no other remedy'.

A thorough search was initiated. Finally it was traced to Sialkot, the parental home of one of the wives of the Datta family, who appeared to be pregnant at the time of the battle that demolished her family. She fled to Sialkot where she gave birth to twin boys. Their maternal uncle gave them protection in secrecy for fear of

198 *The Many Worlds of Sarala Devi*

their life. The Nawab's emissaries seized them and carried them away to Lahore. In the Nawab's bedroom, the *hakim* (physician) ordered them to spit into the Nawab's ears. The twins froze in fear, but after much threat and pursuasion they spat into the Nawab's ears. The Nawab got well soon thereafter. He then mounted the two boys on two horses and instructed his men to take them to two opposite directions, and the area of land covered by each in the next twenty four hours was given to them, free of any levies. One of the horses pushed towards Sialkot in the district of Daffarwal, and the other towards Kanjrur in the district of Gurudaspur. And the two Datta families were re-established once again in these two places.

Even after the re-settlement, the Dattas of Kanjrur had been involved in many battles. They hardly ever enjoyed a peaceful life for any length of time. To die in battlefields was a common occurrence in this family, like death in one's bed after a period of illness for normal people. One who sacrificed his life during war after displaying conspicuous bravery was entitled to be called a *shaheed*, a martyr. This is comparable to some extent like the present day award of the Victoria Cross.

An ancestor of the Kanjrur Dattas became a martyr when giving fight to the invaders. His name was Baba Atal Khan. There is a shrine in Kanjrur commemorating him, a mud-built cairn, surrounded by a low wall. In the evenings men and women, from both Hindu and Muslim communities, arrive from the villages around and light lamps. On every social or religious occasion, such as, the ceremonial first shaving of a child's hair, sacred thread rites or marriages, heads of the Datta family, members of the family, men and women, must visit the shrine, and after prostrating themselves, offer homages of food and flowers. This is obligatory, otherwise no social functions are regarded as complete.

My husband approached me with some hesitation. 'Will you follow this tradition of our family? The custom of a newly married wife in the family to prostrate at the shrine? If you do not wish to conform on the ground that it is a superstitious practice, I will understand and will not insist.'

My reply was firm. 'How do you mean a superstitious rite? I consider it a matter of pride that I am married into a family which can boast of such a heroic person, and who is still revered as a martyr, and whose memory continues to be a matter of such pride and joy for his descendants.'

A date was fixed for our visit to Kanjrur. It was a rather a complicated journey; by railway from Lahore to Amritsar, and then change into another train. The rail journey terminates at Batala, from where one has to ride a horse drawn *tonga* or *ekka* (two wheeler carts) till one reaches the river Ravi, which has to be forded by ferry. These ferry boats are pretty large and able to accommodate men and horses and cattle. We were soon on the other side, where horses were waiting for men to ride, and for me a *doli*, covered on top but otherwise open, as no palanquins were available there. Carried in a *doli* as a bashful wife for about ten miles we reached a shallow stream, called Basanta, on the other side of which was the village Kanjrur. The bearers carried the *doli* walking across the shallow stream, as did the horses. Lined up on the other side were a host of relations and a large contingent of villagers. When the *doli* was put down they performed the customary rituals of welcoming me. Blowing on conch shells or ululations had no place in their conventions; the ceremony was performed just with lamps.

I rested for a while on reaching the house, but the relatives hardly left me alone. By early evening I had to get ready. Streams of people from the neighbourhood villaged arrived to see me—the newly married wife of Chaudhuri Sahib, a girl from faraway Calcutta and on top of that a graduate with a B.A. degree! It came as a surprise to them that such a highly educated woman had agreed to visit the small village of the in-laws just to offer homage at the 'Baba Thakkar Mahal' by prostrating herself.

This episode had created much stir in Lahore. The elder relatives of girls belonging to the Punjab Brahmo Samaj put me up as an ideal for them to follow. Citing my action they were told that just being Brahmos they did not necessarily have to abandon all traditional customs of a family. We visited the shrine the following day carrying with us a huge quantity of prasadas, after circumnavigating the shrine a few times we lit the lamps, and offered our homage and distributed the prasada.

The mud work wall protecting the shrine gets washed up each monsoon. The keeper of the shrine appealed to me to build a brick wall. I agreed and asked for an estimate of the cost to be sent to me; meanwhile I gave him two hundred rupees as an advance to commence the work. I stayed at Kanjrur for five days, and got to know all the relatives connected with my in-laws. I returned to Lahore loaded with their good wishes.

200 *The Many Worlds of Sarala Devi*

I have said earlier that in Punjab, each caste is like a clan. Each clan has its special features, customs, social conducts, handed down unchanged through the generations. These distinctive features continue to be religiously guarded. No distinction, none whatever, is made between the rich and the poor at social gatherings. A High Court judge and a postal peon are treated on equal footing on such occasions. Expenses that can be incurred for marriages of children are specified, so that a rich person does not splurge for his daughter's wedding in a way which cannot be matched by a poor person. Gifts are fixed: so many silk saris, so many cottons; also the standard of feeding the groom's party. Similarly, the groom's people cannot ask for dowry from the bride's family. This is considered as selling one's daughter, a most despicable practice.

Each clan has attached to it a group of professional singers of eulogies, like Scottish pipers. They are not heralds as we understand the term; they are known as *mirasis*. They were once Hindus, but under Islamic influence, converted to Islamic faith. On social occasions, such as marriages, their dues are an item of specified expenditure. When guests congregrate the *mirasis* sing the the songs of glory of the clan they are attached to, which fills the listeners with pride and joy. The past deeds of glory of each client are recorded in the books in details so that there are no confusions or mistakes. But with the growing families of the *mirasis*, the payments from the clients are not enough to sustain them. Not unexpectedly their children have fanned out to various parts of Punjab in search of jobs and livelihoods. Many families of *mirasis* still continue to live in Kanjrur. On my arrival a *mirasi* attached to my in-laws' family, called Gauhar, started singing the songs of praise of the Datta clan to welcome me. It is not customary to do so for a woman, but an exception was made for me. This was the very first occasion when a lady of the family was counted as equal to the men.

Glossary

Kinship terms used:

Baba	Father
Ma	Mother
Mama	Mother's brother or her male cousin
Mami(ma)	Wife of a mama
Mashi(ma)	Mother's sister or her female cousin
Dada	Elder brother or elder male cousin
Didi	Elder sister or elder female cousin
Bouthan	Wife of elder brother or elder male cousin

Seniority terms in kinship:

Baro	Eldest
Mejo	Second
Sejo	Third
Naw	Fourth
Natun	Fifth

Other words:

Annaprasan	A ritual to mark the occasion of an infant's first intake of solid food
Ayah	A child minder
Anna	Old Indian coin — one-sixteenth of a rupee
Babu	A gentleman: also used as a suffix after a man's name as a mark of respect

202 *Glossary*

Brahmo	A new monotheistic faith propagated by Raja Ram Mohun Roy in 1830s
Brahma	One of the Gods of Hindu trinity
Bejoya Dashami	Fourth and the last day of the major Bengali Hindu festival of Durga Puja
Dai	A midwife or a children's nurse
Durga	A major Hindu goddess
Ghat	A landing stage on a river bank or a built up structure on river banks or on the edges of ponds for use of bathers
Hookah	Smoking hubble-bubble
Krishna	A major Hindu god
Kali	A major Hindu goddess
Luchi	Bengali speciality kind of fried bread
Luxmi	Hindu goddess of wealth and grace
Maharshi	A sage: Debendranath Tagore was revered as one
Panditmashai	A teacher
Patkhir	A Bengali delicacy made from milk
Puja	Worship/Prayer
Ragas	Forms of Indian classical music
Saraswati	Hindu goddess of muses
Shiva	One of the Gods of Hindu trinity
Tantra	A religious cult
Vina	A stringed musical instrument

Bengali calendar months quoted:

Baisakh	First month of Bengali calendar — corr. April/May
Asadh	Third month — corr. June/July
Bhadra	Fifth month — corr. August/September
Aswin	Sixth month — corr. September/October
Agrahayan	Eighth month — corr. November/December
Poush	Ninth month — corr. December/January
Magh	Tenth month — January/February

THE TAGORES AND SARTORIAL STYLES

A PHOTO ESSAY

MALAVIKA KARLEKAR

Till the late 18th century, the undivided Tagore family lived in Pathuriaghata, on the banks of the Ganga; in 1784, Nilmoni, grandfather of Dwarakanath Tagore, established himself in a modest abode in what was then Mechhuabazar. This was to later become Jorasanko and with increasing affluence, the 'hut', grew into the famed mansion of the much better known line of the Jorasanko Tagores. An enterprising zamindar with compradorial instincts who became a much-favoured banian (a Bengali intermediary of the British in trade and commerce) with the East India Company, Dwarakanath Tagore (1794–1846) was a successful entrepreneur in indigo and silk, amassing large fortunes and property in and around Calcutta. In 1834, Dwarakanath who was also well-versed in law, set up Messers. Carr, Tagore and Company as well as purchased coal mines in Raniganj. Though known for his opulent style of life and extravagant parties at which he entertained Europeans lavishly, Dwarakanath was careful to observe the rules of Brahmin commensality and never ate with his guests (see Kripalani 1981).

A follower of Rammohun Roy,[1] Dwarakanath was closely involved with the establishment of the Calcutta Medical College in 1835. Earlier, in 1833, together with Rasamoy Dutt, Ashutosh Deb and others, he was chosen to serve on mixed race juries for certain cases in the Supreme Court. His eldest son, Debendranath was quite unlike his father and chose the path of the ascetic.[2]

Educated at Hindu College, he had been initiated into the family business, though Messers. Carr, Tagore and Company did not survive long after the death of its founder. Debendranath established *Tattvabodhini Sabha* with the aim of spreading the knowledge of Indian and European literature and science through Bengali and in 1843, was instrumental in the establishment of the Brahmo Samaj.[3]

*All photographs are from Rabindra Bhawan at Viswabharati, Shantiniketan that has an extensive collection of documents and photographs on and of the Tagore family. I am grateful to Prof Rajat Ray, Vice Chancellor, Viswabharati and to Mr Swapan Mazumdar and his colleagues, Director of the Rabindra Bhawan, Shantiniketan for providing us with copies of photographs used in this essay.

'Maharaja' Sir Jotindramohan Tagore of the Pathuriaghata branch of the Tagore family

Jotindramohan wears a brocade *kurta* (men's loose stitched upper garment) tied with a *patka* (sash) that has *kiran* (gold or sliver fringes), matching *pyjamas* (loose stitched lower garment) and a *choga* (crossover robe) on top. The sword in the scabbard, long pearl necklace with an enamel pendant and *pagri* with a *sarpech* (plume) were all indications of princely as well as high zamindari status. (See Ritu Kumar [n.d.] for an elaborately illustrated and informed account of dress styles of the 'native' princes and zamindars).

With prominent lives outside the home, it could only be expected that men of the Tagore family would dress in what was *de rigueur* for those from their social class: in fact, among the landed gentry, there appears to have been a certain uniformity across regions as styles of several items of clothing, jewels and accoutrements were modelled on those worn by members of the princely states. For instance in photograph 1, 'Maharaja' Sir Jotindramohan Tagore of the Pathuriaghata branch of the Tagore family is dressed in the style of a 'native' prince. Jotindramohan was an aficionado of Indian classical music and of the growing Bengali theatre, organising soirees at his impressive palace.

Dwarakanath Tagore   **Debendranath Tagore**

While Dwarakanath wears a gold-embroidered *angarkha* (long sleeved full-skirted tunic), his son's apparel is more modest though he drapes a *jamavaar*—the finely embroidered Kashmiri shawl, a hallmark of the Bengali elite of the times around his shoulders. Undoubtedly, Debendranath's reformist tendencies led to a more austere presentation of the self.

Though Jotindramohan was given to calling himself Maharaja, the Tagores of Pathuriaghata were not hereditary royalty and the scion was bestowed the title of 'raja' by the British. There were only three hereditary Maharajas in Bengal and who pre-dated the British, those of Cooch Behar, Burdwan and Shushang.

Though men kept themselves up to date on changing sartorial styles, for women the question of dress had very different implications and women of the Tagore family were deeply involved with working towards appropriate styles. Traditionally, Bengali women wore only a single piece of cloth wound dexterously around their bodies; there were no undergarments but elaborate ornaments were not unusual. After the middle of the nineteenth century, Bengali reformers were greatly concerned with upper and middle-class women's situation now referred to by that convenient hold all term, the 'status of women': Rammohan Roy's stand on sati, debates on the age of consent, Iswarchandra Vidyasagar's campaign for widow remarriage, acrimonious discussions around upper-caste kulin polygamy, and, more positively, the need to educate girls and indeed women, occupied the *bhadralok*, or the gentry, of a rapidly urbanising Bengal. For the subjects of such prolix debates, to be visible in an ambience that now stressed decorum and respectability, it would not do to be seen only in a length of material!

Thus, female dress reform became an issue, a 'movement' about which little was known until quite recently. Apart from accepting the new wisdom on norms of decency, reformers were aware that girls' and women's education and their exposure to the world outside the home were severely impaired by what was deemed to be inappropriate and inadequate attire (see Bannerji 2001; Borthwick 1984). The reformist Debendranath Tagore worried about how women and girls from his family and others similarly placed were to be presented in public. In the 1870s, his apprehensions were considerably allayed with

Jnanadanandini Debi, c. early 1870s

Here Jnanadanandini is dressed in a variation of the reformed attire that combines a more traditional way of draping the *giley kara paar* sari (that had fine pleats along the border) with the modern blouse with high neck and full sleeves with cuffs.

Malavika Karlekar 209

the return of daughter-in-law Jnanadanandini from Bombay 'dressed in a civil and elegant attire in imitation of Gujarati women', quoted in Bannerji 2001: 103). Wife of Satyendranath Tagore, first Indian member of the I.C.S., Jnanadanandini had been a child bride (she was married at 7) and had grown up in the rambling Tagore home in Calcutta's Jorasanko (Karlekar 1991, 2005). She did much to introduce women of the large extended Tagore family to a new dress code and, with a few others, was soon at the forefront of the sartorial reform movement.

Jnanadanandini Devi was deeply influenced by the newly-introduced Parsi *garo*: by the latter part of the 19th century, the Parsi *gara* or *garo* – sari with Chinese embroidery in white or variegated silk threads was introduced in India. These were either originals or based on the all-over hand-embroidered *garas* brought back by Parsi traders from China in the 1850s. Either fully embroidered, the peony, cock and butterfly being favourite motifs, or only with heavily worked borders that were attached, they soon became eponymous with a type (Parsi-border sari) that spread throughout India. Not long after its introduction, crafts people in Surat started copying the *gara* as well as fine borders and supplying rapidly expanding markets in the urban areas of Bombay and Bengal Presidencies, and in time, some parts of Madras Presidency as well as north India and the more westernised among the princely states.

The introduction of the sari blouse *(jama*, often modelled on western styles), and petticoat *(shaya)* was essential before upper and middle-class Bengali women could come out in public; in an article purported to have been written by Jnanadanandini (using a pseudonym) in *Bamabodhini Patrika*, a women's magazine popular in reformist circles, the author commented on a new mode of dress that took from English, Muslim and Bengali traditions and yet retained a Bengali essence. For instance, the author wrote of how she now wore shoes, stockings, bodice *(angiya cachali* in place of the Parsi *sudreh* or undershirt), blouse, a short skirt-like petticoatwith a sari draped over it; when she went out she wore a *chador* that could be used to cover her head if necessary (Borthwick 1984: 248).

Blouses were elaborate, modelled on current styles of gowns and blouses prevalent in the West: thus high collars with ribbons, frills, jabots and brooches were popular from the 1870s till the turn of century and a few women also wore mutton chop sleeves, peaked at the shoulder. Shawls draped elegantly over one shoulder, closed shoes, brooches and hair ornaments completed the ritual of westernised elite female dress.

Sarala Devi (seated) with sister Hironmoyee

Both sisters are dressed in elaborate Parsi-border saris and Sarala's blouse has mutton chop sleeves. Both sisters wear *tiklis* (small pendants on chains) on their foreheads. As both saris appear to be of heavy silk, it would be safe to surmise that the visit to the studio was in winter, at a time when it was possible to wear such attire with a certain degree of comfort.

Later, while those from the Brahmo Samaj referred to the new style of wearing the sari with blouse and *chador* as the 'Thakurbarir sari' (sari worn in the style of the Tagores, a leading Brahmo family), as more and more Brahmos started wearing the sari in this manner, it came to be popularly known as the 'Brahmika sari' throughout

India (Sarala Devi Chaudhurani 1982: 54). Children too were dressed in clothes in vogue for British children of the times. As for the young unmarried girls in the family, it was acceptable for them to wear the 'English frock' (Sarala Devi Chaudhurani 1982: 53).

Saroja Devi, daughter of Dwijendranath, Sarala Devi's eldest maternal uncle, with her son

The little boy is dressed in a variant of Little Lord Fauntleroy suit—quite the fashion at the end of the nineteenth century and the early twentieth. Such suits—so called after the character in Frances Hobson Burnett's 1886 book of the same name—were of expensive velvet with fancy collars often with trim; here, it appears to be gold braid. The child also wears socks and buttoned-up leather shoes decorated with a bow and flower.

To go to a studio to be photographed after the wedding became increasingly popular after the 1870s; it was also an occasion for impressive sartorial displays.

Rabindranath Tagore with 10-year-old bride Bhabatarini (Mrinalini), 1883

In this somewhat formulaic after-the-wedding studio composition at Bourne & Shepherd, shortly after the marriage ceremony that was in Calcutta, litterateur Rabindranath wears a jamavaar over his kurta, while Mrinalini has a net veil draped over her elaborate Parsi-style Brahmika sari from under which a closed court shoe peeps out. The expensive clothes of both and the draping of these reflect the western-educated zamindari style of the times. A confident Rabindranath strikes a pose with a hand on his hip; the young bride is perched somewhat tentatively on the parapet-like seat. Her eyes have a slightly glazed look, hardly surprising as she must surely have been in a state of some shock following her marriage into the eminent family with its many and varied characters, including strong-minded and talented women.

In keeping with the dominant patriarchal tradition in upper-class homes of re-naming a bride (in effect effacing her earlier identity), Bhabatarini was renamed Mrinalini and within a month of her marriage, was dispatched to live with Rabindranath's older brother Satyendranath's wife Jnanadanandini in her home in central Calcutta. The young girl was schooled at the nearby Loreto Convent and trained in various other social and housewifely skills by her much older and sophisticated sister-in-law (Dutta and Robinson 1995: 86–7).

Interestingly, the marriage was held in Calcutta, and not in Jessore district, the home of the bride as is customary; this change in venue may have been out of deference to the wishes of the high-status and influential Tagores. Rabindranath Tagore was Debendranath and Sharada Devi's youngest son, outstanding for his literary excellence, powerful insights into the nature of colonialism and sensitivity to changing gender relations, the

Swarnakumari Devi wearing the *chador* over a *mukut* (crown), c. 1880s

Swarnakumari, fifth daughter of Debendranath Tagore, was Sarala Devi's mother and became a writer of some repute, the first Bengali woman novelist. She also edited the family journal *Bharati*. The photograph is probably taken in the 1880s as she is wearing a high-necked blouse, Parsi border sari and brooches.

214 *The Tagores and Sartorial Styles*

family and conjugality. He was close to his niece Sarala Devi and appreciative of her musical talent.

The extended Tagore family was a much-photographed community, with images recording different life stages of most members. The following photographs introduce us to a number of amazing women from this family, some more Anglicised than others, as well as document sartorial innovations.

Protibha Devi (1865–1912), a granddaughter of Debendranath Tagore, early 1880s

Protibha Devi has obviously been photographed before an important social occasion. She is wearing the all-over embroidered sari in the style of the Parsi garo, velvet blouse with gold work and has an elaborate coiffeure, long earrings and holds a fan in her hand. The fan and earrings of this kind were much in fashion. Not uncommonly, accoutrements such as the fan and straw hat, indicative of the individual's social position (often reflecting styles used by those similarly placed in Britain) and used on special occasions, were strategically placed within the frame.

While sometimes these used to be supplied by the studio, in the case of the Tagore women, these would almost certainly have been their own.

Indumati, another granddaughter of Debendranath Tagore

Indumati was the only Tagore woman of that generation to wear a gown as her usual dress. Wife of Dr. Nityananda Chattopadhyay, Indumati lived in Madras. To be photographed dressed in western gown with pin tucks and frills, reading, and then with a racquet in hand were to convey to the viewer that Indumati was an educated woman, interested in sports and a life outside the home. Well-known film actress Devika Rani was her granddaughter.

There are many photographs still available of Sarala Devi, each recording occasions and phases in her eventful life; many of these have been described by her in *Jeevaner Jharapata*.

Sarala Devi at around age 18

Here Sarala wears an elaborate blouse that is modelled on the upper half of a western gown with a brooch at the middle of the high neck and long sleeves that have ruffs at the end. She has draped her sari in the new style introduced by her aunt, Jnanadanandini Devi.

A proud graduate

It is possible that both this photograph as well as the earlier one were taken after Sarala's graduation (the sari and studio props appear the same). In this pose she is wearing the graduate's gown and mortar board and of course holds a book in her right hand. Here however, she is not engaging with the camera, but rather looking in to the middle distance.

Clearly then, Sarala Devi—like many other Tagore women—experimented with sartorial styles; her interesting life allowed her the space to do so. These photographs help provide a visual context to this life as Sarala Devi was completely at ease before the camera. In fact, that the Tagores were so taken with photography has been invaluable for those studying their changing life style. Understanding sartorial style without a visual aspect would have been very different indeed!

Sarala spinning, perhaps taken in Dehra Dun in the 1920s

Sarala spins at a rather elaborate *charkha*. She is obviously posing for the photograph that may have been taken in a studio or even at home. Her dark Parsi-border sari is fastened at the shoulder with a large brooch, and she has one ear exposed very much the style introduced by Parsi women from similar backgrounds, who would usually wear an expensive ear ornament as well. It would not be unreasonable to surmise that the photograph may have been taken when M.K. Gandhi was staying in the Chaudhuri home. *Khadi* was just being talked about and *khaddar* saris were still a while away. Some months later, at the 1921 session of the AICC at Vijayawada, it was resolved that by 30 June, two million *charkhas* should be in operation. Gandhi encouraged women, rich and poor, young and old, to spend at least an hour in the day at the spinning wheel, producing *khadi* yarn.

Sarala Devi in later life, perhaps after her return to Calcutta as she is dressed in widow's weeds

218 *The Tagores and Sartorial Styles*

NOTES

1. Best known as the founder of Brahmo Sabha, social and religious reformer Rammohun was committed to changing traditional society and the man responsible for Governor General Lord Bentinck passing the Sati Regulation XVII of 1829; this had the status of law and banned the practice. Apart from fluency in Bengali and English, Rammohun was well versed in Persian, Arabic and Sanskrit.

2. In his *Swarachit Jiban Charit* (Self-written Life or Autobiography), Debendranath described in great detail his semi-mystical experiences and commitment to the formless God. Both Debendranath and his father Dwarakanath however, were unmindful of their wives' feelings and Debendranath thought little of leaving his wife with their 14 children and going to the mountains for months on end. Interestingly, the advocate of women's emancipation did not extend his concern to his wife though he did encourage the education of his daughters (see Karlekar 1991).

3. The Brahmo Samaj was established in 1843 by Debendranath Tagore and emerged out of Rammohun Roy's Brahmo Sabha (1830); deeply influenced by Unitarianism, it was committed to rational worship as the basis of religion, social reform and active work among the poor.

REFERENCES

Bannerji, Himani, 2001. 'Attired in Virtue: Discourse on Shame *(lajja)* and Clothing of the Gentlewoman *(bhadramahila)* in Colonial Bengal' in *Inventing Subjects: Studies in Hegemony, Patriarchy and Colonialism*, New Delhi: Tulika, 99–134.

Borthwick, Meredith, 1984. *The Changing Role of Women in Bengal, 1849–1905*, Princeton: Princeton University Press.

Dutta, Krishna and Andrew Robinson, 1995. *Rabindranath Tagore: The Myriad-minded Man*, New Delhi: Rupa.

Karlekar, Malavika, 1991. *Voices from Within: Early Personal Narratives of Bengali Women*, New Delhi: Oxford University Press.

_____, 2005. *Re-visioning the Past: Early Photography in Bengal 1875–1915*. New Delhi: Oxford University Press.

Kripalani, Krishna, 1981. *Dwarakanath Tagore*, New Delhi: National Book Trust.

Kumar, Ritu, n.d. *Costumes of Princely India*, London: Christie's Books.